EUROPE
for
BIKERS

Simon Weir

Published by Geographers'
A-Z Map Company Limited
An imprint of HarperCollins Publishers
Westerhill Road
Bishopbriggs
Glasgow
G64 2QT

HarperCollinsPublishers
Macken House
39/40 Mayor Street Upper
Dublin 1
D01 C9W8
Ireland

www.az.co.uk
a-z.maps@harpercollins.co.uk

1st edition 2023

Text and routes © Simon Weir 2023
Images pages 3, 4 and 240 © Simon Weir
Cover and all other images © Mark Manning/Bauer
Mapping © Collins Bartholomew Ltd 2023

A catalogue record for this book
is available from the British Library.

ISBN 978-0-00-854783-7

10 9 8 7 6 5 4 3 2

Printed in Malaysia

welcome

Welcome to *Europe for Bikers*, which brings together my 100 favourite motorcycle routes in one easy-to-use volume, with a tankbag-friendly spiral binding and high-quality A-Z mapping.

This collection of routes took a long time to pull together. I've been exploring Europe on two wheels for almost as long as I've been riding – more than thirty years. I was fortunate that, during my ten years on *RiDE* magazine, I was able to revisit favourite places with photographer Mark 'Weeble' Manning, capturing many of the images used here.

Really, this book is a product of obsession – and not just one. At one point, I was fixated on finding the best non-motorway routes across the Continent. At another time, I was a devoted pass-bagger, visiting the mountains to tick off first the famous roads, then the highest roads, then the obscure ones… before I turned my attention to collecting gorges, then castles, then Roman ruins – as well as riding to visit friends or music festivals or biking events in Europe.

No matter what flimsy excuse took me to Europe, the golden rule was always the same: never ride a boring road (if at all possible). Of course, I've spent more than my fair share of time on motorways trying to cross the Continent quickly, but those miles don't make memories. Getting off the beaten track does – and that's the obsession that fills these pages.

And I'm not the only one to have that passion for finding great biking roads. So many people have helped me over the years, sharing with me their favourite roads, favourite places to visit and even their favourite cafés – and with *Europe for Bikers*, I'm sharing the best of everything I've learnt with you, as you must surely share that passion too.

Enjoy *Europe for Bikers* – and the rides it leads you on!

Simon Weir
www.simonweir.co.uk

how to use this book

The 100 routes in this book are divided into chapters by country. Interspersed with these are pages with additional information, including how to get your bike to Spain and Portugal, Europe's highest paved roads, speed limits by country and Mediterranean islands. The introductory section contains details of what you need to know when planning and preparing for your trip, and when riding in Europe.

Riding times

In broad terms, each of the routes is a day's ride. Some are short days, some are long days, but all are presented with the distances and an estimated riding time. This is based on observing local speed limits but does NOT include time for stops – though places for coffee and lunch are suggested along the way (marked on the maps). However, these are just suggested stops: if you spot somewhere on the way that takes your fancy, stop there.

When planning your ride, remember to allow time for stopping – half an hour each for morning and afternoon coffee stops, an hour for a relaxed lunch and time for filling up. If a route has six hours of riding, with stops you're likely to be on the road for eight and a half hours. That means leaving your hotel at 9 a.m. and getting back to it around 5.30 p.m. Longer rides will either need an earlier start or a later finish.

Navigation

Please review the map and notes before setting off on any ride: if they help you get the route straight in your head, your ride will be much smoother and more enjoyable. The spiral-bound format is designed for fitting in a tankbag, but don't take your eyes off the road to read the map while riding: find a safe place to stop and confirm the next leg of the ride.

Routes are also available as GPX downloads for sat nav from www.simonweir.co.uk – but even if using one of those, it's so important to use the book to get familiar with the route before riding it, so the sat nav is just an aid – not a lifeline.

If you ever think you've gone astray, please find somewhere safe to stop and check the map and the directions in the book. It will help you get back on track. Almost all the routes in the book are 100 per cent tarmac – you'll know before setting off if you've selected one that includes some unpaved roads. So if a sat nav suggests turning onto a gravel road, it can be ignored: it will recalculate. If you're purely using the map to navigate, you wouldn't turn onto an unmade road, so don't do it just because the sat nav wants a muddy short cut! But maybe stop and check the map to make sure you haven't left the planned route.

Some motorway tolls are paid as you go, but for Switzerland (left) and Austria (right) you need to display a vignette sticker

Some French cities require a Crit'Air sticker for the bike

planning your trip

When to go
The earlier in the year you want to go, the further south you should head. Southern Spain and Portugal and – if you can get there – southern Italy can often be great in November, February and March… though April or May are the more realistic times to start touring. The less mountainous parts of Northern Europe can be fantastic in spring.

If you're planning on riding any high alpine routes, you have a more limited window. The highest passes normally open in early June and start closing at the end of October.

If going to France in July, check where the Tour de France will be. Not only will the roads it uses be closed on the day it passes through a region (potentially derailing your route) but also those roads will be busy with set-up/take-down for the race and thronged with amateur cyclists following the Tour for a few days either side.

August is normally best avoided, if possible, as not only is it the hottest time of year to be sitting at traffic lights or carrying bags into hotels while wearing bike kit but also much of Europe is on holiday, so the roads are at their busiest.

Generally, the best time to ride the high Alps is September or even early October. The weather is usually still glorious, and the roads are quieter and in good condition.

Bike insurance
Make sure you inform your insurer before making the trip. You don't need a green card, but some policies may offer only the legal minimum (third-party only) cover unless you declare the trip to the insurer. Breakdown insurance that includes repatriation is a good idea.

Health insurance
British travellers need the new Global Health Insurance Card but I would strongly recommend getting separate travel/medical cover (check any policy to make sure it covers riding motorcycles over 125cc). Make sure the policy includes repatriation cover to get you home.

To book or not to book?
That is the question. If you're confident, you can ride without a plan and at 3 or 4 p.m., use Booking.com to find a hotel somewhere two hours down the road. It gives flexibility and heightens the sense of exploring. To be certain of getting somewhere in the right place to ride the best roads, plan ahead and prebook – you'll often get a slightly better rate as well.

Motorway tolls
Some countries require a vignette (toll sticker). For Switzerland, this is a fairly expensive sticker, good for an entire year. It can be ordered online in advance of a trip. In Austria and Slovenia you can buy a 10-day tourist vignette (a sticker in Austria; in Slovenia it's electronic and your reg is entered into a database).

Crit'Air sticker
In France, bikes need a Crit'Air sticker to pass through some cities. It's cheap and shows you're considerate of local laws… but it takes about 8–10 days to arrive. Order it here: www.certificat-air.gouv.fr/en/

Bike prep
Before any touring holiday, make sure your bike is in good order – and particularly make sure you have more than enough life in your tyres for the planned journey. Nothing will derail it faster than having to find replacement rubber halfway round.

what to take

Documents
Make sure you have your original V5 registration and insurance certificate with you. Some people take copies as well – it's probably good practice but in Europe I've never needed them.

National identity
Bikes from Britain should now display a UK (not a GB) sticker.

Must-carry items
In France, every rider or pillion needs to have a hi-vis vest: not to be worn when riding, but to be worn when standing on the roadside. They also need CE gloves (NB: it's illegal to ride without gloves in France). You don't need to carry spare bulbs, a warning triangle or a fire extinguisher as you might in a car or motorhome. You don't need breathalysers (that law's been scrapped) or reflective stickers on your crash helmet (unless it was bought in France). In Spain, if you wear corrective lenses to ride, you are expected to have a spare set with you.

What to pack
Travel light. Shorts and flip-flops when you're off the bike. Take base layers and other clothing that can be rinsed/washed through in the evening and will be dry by the next morning. If you're on a well-prepped modern bike, you shouldn't need to carry spares. A puncture repair kit that you know how to use is a good idea.

Know your tech
Don't try to learn to use gadgets while you're on the road – you'll waste time and not get the best out of them. This is especially true if using a new sat nav or phone app like Scenic or Calimoto. Try them out on at least a few rides close to home, to get used to following their directions.

What to wear
Always, always have something waterproof – whether that's a textile suit or a set of waterproofs in the topbox. Better to carry them and not need them than have one wet afternoon soak you to the bone and spoil your trip.

If wearing a textile suit, it should have good venting. Despite the note of waterproof caution, you're more likely to get day after day of hot and sunny weather. If going somewhere seriously hot, consider a layer system: base layer, a windproof liner if it gets cold, an armoured mesh jacket, and waterproofs to keep you dry and add another windproof layer.

Final checklist
Don't overlook the basics when packing. Things I've been known to forget include:
- Sunglasses
- Sun cream
- Phone charger
- Power adaptor (top tip: I now take one adapter and a four-gang extension lead so I can charge phone, Bluetooth headset and GoPros from one power socket)
- Hayfever pills (or any meds).

Plus of course make sure you have your driving licence and passport with you before leaving the house…

riding advice

Riding on the right
Relax – it's no big deal. But. Take care when pulling away, especially from petrol stations… if you're going to head off on the wrong side of the road, that's when it's most likely to happen.

Priorité à droite
In France, if you see a yellow diamond with a black line through it as you come into a village, it means you have to give way to traffic from side roads. Yes, they can legally pull out on you.

Speed limits
There is normally a sign, when crossing a border, confirming the speed limits in the country you've entered. They do vary, especially for motorways and for country roads, so be very clear on the limit in the country you're visiting. Most of France has an 80 kph limit on single-track roads, but some areas are returning some roads to 90 kph: these will be signposted. Some areas of Germany and Austria now have lowered 70 kph limits. In Spain, limits are often lowered around junctions.

Village name signs indicate the start of 50 kph limits (which end with the sign where the name is crossed out). There are increasing numbers of 30 kph limits in urban areas (and some 40s or even 45s), so watch the signs carefully.

Large sections of German autobahns are derestricted, though some stretches have a 130 kph limit – and if there's a lot of traffic, there is an advisory 130 kph limit, so you could face a ticket if going faster on a crowded road. Note when crossing from Germany to Austria that the Austrian motorways are NOT derestricted…

Speeding
Most European countries have on-the-spot fines for speeding that increase quite rapidly. In several countries, the police can impound your bike and ban you on the spot if you're caught doing a spectacular speed (generally 50 kph over any speed limit). There are cameras on some open roads as well as in villages – and despite Brexit, it looks like fines will follow British bikers home.

Speed camera warnings
If using a sat nav, it should adapt to local laws: in some countries, it will show you where cameras are. In France you'll get a (subtle) warning that you're in a 'hazardous road section': somewhere in there is a speed camera.

riding advice

Noise limits

Increasing numbers of roads in Germany and Austria have 95 dB limits, with noise cameras to catch bikes with loud exhausts. There will be a sign at the start of these roads. If you have the bike's stock exhaust, its dB rating will be on the V5; if you have a replacement exhaust (especially without the baffles) chances are you'll be fined on those roads...

Motorway tolls

Some countries have toll motorways. In France, the tolls are paid at booths (contactless cards are the easiest way), while for other countries, the tolls may be paid in advance (see page 5).

Know your range

Be very clear on your bike's tank range (which may be lower when two-up and fully loaded). Fill up at the first opportunity after using two-thirds of it. If travelling in a group, always make sure all the bikes fill up at the same time, every time.

Make time for stops

You'll enjoy the riding more – and the whole holiday – if you're not tired. Having 5 minutes off the bike every 60–90 minutes will stop aches before they can start, and keep you feeling fresh.

Drink a lot

In this case, water – not just coffee. Getting dehydrated in hot climates or at altitude can lead to a lack of concentration, which leads to mistakes... and mistakes on a bike are A Bad Thing.

Don't take on too much

Europe's a big place. Don't try to pack too many miles into a day – especially on the final day of a tour, when you're likely to be most tired.

Be flexible

Even the best tour plan should be a guide, not a straitjacket. Don't sweat it if there's a road closure: just follow the diversion. If a road or place catches your eye, investigate it – it might turn out to be the highlight of the trip. Don't become a hostage to the schedule: always be ready to adapt it as you go.

Know where you are

If you think you might be lost, don't keep riding. Stop. Check a map, a phone, a sat nav – better still, ask someone. Even if you confirm that you are on track, that's good.

Keep a bit in hand

Don't ride flat-out on unknown roads. Besides a mechanical breakdown, the two things guaranteed to spoil your bike trip are crashing and getting stopped for speeding. Neither's worth the risk.

route locations

contents

Spain & Portugal

Las Palomas Pass, Spain (route 25, pages 68–9)

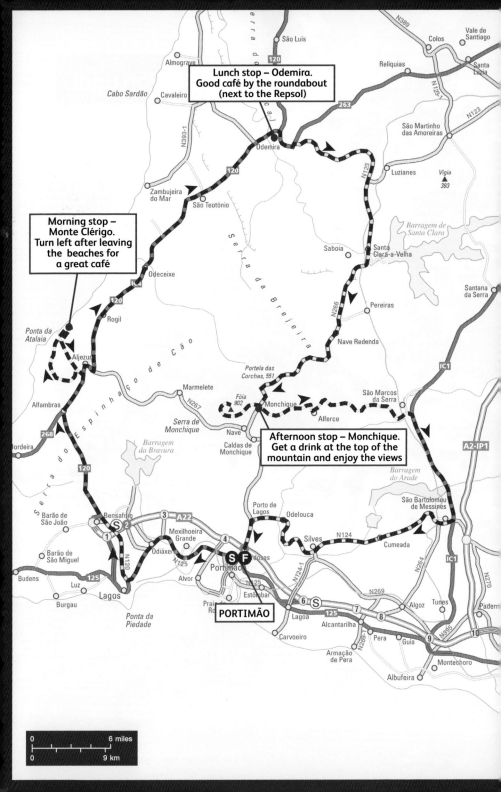

1 Portimão Classic

*The Algarve has a fabulous climate –
even when the rest of Europe is
shivering in winter, it's often great
for riding down here. In fact, it's
often too hot to ride comfortably in
high summer (July and August). But
for an early spring or late autumn
destination, it's unbeatable – perfect
for a fly-ride break. This route heads
from Portimão to the west coast,
then cuts inland and climbs to the*

FROM	**Portimão**
DISTANCE	**165 miles**
ALLOW	**5 hours**

*top of the Serra de Monchique before
returning to the coast. I first came
here on the launch of the KTM 990
SM-T and some of the roads on this
route were used on that ride.*

Route
- Leave Portimão on the N125 to Lagos.
- In Lagos, turn right on the N120 to Bensafrim.
- Go straight over the roundabout in Bensafrim to stay on the N120.
- After 12 miles, turn left to Monte Clérigo.
- At the T-junction, turn left to Vale de Telha.
- Follow the road round in a loop past the beaches, until you return to the T-junction. Go back to the N120 and turn left to continue towards Lisbon.
- In Odemira, turn right at the roundabout to go into the town centre.
- About 1½ miles outside town, turn right on the N123 to Luzianes.
- Keep going straight in Luzianes as the road becomes the N266 to Portimão.
- At the roundabout in Monchique, take the second exit to Fóia and the 'Estação Radar'.
- Follow this twisting, narrow road up to the summit of Fóia for the views, then return to Monchique.

- Turn right to continue towards Portimão.
- At the next roundabout (by the petrol station), turn left on the N267 to Alferce.
- At the IC1, turn right to Portimão.
- Take the exit signed for the A2 motorway and the N124.
- Follow the N124 to Silves – and follow it all the way back to Portimão.

Fly-ride it
You don't have to ride all the way
to the Algarve (unless you want to).
You can fly to Faro and hire a bike –
several companies operate down here,
including Hertz. www.hertzride.com

Racing at Portimão
World Superbikes regularly race at
Portimão and MotoGP first visited the
circuit in 2020. For info and tickets see
www.autodromoalgarve.com.

Fóia, Monchique
At 902 m, Fóia is the tallest peak in
the Monchique range and the highest
point in southern Portugal. No wonder
the view's great.

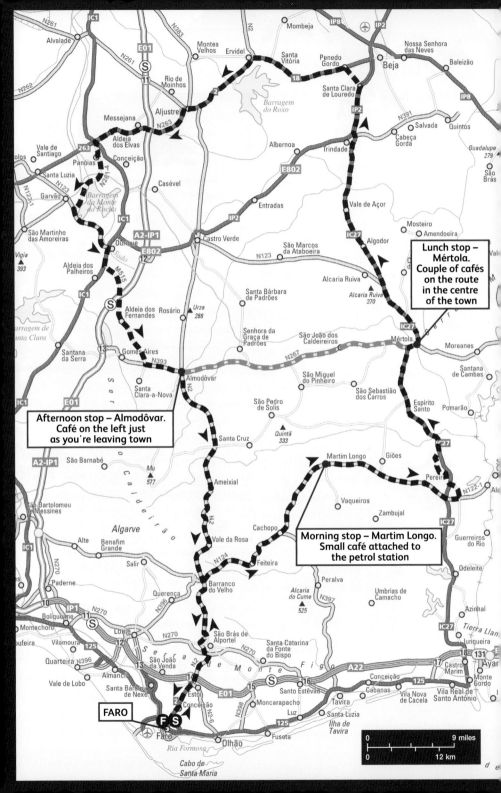

Lunch stop –
Mértola.
Couple of cafés
on the route
in the centre
of the town

Afternoon stop – Almodôvar.
Café on the left just
as you're leaving town

Morning stop – Martim Longo.
Small café attached to
the petrol station

FARO

2 Faro's Riches

*When my friend Mark first considered
moving to Faro, he flew out and hired
a bike. I was in the north of Scotland
when he sent me a message, asking
which road to ride. I couldn't give him
one answer. I had to give him two:
the N124 and the N2. Both roads are
on this balloon route, which uses a
single road (the N2) to head out from
the start and back to the finish. It's
a full day's ride on smooth tarmac,
with some relaxing straight stretches
separating some super-twisty roads.*

FROM	Faro
DISTANCE	215 miles
ALLOW	5½ hours

*The route is easily shortened, by
taking the N267 to Almodôvar
(turning left outside Mértola). If you
can't ride all the way down there, do
what Mark did: fly into Faro and hire
a bike. It's a great way to get some
winter sun or to add some bike fun to
a family Algarve holiday.*

Route

- Leave Faro on the N2, heading north.
- Stick with the N2 towards Almodôvar through São Brás de Alportel.
- After 8 miles, turn right on the N124 to Alcoutim.
- Go straight over the IC27 and turn left at the roundabout on the N122 to Beja.
- At the IC27, turn left to Mértola.
- Go through Mértola, following the IC27 towards Beja.
- Join the IP2 to Beja.
- After 4½ miles, take exit 42 for Santa Clara.
- Turn left at the roundabout for Gordo.

- At the traffic lights, turn left on the N18 to Ervidel.
- In Ervidel, turn left on the N2 to Aljustrel.
- Go through Aljustrel town centre and pick up the N263 to Messejana.
- Go straight over the IC1 and take the first left for the N261-4 to Garvão.
- At the N123, turn left to Ourique.
- In Ourique, join the IC1 to Faro.
- After a mile, turn left on the M515 to Almodôvar.
- Turn left on the N393 to Almodôvar.
- In Almodôvar, turn right on the N2 to return to Faro.

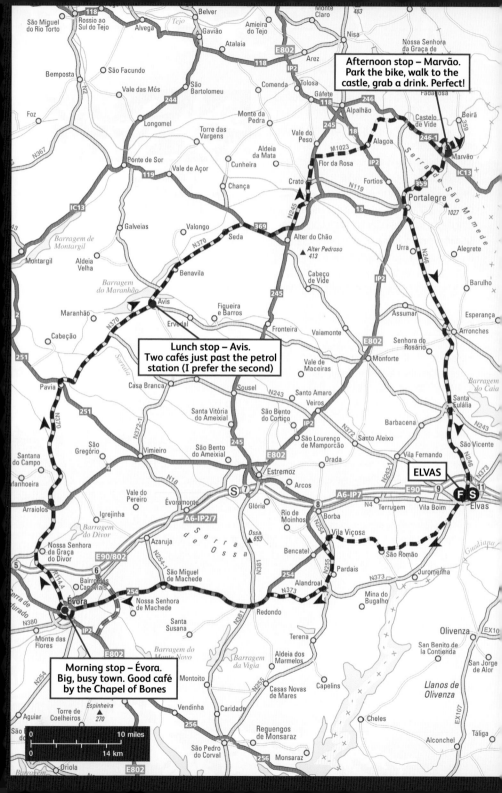

Afternoon stop – Marvão. Park the bike, walk to the castle, grab a drink. Perfect!

Lunch stop – Avis. Two cafés just past the petrol station (I prefer the second)

ELVAS

Morning stop – Évora. Big, busy town. Good café by the Chapel of Bones

3 Elvas Greatest Hits

You can see the fingerprints of history all over this corner of Portugal, hard by the Spanish border. But as well as castles and defensive cities, like the star-shaped citadel of Elvas, there's also the majestic ducal palace in Vila Viçosa to visit, and the eerie but fascinating Chapel of Bones in Évora. There's plenty of good riding, too – heading across the plains to the hills

FROM	Elvas
DISTANCE	200 miles
ALLOW	5½ hours

on the border and one of Portugal's most famous scenic villages. Marvão is perched high on a hill, girdled by battlements, with amazing views.

Route

- Leave Elvas on the N373 to Alandroal.
- Don't miss the right turn for the minor road to São Romão, two miles from the last roundabout in Elvas. Take this road all the way to Vila Viçosa.
- Cross Vila Viçosa and turn left on the N255 to Alandroal.
- After 5 miles (as the road bypasses Alandroal), turn right on the N373 to Redondo and Évora.
- At the N254, turn left to Redondo and take it all the way into Évora.
- Leave Évora on the R144.4 to Arraiolos. This becomes the N370. Stay with it through Arraiolos to Pavia.
- In Pavia, turn left on the N251. After 300 m, turn right on the N370 to Avis.
- Turn left in Avis on the N243 then, after crossing the bridge, turn right on the N370 to Seda.
- At the N369 junction, turn right to Portalegre and Alter do Chão. This road then becomes the IC13.
- After 6 miles, take the exit for Alter. At the bottom of the sliproad, turn left on the N245 to Crato.
- Go straight through Crato and pick up the M1023 to Alagoa.
- Turn left when this road hits a T-junction on the far side of Alagoa, then turn right on the N246 to Portalegre. Keep going straight as it becomes the N246-1 to Castelo de Vide.
- Turn left at the N359 T-junction, then turn left at the roundabout to take the N359 to Beirã and Marvão.
- Don't miss the right turn, 2 miles later, to go into Marvão itself.
- Backtrack to the N359 and take it all the way to Portalegre.
- From Portalegre take the N246 to Elvas.

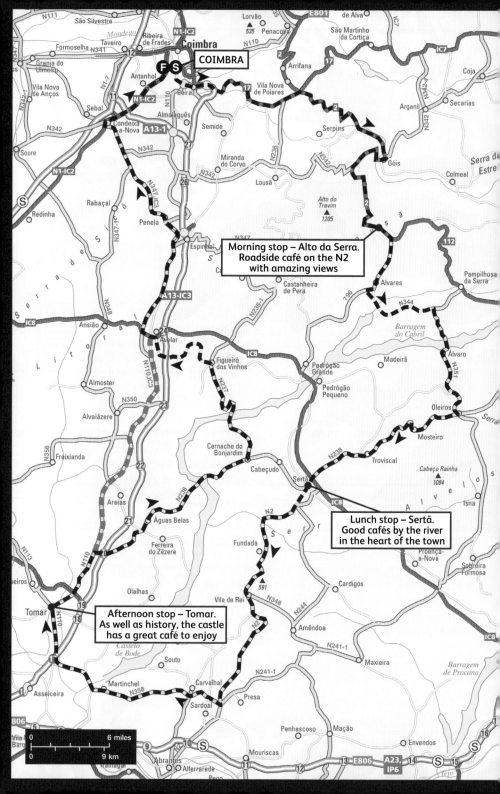

COIMBRA

Morning stop – Alto da Serra.
Roadside café on the N2
with amazing views

Lunch stop – Sertã.
Good cafés by the river
in the heart of the town

Afternoon stop – Tomar.
As well as history, the castle
has a great café to enjoy

4 Coimbra and Tomar

I'm a sucker for a good castle, especially one with a story attached – and they don't come much better than the Convent of Christ in Tomar, once the stronghold of the Knights Templar. This route starts from the arguably even more fascinating and charming small city of Coimbra, which for several hundred years was the capital of Portugal. In between, there

FROM	Coimbra
DISTANCE	195 miles
ALLOW	6 hours

are miles of the amazing flowing roads that make the country such a paradise for motorcyclists (but you can cut the route short if you spend too long exploring Tomar).

Route

- Leave Coimbra on the N17 towards Lousã and Vila Nova de Poiares.
- At the N2 roundabout turn right to Góis.
- Turn left at the roundabout 2½ miles after Góis to stay on the N2, towards Pampilhosa da Serra and Castelo Branco.
- Don't miss the right turn 8 miles later (a mile after the Alto da Serra café) to stay on the N2 to Alvares.
- Go through Alvares and, about half a mile after the village, turn left on the N344 to Pampilhosa da Serra and Oleiros.
- After 8½ miles, turn right on the N351 to Oleiros.
- At the N238 T-junction turn right to Sertã.
- Cross Sertã and rejoin the N2 towards Abrantes and Vila de Rei.
- After 22 miles, at a traffic-light-controlled junction, turn right on the N358 to Carvalhal.
- Turn right at the T-junction after Martinchel to stay on the N358 to Tomar.

- At the A13 roundabout, go straight over on the N110 to Tomar.
- Leave Tomar on the N110 to Coimbra.
- *Short of time? If you spent too long looking around Tomar, pick up the IC3 (or if you have the electronic toll tag, the A13) to get back to Coimbra quickly.*
- For the full route go straight ahead on the N238 to Alviobeira and Sertã.
- In Cernache do Bonjardim, turn left on the N237 to Coimbra and Figueiró dos Vinhos.
- Stick with the N237 through the centre of Figueiró dos Vinhos.
- Don't miss the left turn – a mile outside Figueiró – to stay on the N237 to Aldeia de Ana de Aviz and Avelar.
- On the edge of Avelar, turn left on the IC8 for one junction, then take the IC3 to Coimbra and Penela.
- At Condeixa a Nova, join the IC2 to return to Coimbra.

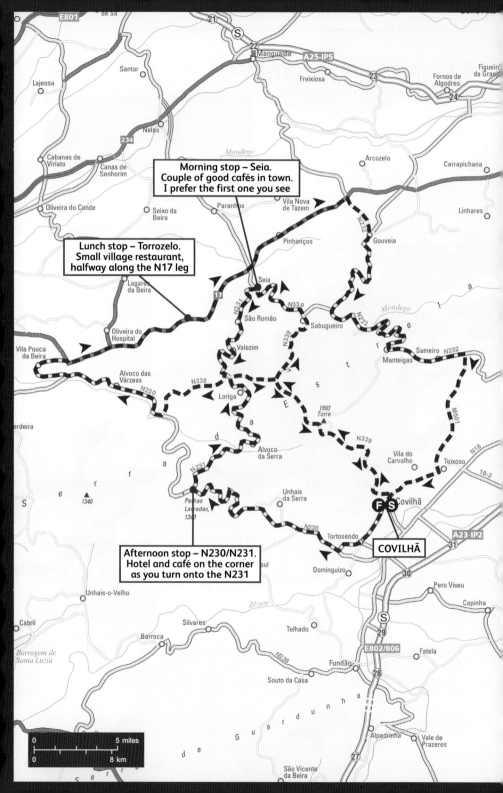

Morning stop – Seia.
Couple of good cafés in town.
I prefer the first one you see

Lunch stop – Torrozelo.
Small village restaurant,
halfway along the N17 leg

Afternoon stop – N230/N231.
Hotel and café on the corner
as you turn onto the N231

5 The Portuguese Stelvio

I first came to Portugal's Serra da Estrela mountains chasing rumours of a single road: the one known as the Portuguese Stelvio. While I love the challenging Stelvio Pass, which is the highest in Italy, could these far-lower mountains really have a route to match it? The road I discovered here turned out to be quite different but every bit as brilliant, in its own way... and far quieter than the often-busy Stelvio. I've been back several times and have spent a long time trying to

FROM	Covilhã
DISTANCE	195 miles
ALLOW	6 hours

perfect this route. The heart of it is the N339, the famed Portuguese Stelvio. I still can't decide whether it's best when ridden from Covilhã or towards it... so it's both the first and the last road on this full day's ride which means you get to enjoy it in both directions.

Route
- From Covilhã, take the N339 to the Serra da Estrela and Torre.
- In Seia, turn left (to the centre) and take the N231 to São Romão.
- 7 miles after São Romão, turn right on the N338 to Vide (the turn before the roundabout; though you can take the M518 from the roundabout to Vide as well).
- In Vide, turn right on the N230 to Coimbra.
- At the lights in Nogueira do Cravo, turn right on the N17 towards Oliveira do Hospital.
- Stick with the N17 for 20 miles (go right then left to stay on the N17 when it meets the N231).
- At the N232, turn right to Gouveia and stay with it through Manteigas.
- Don't miss the right turn, 5 miles after leaving Manteigas, for the M501 to Teixoso.
- At the N18, turn right to bypass Covilhã.
- After 6 miles, turn right at the roundabout, towards Covilhã and follow signs for the hospital.
- At the roundabout with the fountains, pick up the N230 to Coimbra.
- After 20 miles, turn right on the N231 to Seia.
- At the next roundabout, turn right to climb up into the Serra da Estrela again.
- At the N339, turn right to return to Covilhã and complete the loop.

Torre
Portugal's highest mountain is in the Serra da Estrela. You can ride right up to the summit, which has an observatory and a café... how civilized!

Senhora do Boa Estrela
Just down from the observatory, with a large parking area off the N339, is a shrine with a life-size madonna carved into the rocks.

Toy Museum, Seia
A compact museum offering an insight into what it would have been like growing up in Portugal in years gone by, with a huge collection of old toys.

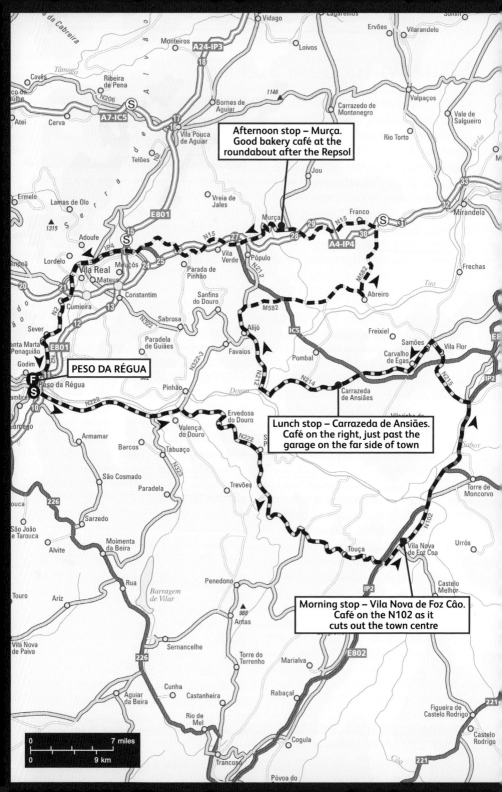

Afternoon stop – Murça.
Good bakery café at the
roundabout after the Repsol

PESO DA RÉGUA

Lunch stop – Carrazeda de Ansiães.
Café on the right, just past the
garage on the far side of town

Morning stop – Vila Nova de Foz Côa.
Café on the N102 as it
cuts out the town centre

6 Port Country

As with the Portuguese Stelvio (route 5), my first trip to the port-growing Douro Valley was to find a road with a big reputation. Scientists working for a car hire company had calculated that the best driving road in Europe was the N222 from Peso da Régua to Pinhão. I had to see it. Frankly, I was underwhelmed. Oh, it is pretty enough, but it's flat and mostly straight… Whereas the next stretch of the road is hilly, packed with brilliant bends and wonderful views across

FROM	Peso da Régua
DISTANCE	180 miles
ALLOW	5½ hours

the terraced slopes. This route warms up with that basic bit of the N222, but builds up to the best roads in the region for a full day on some of the quietest, twistiest tarmac in Portugal. Solo, two-up or in a group, it's a fantastic ride.

Route

- From Peso da Régua, take the N2 bridge across the River Douro.
- Turn right on the N222 towards Pinhão and São João da Pesqueira.
- At the IP2 roundabout, go straight over on the N102 to Vila Nova de Foz Côa.
- At the next roundabout, go straight over on the IP2 towards Bragança.
- After 11 miles – as soon as it starts to become a dual carriageway – take the exit for the N102 and N215 (J9) to Junqueira.
- Turn left at the roundabout (under the dual carriageway).
- Don't miss the left turn for the N215 to Vila Flor.
- Go straight through Vila Flor and at the roundabout (just after the short dual carriageway and the garage), turn left on the N214 to Carrazeda de Ansiães.
- At the IC5 roundabout, carry straight on, along the N214 to Carrazeda de Ansiães.
- At the T-junction, turn right towards Tua and Alijó on the N212.
- Turn right in Alijó to stay on the N212.
- Don't miss the right turn 3 miles later for Carlão.
- Go straight over the roundabout, to Chã.
- In Chã, turn right (by the café) to Sobreira on the M582.
- At the N314 turn left towards Abreiro.
- After 5 miles, turn left on the M582 to Mirandela.
- At the N15, turn left to Franco.
- Stick with the N15 for 30 miles, as it runs parallel to – and criss-crosses – the A4.
- At Vila Real, join the IP4 towards Porto. This is just to bypass the town.
- Leave the IP4 at J24 and pick up the N2 to Peso da Régua.
- Stay on the N2 to complete the loop.

Port tasting

The slopes around the Douro are terraced and planted with vines, for producing port. Take a day off the bike to enjoy a tasting at one of the vineyards.

7 Bragança Circuit

My good friend John Cundiff of Alpine TT had been bringing tour groups to Northern Spain and Portugal for years, so kept telling me how good the roads were – especially the N103 from Bragança to Chaves in Northern Portugal. I knew I could trust John's recommendations, but I was still blown away when I rode it. Then I found the N206 – broadly parallel and just as good... Never mind doubling

FROM	Bragança
DISTANCE	185 miles
ALLOW	5½ hours

the road numbers, combining these two roads into a one-day ride doubles the fun: miles of broad, smooth, seriously twisty roads with fabulous surfaces and virtually no traffic. Epic!

Route

- Leave Bragança on the N103 to Chaves.
- Follow the N103 through Chaves, following signs for Braga and the A24.

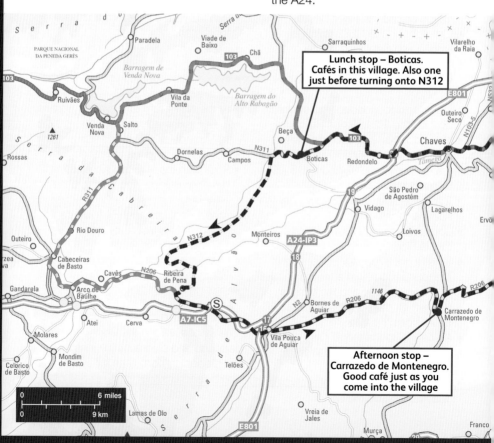

Lunch stop – Boticas. Cafés in this village. Also one just before turning onto N312

Afternoon stop – Carrazedo de Montenegro. Good café just as you come into the village

- Don't get on the motorway: carry on along the N103.
- In Sapiãos, turn left towards Boticas on the N312.
- In Boticas, turn right towards Cabeceiras on the R311.
- 3 miles later, turn left at the roundabout on the N312 to Ribeira de Pena.
- Go through Ribeira de Pena and turn left on the N206 towards Vila Real and the motorways.
- At the A7 / A24 roundabout, don't get on the motorway: go straight across to stick with the N206.
- Cross Vila Pouca de Aguiar following signs for Valpaços and the Roman mines ('Minas Romanas', on a brown sign) as the road becomes the R206.

- This road (which becomes the N206 again in Torre de Dona Chama) will take you all the way back to Bragança.

Want more?

This route is easily extended, for high-mile riders wanting a longer day.
- Rather than turning in Sapiãos, stay on the N103 for another 29 miles.
- Coming into Venda Nova, turn left towards Salto on the R311-1.
- In Cabeceiras de Basto, pick up the N205 towards the motorway.
- After 2 miles, join the N206 that leads to Ribeira de Pena and Bela Vista.

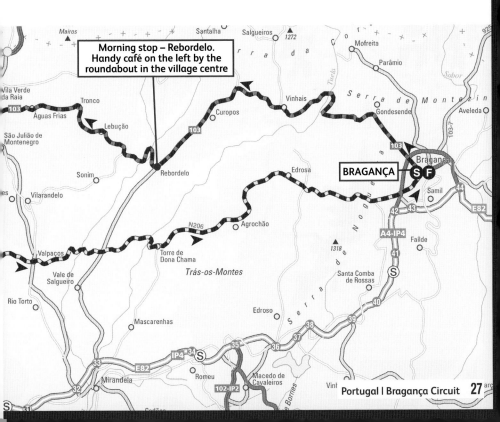

Morning stop – Rebordelo.
Handy café on the left by the roundabout in the village centre

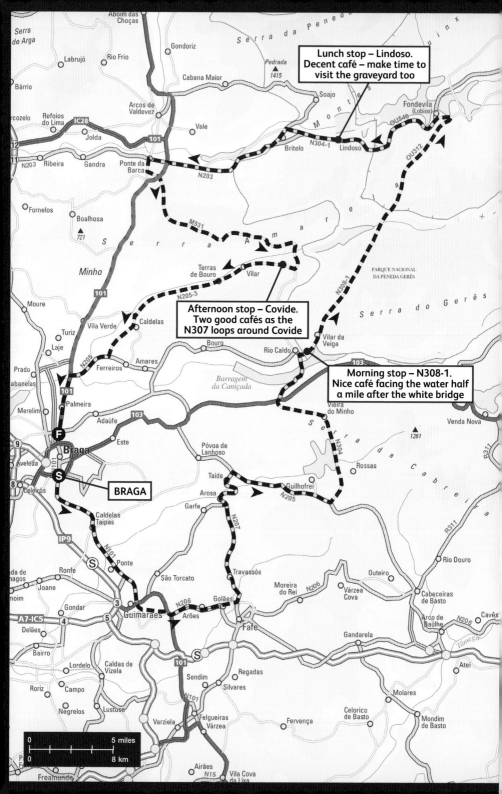

8 Gerês and Guimarães

There's a wild, untamed beauty to the Gerês National Park in northwest Portugal, by the Spanish border. The riding is equally beautiful: miles of quiet roads in an epic landscape. This route from the compact city of Braga heads out to historic Guimarães, dominated by an enormous

FROM	Braga
DISTANCE	145 miles
ALLOW	5½ hours

10th-century castle; if you spend too long exploring that, you may need to short-cut the afternoon ride.

Route

- Leave Braga on the N101 to Guimarães.
- Look around Guimarães, then rejoin the N101 to Fafe. This road becomes the N206.
- After about 6 miles, take the exit for Fafe and the N207 / R207.
- At the bottom of the slip road, turn left to Póvoa de Lanhoso on the N207.
- Don't miss the right turn, on the way out of Porto de Ave, for the N205 to Cabeceiras de Basto. This surface may be patchy in places.
- After 8½ miles, turn left (by a petrol station) on the N304 to Vieira do Minho.
- At the N103 roundabout, turn right to Chaves, then after 500 m turn left to continue on the N304 towards Rio Caldo and the Gerês National Park.
- Go over the bridge and turn right on the N308-1 to Spain. This becomes the OU312 when it crosses the border.
- Don't miss the left turn in the centre of Lobios to stay on the OU312 towards Ourense, also signed for Portugal.

- At the T-junction turn left on the OU540 to Portugal. It's called the N304-1 when it crosses the border, then becomes the N203.
- *Short of time? Take the N101 back to Braga from Ponte da Barca.*
- Go into the centre of Ponte da Barca and pick up the M531 – it's not well signed, so look for the brown sign to Castelo da Nóbrega. This road becomes the M548.
- Don't miss the left turn as you leave Azias Santa Maria (next to a bar) for the minor road to Valdreu, which is signed for 'Santuário Sto António'.
- When this road meets the CM1149, turn left to Brufe.
- At the M531 T-junction, turn left to go into Brufe. The road becomes the N307 when it crosses the dam.
- When the road forks, bear right towards Braga and Covide.
- In Terras de Bouro, turn right at the roundabout on the N205-3 to Braga.
- At the N205 roundabout, turn right to Vila Verde and Braga.
- At the N101 roundabout, turn left to return to Braga.

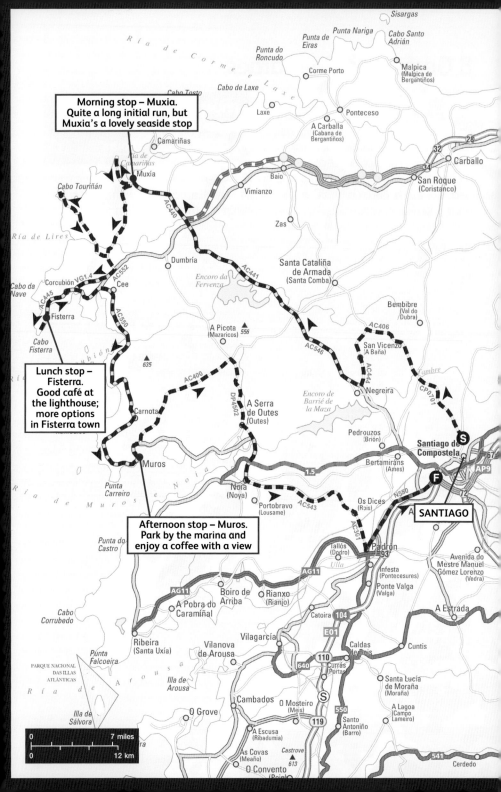

Morning stop – Muxia.
Quite a long initial run, but
Muxia's a lovely seaside stop

Lunch stop –
Fisterra.
Good café at
the lighthouse;
more options
in Fisterra town

Afternoon stop – Muros.
Park by the marina and
enjoy a coffee with a view

SANTIAGO

9 Finisterre and Friends

This route around the pilgrimage city of Santiago de Compostela heads out to Muxia, one of the most charming towns on the Costa Muerte (yes, Coast of Death...). From there it loops out to the lighthouse on Cape Touriñán, before making its way to Cape Finisterre – once thought to be the most westerly point of the European mainland, though in fact Touriñán is more westerly… and Cabo de Roca in Portugal trumps them both.

FROM	Santiago de Compostela
DISTANCE	180 miles
ALLOW	6 hours

Route

- Leave Santiago de Compostela on the CP0701 towards Bembibre.
- Go through Portomouro and look for the left turn for the AC406 to Santa Comba.
- Don't miss the left turn after 6½ miles for the AC444 to A Baña.
- At the roundabout on the edge of Negreira, turn right on the A544 and then pick up the AC546 to A Pereira and Muxia.
- Keep going straight to Muxia, as the road becomes the AC441 and then the AC440.
- From Muxia, backtrack to Os Muiños and pick up the DP2303 to Cee.
- Don't miss the right turn in Bernum for the road to Cape Touriñan.
- After visiting the cape, backtrack to Bernum and turn right to go into Cee.
- Turn right on the AC552 then go right at the roundabout on the VG1.4 to Fisterra.
- Turn right on the AC445 and follow it all the way to the lighthouse at Cape Finisterre (Cabo Fisterra).

- Backtrack along the AC445 to Cee and pick up the AC550 that runs along the coast.
- Go through Muros and pick up the AC400 to Santa Comba.
- At the roundabout in Pino do Val, turn right to Serra de Outes on the CP3404 (which becomes the DP4502).
- In Serra de Outes pick up the AC550.
- *Short of time? Cross the river and jump on the main CG1.5 back to Santiago.*
- For the full route, go over the CG1.5 roundabout and take the left turn to Bertamirans and Santiago on the AC543.
- After about 8 miles, turn right at the roundabout on the AC301 to Rois.
- Don't miss the left turn (at the roundabout under the bridge) to stay on the AC301 to Padrón.
- On the outskirts of Padrón, turn left on the N550 to return to Santiago.

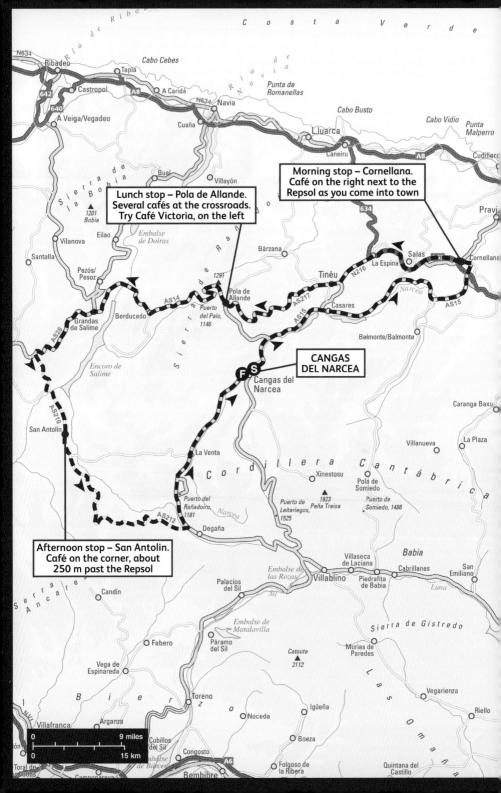

10 Asturias Ways

The north coast of Spain is chock full of spectacular riding. This route has taken me some time to refine, because on my first few trips here I kept basing myself in the quaint coastal town of Lluarca. Which is lovely... but moving inland to the oldest town in Asturias, Cangas del Narcea, is what finally brought it all together. Riders from northern Europe – particularly Belgium, Britain, Germany and Holland – may find these roads unnaturally empty, especially as they're so good. It's hard to believe they're not packed

FROM	Cangas del Narcea
DISTANCE	185 miles
ALLOW	5½ hours

with bikers. You find yourself asking: 'Where is everyone?' Which is why I'm encouraging people to visit. When I sent my friend Andy T. along some of these roads, he came back smiling. 'That AS14 might just be the best road ever,' he said. See for yourself on this route.

Route
- Leave Cangas del Narcea on the AS15 towards Soto de la Barca.
- At Cornellana, turn left on the N634 to La Espina. This runs parallel to the motorway (don't get on that – stick with the N634).
- In La Espina, turn left on the N216 signed for Cangas del Narcea.
- In Tinéu, go straight ahead on the AS217 to Pola de Allande.
- In Pola de Allande, go straight over the crossroads, on the AS14, towards Grandas and Puerto del Palo (Palo Pass).
- In Grandas de Salime, turn left by the church on the AS28 towards Lugo.
- After 9 miles, coming into O Acevo, turn left on the LU-P3601 to Negueira de Muñiz. Take care when – for about 2 miles – it becomes a single-lane road.

- Just follow the road (which changes number several times: from LU702 to AS210, AS348 and then AS212).
- At the AS15 T-junction, turn left to return to Cangas del Narcea.

Cider
The local tipple here in Asturias is a flat cider. Locals pour it from above their heads to add bubbles... Try it!

Pilgrims
Parts of this route track the Camino, the pilgrimage route to Santiago. You'll see signs and probably pilgrims.

Waterproofs
This is the greenest bit of Spain and even though summer is normally hot and dry, always pack waterproofs... just in case.

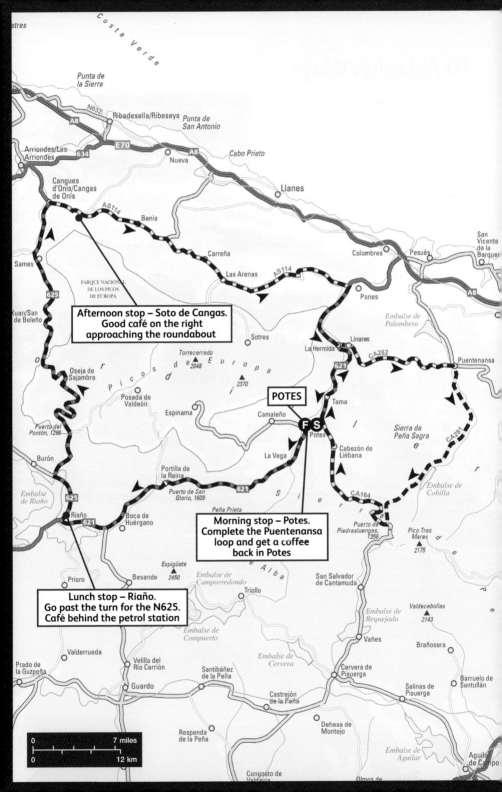

11 Picos Hourglass

The Picos de Europa mountains are super-scenic, full of great roads and, especially compared with the Alps, there's hardly anyone here. It's a great place to ride a bike. Potes is really easy to reach from Santander, so this tends to be the area where you see most British bikers. I first came here with my friend John Cundiff on an Alpine TT tour and have been visiting regularly ever since. The heart of this route is one of the classic European touring rides, the Potes triangle: over the San Glorio Pass to Riaño (stopping for a picture at the Mirador), then over the Pontón Pass

FROM	Potes
DISTANCE	190 miles
ALLOW	5½ hours

to Cangas de Onís, along the epic AS114 to Panes and back to Potes through the La Hermida Gorge. It has everything: the views, the bends, the perfect tarmac... but for me, it's a bit short for a day's ride. For a fuller trip, I warm up with a second loop around Potes, heading to Puentenansa and the Cohilla Reservoir – which means riding the La Hermida gorge once in each direction.

Route

- Leave Potes on the N621 towards Unquera and Panes. This will lead you into the La Hermida Gorge.
- In La Hermida village, turn right on the CA282 to Linares.
- In Puentenansa, turn right on the CA281 to Cosío.
- At the CA184, turn right to Valdepradó.
- Back in Potes, turn left at the roundabout on the N621 to Riaño.
- Don't miss the left turn – half a mile later, in the town centre – to stay on the N621 over San Glorio Pass.
- Approaching Riaño, turn right on the N625 to Cangas de Onís. This will take you over the Pontón Pass and through the Los Beyos Gorge.
- In Cangas de Onís, turn right on the AS114 to Panes.
- In Panes, turn right on the N621 to return, through the La Hermida Gorge, to Potes.

Want it shorter? Simply head directly from Potes to Riaño on the N621, lopping off the Puentenansa loop, for a short but rewarding day's ride.

Covadonga
Just outside Cangas de Onís is the spectacular Covadonga Basilica, with its chapel built into a cave. Allow an hour for a visit.

Fuente Dé
Head into the mountains from Potes and you'll find Fuente Dé: a huge cirque, with a cable car to carry you to the top of the peak... pack a head for heights.

Seaside detours
The coast is very close to the Picos, with several lovely fishing towns to visit. Take the N625 from Cangas de Onís, and then the AS260 at Arriondas to Mirador del Fitu.

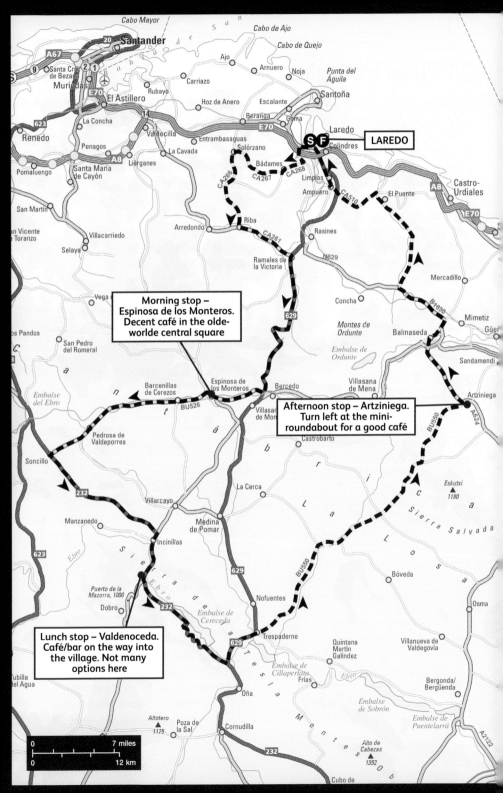

LAREDO

Morning stop – Espinosa de los Monteros. Decent café in the olde-worlde central square

Afternoon stop – Artziniega. Turn left at the mini-roundabout for a good café

Lunch stop – Valdenoceda. Café/bar on the way into the village. Not many options here

12 Cantabrian Classic

Laredo is a resort town halfway between Santander and Bilbao – just over half an hour from both, which is handy if your ferry arrives in the evening. It's a proper seaside holiday town if you want a day on the beach, but it's also at the foot of the spectacular Cantabrian Mountains. There are roads here to suit all kinds of riders, so it's a mystery to me that so few come here: most seem to

FROM	Laredo
DISTANCE	175 miles
ALLOW	5½ hours

head straight past, hurrying off to the famous bits of the Picos or going east to the Pyrenees. They don't know what they're missing, as the riding here is some of the finest in Spain.

Route

- Leave Laredo on the N634 to Colindres.
- Turn right in Colindres to stay on the N634 towards Treto.
- In Treto, turn left on the CA268 to Bádames.
- In Bádames, turn right on the CA267 to Secadura.
- In Solórzano, turn left on the CA266 to Matienzo.
- At the T-junction in Riba, turn left on the CA261 to Lastres.
- In Ramales de la Victoria, turn right on the N629 to Burgos.
- In Bercedo, turn right on the BU526 to Espinosa de los Monteros.
- Don't miss the left turn in Espinosa to stay on the BU526 towards Reinosa.
- In Soncillo, turn left on the N232 to Logroño.
- After 30 miles, turn left on the N629 to Trespaderne and Santander.
- In Trespaderne, turn right on to the BU550 to Artziniega (also spelt Arceniega on signs).
- In Artziniega, pick up the A624 to Balmaseda.
- At Balmaseda, join the BI636 towards Bilbao for one junction (to bypass the town centre) then take the BI630 towards Ramales.
- In Valle de Villaverde, turn right on the CA153 to Trucios.
- At the roundabout in El Puente, turn left on the CA510 to Ampuero.
- In Ampuero, join the N629 to return to Laredo.

Getting your bike to Spain and Portugal

Ferries sail to Bilbao and Santander from the UK, taking 24–36 hours, depending on the crossing you select. When boarding the ship, follow the directions of the crew to park in the right place.

All you have to do is leave the bike in gear and take everything you'll need for your time on board. The crew have all the necessary straps and will secure your bike for you.

When planning your trip, remember to get to the port in time to check in before the sailing time… and accept that you may not disembark and get through passport control for an hour after the scheduled docking time. Also be prepared for the fact that, sometimes, adverse sea conditions may delay arrival or departure times. However, sailing to these north coast ports makes Spain and Portugal easy to reach on great roads…

Of course, it is also possible to ride down to the Iberian Peninsula from anywhere in Europe. However, getting to Spain means crossing France which, not to put too fine a point on it, is a large country. Traversing it usually means either two days with a lot of toll motorway, or several days on better roads. If you have only a week or ten days for your tour, riding down can mean spending more time in France than Spain, and getting to Portugal probably isn't realistic.

N621 in the Picos de Europa (route 11, pages 34–5)

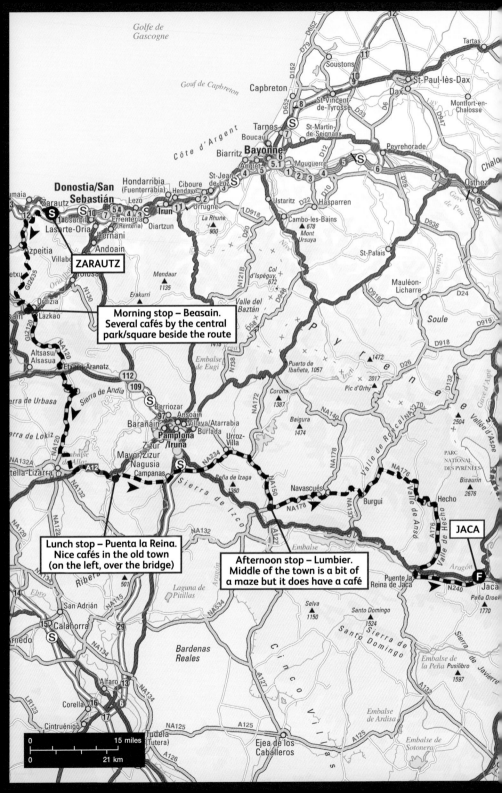

ZARAUTZ

Morning stop – Beasain.
Several cafés by the central
park/square beside the route

JACA

Lunch stop – Puenta la Reina.
Nice cafés in the old town
(on the left, over the bridge)

Afternoon stop – Lumbier.
Middle of the town is a bit of
a maze but it does have a café

13 Coast to Coast (day one)

This three-day trip is all about one of the most famous roads in Spain, the N260. It runs along the foot of the Pyrenees and has introduced countless riders to the joys of mountain riding. My route starts on the Atlantic coast in the Basque resort of Zarautz – handy for Santander

FROM	Zarautz
TO	Jaca
DISTANCE	190 miles
ALLOW	5½ hours

and Bilbao – to deliver the maximum amount of great riding.

Route

- Leave Zarautz on the GI2633 to Aizarnazabal.
- In Iraeta, turn left on the GI631 to Zestoa.
- In Azpetia, pick up the GI2635 to Urrestilla. It isn't well signed.
- Go through Beasain and pick up the GI2120 to Lazkao. This becomes the NA120.
- Stick with the NA120 through Etxarri-Aranatz, under the motorway, to Lizarraga.
- Don't miss the left turn 20 miles later for the NA700 to Murugarren.
- In 750 m, go straight on (a right turn as the road goes left) on the NA7008 to Zurucuáin.
- At the NA1110, turn left to Pamplona.
- Jump on the A12 motorway for five junctions/8 miles, leaving at J24, then take the NA1110 through to Puenta la Reina.
- Turn right on the NA6064 to Obanos.
- At the NA601, turn right to Campanas.
- When the NA601 meets the A15 don't get on the motorway: take the parallel N121 towards Campanas.

- Don't miss the right turn – just after Campanas – for the NA234 to Tiebas and Urroz. Go straight over the A21 motorway on the NA234.
- In Urroz-Villa, turn right on the NA150 to Aoiz.
- In Lumbier, turn sharply left on the NA178 to Navascués.
- After 6 miles, turn right following the sign for Foz de Arabayun – a good photo point to make people on social media jealous.
- Carry on to rejoin the NA178 at the bottom of the hill.
- In Navascués, turn right on the NA214 to Burgui.
- In Burgui, go straight over the roundabout on the NA137 to Isaba.
- Don't miss the right turn 5 miles later for the NA176 to Garde.
- Stick with the NA176 all the way through Ansó, to Hecho. One stretch of this road was quite rough last time I rode it; the rest was amazing… so take it steady and bear with the rougher bit.
- In Puente la Reina de Jaca you have a choice: you could join the motorway to Jaca for 10 miles or ride past it and turn left on the N240 and take that to Jaca instead.

13 Coast to Coast (day two)

This day starts with a short but dull stretch on the plain from Jaca to Sabiñánigo: don't be fooled by it. The riding clicks up a gear as the road heads into the mountains – and from Biescas on, it's fantastic all the way. This is the stuff that makes the N260 such a popular road. For me, what's so great about the N260 is that it's surrounded by loads of equally brilliant roads. This means you can stop a few nights at any of the towns along this central stretch

FROM	Jaca
TO	La Seu d'Urgell
DISTANCE	185 miles
ALLOW	5 hours

and have a fabulous few days' riding. I've included one of my favourite Pyrenean roads as an alternative, swapping a section of the N260 for the climb to the French border, then back over Bonaigua Pass.

Route

- Leave Jaca heading east on the N330. You have a parallel motorway option if you want it – and it's only 6½ miles.

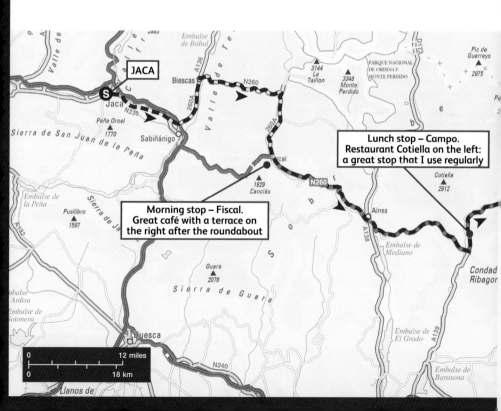

Morning stop – Fiscal.
Great café with a terrace on the right after the roundabout

Lunch stop – Campo.
Restaurant Cotiella on the left: a great stop that I use regularly

- At the roundabout, go straight (that's if you took the N330; turn left if you took the motorway) on the N330 to Huesca, also signed for the N260 to Biescas.
- After a mile and a half, take the slip road for the N260 to Biescas.
- Don't miss the right turn in Biescas by the garage to stay on the N260 (or you'll end up in France).
- It's a good uninterrupted run on the N260 for the next 60 miles.
- At the N230 T-junction, turn right to El Pont de Suert.
- Turn left after the garage in El Pont de Suert on the N260 to La Pobla de Segur.
- At the roundabout in La Pobla de Segur, turn left for the town centre and the N260.

- In Sort, turn right in the town centre to stay on the N260 to La Seu d'Urgell.

Want more?

This is quite a relaxed day. For a fuller day in the saddle – and to ride one of the most amazing passes in the Pyrenees – change the route after lunch (this adds about 45 mins to the day's ride).
- At the N230 junction, turn left to Vielha and France.
- In Vielha, turn right for the town centre and take the C28 over the Bonaigua Pass, with one of the most spectacular runs of hairpins in the Pyrenees. There is a café there with a great view over them.
- Turn left in Sort to rejoin the core route on the N260.

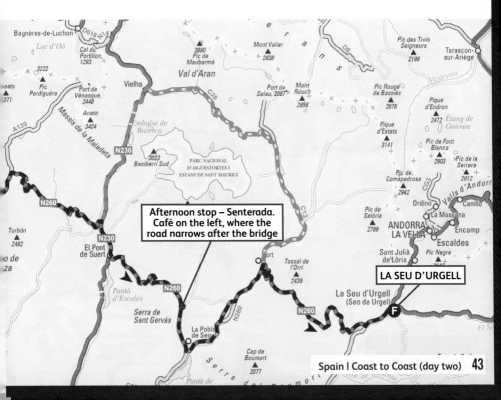

Afternoon stop – Senterada.
Café on the left, where the road narrows after the bridge

LA SEU D'URGELL

13 Coast to Coast (day three)

I remember coming to this area on a touring-bike test for RiDE. *I'd intended to go to the Alps but, as the day of departure loomed, the forecast there was awful... so I cancelled all the hotels and set off with no more plan than to get to the Pyrenees, which promised to be dry. It was my first visit for about ten years and I'd forgotten how beautiful these mountains were, how quiet the roads were, how friendly the people were*

FROM	La Seu d'Urgell
TO	Colera
DISTANCE	170 miles
ALLOW	5 hours

and just how good the food was. I've been coming back regularly ever since. This day's ride uses all the roads we rode on that test – and they're still every bit as brilliant today.

Route

- Leave La Seu d'Urgell on the N260 heading towards Puigcerdà.
- Turn left at the roundabout in Bellver de Cerdanya to stay on the N260.
- At the next roundabout, turn right towards Barcelona on the N1411.
- Keep going straight as the road becomes the LP4033b to Alp.
- At the E9 roundabout, turn left towards Puigcerdà.
- Don't miss the exit 2 miles later for the GIV4034 to Urtx, a single-lane short-cut.

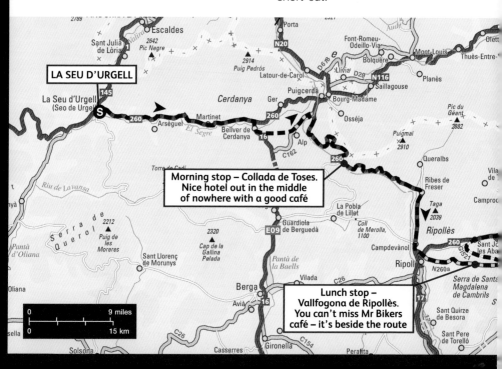

Morning stop – Collada de Toses. Nice hotel out in the middle of nowhere with a good café

Lunch stop – Vallfogona de Ripollès. You can't miss Mr Bikers café – it's beside the route

- Turn right at the crossroads to rejoin the N260. This stretch is one of my favourites.
- In Ripoll, turn left into the centre, following the signs for the N260. Cross the town centre and take the N260a to Vallfogona de Ripollès.
- Don't miss the sharp left turn about 4 miles after Vallfogona for the GI521 to St Joan de les Abadesses.
- In St Joan, turn right on the N260 again, now signed for Girona.
- At the roundabout, go straight over on the C38 towards St Pau de Segúries. When it crosses the border into France at Col d'Ares, the road becomes the D115.

- Don't miss the right turn, 4 miles after the village of Le Tech, for the D3 to Figueres. When it crosses the border back to Spain, it becomes the GI503, then the GI502.
- At the N-II, turn left towards Perpignan.
- Go over the motorway and turn right on the GI602 to Capmany.
- Follow the GI602 to Espolla, where it becomes the GI603.
- After 6 miles, go under the N260, then turn left to join it, heading for Llanca and Colera – where the route ends. If you have time, the last miles of the N260 to the French border are epic (just don't take the tunnel).

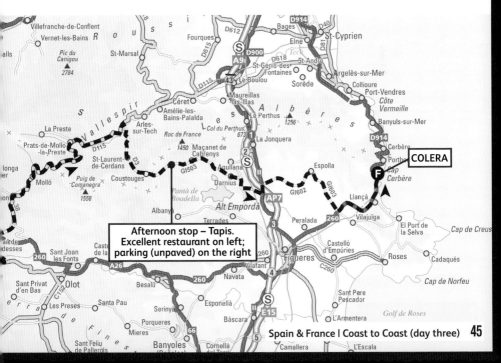

Afternoon stop – Tapis.
Excellent restaurant on left;
parking (unpaved) on the right

COLERA

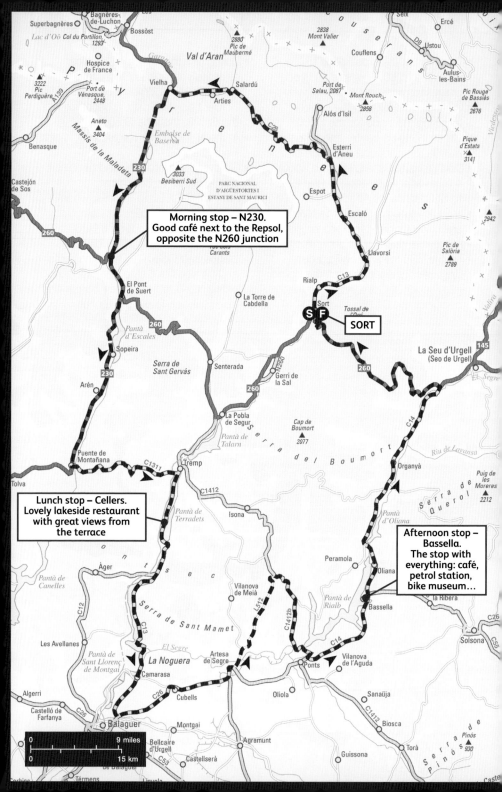

Morning stop – N230.
Good café next to the Repsol, opposite the N260 junction

SORT

Lunch stop – Cellers.
Lovely lakeside restaurant with great views from the terrace

Afternoon stop – Bassella.
The stop with everything: café, petrol station, bike museum…

14 The Best Sort

There are so many wonderful roads in the Spanish Pyrenees that you're spoilt for choice… and when it comes to spectacular scenery, this is definitely one of the best places in Europe to ride a motorcycle. Once you get past the N260, running east/west along the length of the mountains, there's a whole world of brilliant riding to be discovered. This route around the small town of Sort starts with the spectacular climb over the Bonaigua Pass to Vielha. It heads south, hugging rivers and lakes, scaling more

FROM	Sort
DISTANCE	240 miles
ALLOW	6½ hours

heights, stopping at Bassella – where there's a quirky, slightly unexpected motorcycle museum (see www. museumoto.com). This is a fairly long day in the saddle, but it can be shortened by taking the N260 from Sort to El Pont de Suert, lopping off the Vielha section, which saves just over an hour.

Route

- Leave Sort on the C13 towards Vielha. The road becomes the C28 as it bypasses Esterri d'Àneu.
- Cross Vielha and turn left on the N230 to Vilaller and Lleida. Stay on it for 45 miles, through El Pont de Suert, all the way to Puente de Montañana.
- Don't miss the left turn (by the war memorial) in Puente de Montañana for the C1311 to Tremp.
- In Tremp, turn right on the C13 to Balaguer and Lleida.
- At the C26 T-junction, turn left to Solsona and Andorra.
- After 15 miles, take the exit signed for Artesa de Segre and Tremp.
- Turn left in Artesa town centre on the L512 to Isona and Tremp.
- Don't miss the right turn 10 miles later for the C1412b to Ponts.
- At the C14 roundabout, turn left to Oliana and Solsona. Stay on this road for 35 miles.
- At the Adrall roundabout, turn left on the N260 to return to Sort.

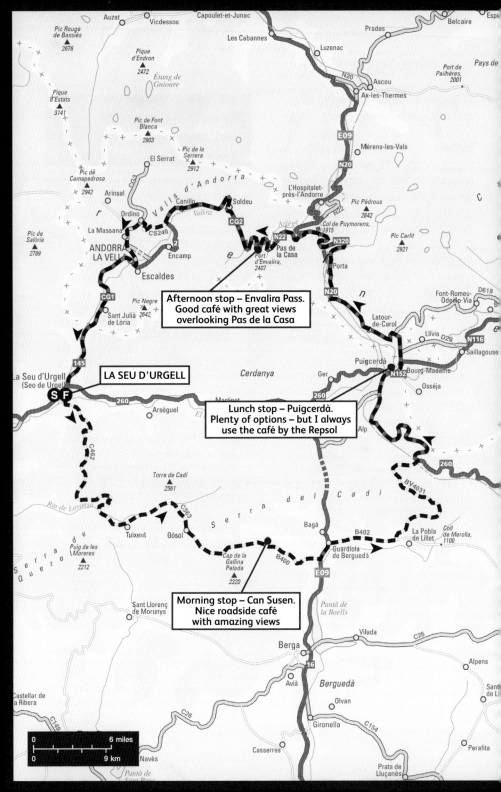

Afternoon stop – Envalira Pass.
Good café with great views
overlooking Pas de la Casa

LA SEU D'URGELL

Lunch stop – Puigcerdà.
Plenty of options – but I always
use the café by the Repsol

Morning stop – Can Susen.
Nice roadside café
with amazing views

0   6 miles
0   9 km

15 Andorra and More

This ride through three countries has everything: massive views, epic corners, ski towns, tax havens… everything. Including a short but brilliant stretch of the famous N260. It's a fairly relaxed day, nipping over the border into France to set up the run through Andorra. It's possible to extend the day by adding in a couple of scenic dead-end roads up to the ski areas above Ordino in Andorra (the

FROM	**La Seu d'Urgell**
DISTANCE	**155 miles**
ALLOW	**5 hours**

GC3 and GC4). The views from the top are spectacular, but will add an hour and a half into the day. Alternatively, stop on the CS240 (Coll d'Ordino) at the Roc del Quer viewpoint and do the 'skywalk' for amazing views.

Route

- Leave La Seu d'Urgell on the C462 to Tuixent. This is narrow in places.
- Don't miss the left turn after about 23 miles (going straight as the road bends right) on the C563 to Gósol – if you get to Tuixent, you've overshot the turn.
- Go straight through Gósol as the road becomes the B400.
- At the C16 junction, turn left to Puigcerdà.
- After about a mile, take the second exit (as the C16 comes out of an underpass) for the B402 to Ripoll and La Pobla de Lillet.
- In La Pobla de Lillet, turn left after the Repsol on the BV4031 to Castellar de n'Hug and La Molina.
- At the GI400 T-junction, turn right towards Ripoll and Girona.
- At the N260 T-junction, turn left to Puigcerdà (what follows is my favourite stretch of this famous road).
- Turn right at the Puigcerdà roundabout on the N152 to cross the border into France.

- Take the N20 towards Andorra and Ur.
- Look out: don't take the N20 through the tunnel (about 9 miles after crossing the border). Peel off to the right and take the N320 to Andorra and Foix.
- At the N22, turn left to Andorra.
- Again, don't take the tunnel: go straight over the first roundabout on the N22 to Pas de la Casa, following the signs for Andorra via the Col d'Envalira.
- Cross Pas de la Casa on the CG2, following signs for Andorra La Vella.
- At the bottom of the pass, turn right to Andorra La Vella.
- Don't miss the right turn in Canillo for the CS240 to Ordino.
- In Ordino, take the CG3 to Andorra La Vella.
- In Andorra La Vella, join the CG1 to Spain, where the road becomes the N145 to La Seu.

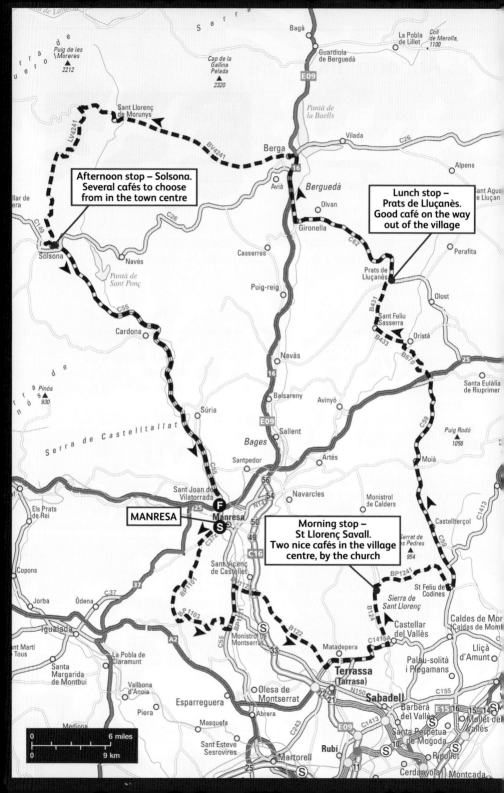

16 Manresa Miles

I did plenty of bike launches in the hills outside Barcelona over the years – everything from the mighty Triumph Thunderbird to the friendly Honda CMX500 Rebel, from the Honda CB650F to the fire-breathing original BMW S1000XR. That was a bike that really made the most of the sublime mixture of roads here, as it had everything you'd need for this route: agility, stability, a beast of a motor and day-long comfort. This is a longer route than we get on most

FROM	Manresa
DISTANCE	180 miles
ALLOW	6 hours

bike launches, packed with twisty tarmac as it heads out from the city to the foothills of the Pyrenees. There's a short stretch of urban riding to be done to get around Terrassa on the edge of the city, but after that it's unspoilt countryside, quiet villages and amazing roads all the way.

Route

- Start on the C37z towards Igualada.
- At the first roundabout turn left on the C37z/BP1101 to El Bruc.
- After 7 miles, turn left on the BP1103 to Montserrat. Go round the hairpin at the monastery to stay on the BP1103.
- At Monistrol, turn left on the BP1121 towards Manresa.
- After 2½ miles, turn right on the BV1123 to Castellbell. Go left at the bottom of the sliproad, cross the river and turn left on the B122 to Rellinars.
- At the B40 roundabout, turn left to Terrassa. Just keep going in a straight line until you pass the industrial area.
- At the roundabout, turn left on the C1415a to Castellar del Vallès.
- At the T-junction in Castellar, turn left on the B124 to St Llorenç Savall.
- Coming into St Llorenç, turn right towards the centre and stay on the BP1241.
- In St Feliu de Codines, turn left on the C59 to Centelles.
- Carry on through Moià and over the C25 as the road becomes the B670.
- In Oristà, turn left on the B433 to Olost.
- Turn right in St Feliu Sasserra on the B431 to Prats de Lluçanès.
- In Prats, turn left on the C62 to Berga. Turn left when the road goes through a cutting to stay on this heading.
- Join the C16 to Berga. After 5 miles, turn left to Berga and St Llorenç de Morunys. Go right at the roundabout then left at the top of the hill for the BV4241 to St Llorenç.
- Turn left at the roundabout at the top of Coll de Jou on the BV4241 to Solsona.
- From Solsana, take the C55 all the way back to Manresa.

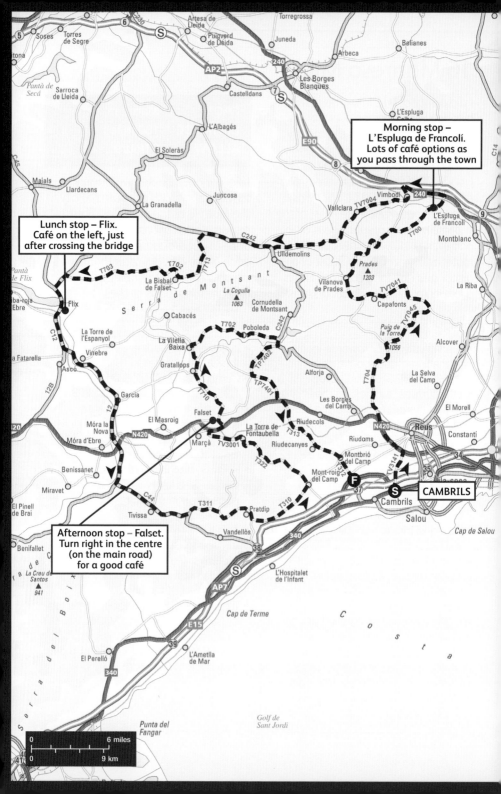

Morning stop – L'Espluga de Francolí. Lots of café options as you pass through the town

Lunch stop – Flix. Café on the left, just after crossing the bridge

Afternoon stop – Falset. Turn right in the centre (on the main road) for a good café

CAMBRILS

17 Cambrils Corners

My colleague Kev Raymond was frothing with excitement when he came into the office after the Suzuki V-Strom launch in Tarragona: 'You won't believe how good the roads are,' he said. I just grinned and held up a pic of me riding here: 'They're amazing,' I agreed. This route is based down the coast at the smaller seaside resort of Cambrils, partly because it offers a bit of off-the-bike beach holiday but mostly because it lets you get straight out on the good

FROM	Cambrils
DISTANCE	190 miles
ALLOW	5½ hours

riding. It uses a lot of the roads from the V-Strom launch – the ones Kev described as 'so twisty you could get seasick', but I'd never get sick of riding them. This is a real 'rider's' route, with more bends than MC Escher's plumbing – all on quiet and beautifully surfaced roads.

Route

- Leave Cambrils on the TV3141 to Reus.
- At Reus, turn left on the N420 to Alcañiz.
- After 2½ miles, take the exit for Reus Nord and take the T704 to Maspujols.
- At Puig de la Torre, turn right on the TV7045. At the T-junction, turn left on the TV7041.
- In Prades, turn right on the T700 to L'Espluga de Francolí.
- Cross L'Espluga and join the N240 to Lleida. After 3 miles take the exit for the TV7004 to Vimbodí.
- Follow the TV7004 through Vallclara.
- At the C242, turn right to Margalef.
- Don't miss the left turn 7 miles later for the T713 to Margalef.
- In La Bisbal de Falset, go straight on at the T-junction, on the T702 to La Palma d'Ebre.
- At the C233, turn left to Flix.
- Turn left on the C12 to Flix and La Móra.

- After 15 miles, turn left on the C44 to Tivissa.
- Take the C44 for 11 miles, then turn left on the T311 to Pratdip (it becomes the T310 after a few miles).
- Turn left at the T-junction to stay on the T310 to Mont-roig del Camp.
- At the Mont-roig roundabout, turn left on the T322 to Colldejou.
- In La Torre de Fontaubella, bear left on the TV3001 to Marçá.
- In Marçá, turn right on the T300 to Falset.
- Cross Falset. Take the T710 to Gratallops.
- At La Vilella Baixa, turn right on the T702 to La Morera de Montsant.
- Turn right at the C242, then right again on the TP7402, then left on the TP7041 to Porrera. Stay on this road towards Tarragona.
- Go straight across the N420 on the T313 to Duesaigües.
- In Montbrió del Camp, pick up the T312 to return to Cambrils.

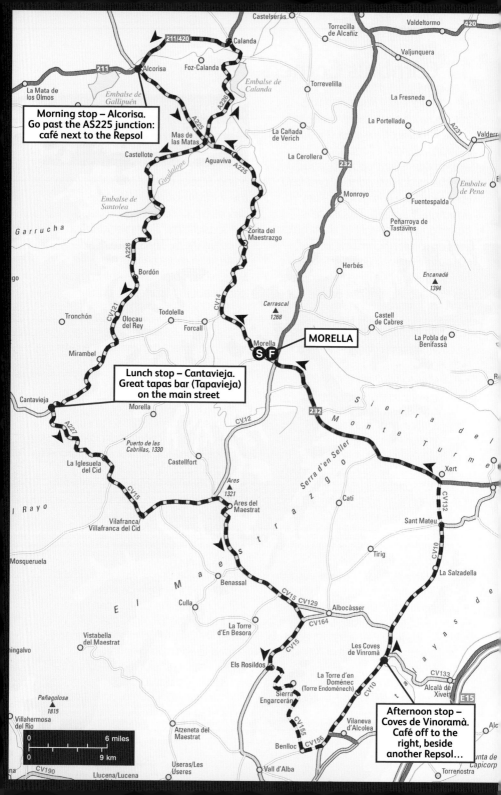

Morning stop – Alcorisa.
Go past the AS225 junction:
café next to the Repsol

MORELLA

Lunch stop – Cantavieja.
Great tapas bar (Tapavieja)
on the main street

Afternoon stop –
Coves de Vinoramà.
Café off to the
right, beside
another Repsol…

18 Majestic Morella

It's perhaps no surprise that when a country contains cultural riches like Madrid and Granada, Seville and Barcelona – not to mention motorcycling honeypots like the Pyrenees and Picos de Europa – that the smaller places tend to be overshadowed. But it is a shame, because if you're only concentrating on the big stuff, it's too easy to miss the smaller treasures, like Morella. I first stopped in this lovely small town with Weeble the photographer because it was a handy halfway point between Murcia and Catalonia. It was

FROM	Morella
DISTANCE	185 miles
ALLOW	5 hours

a good (or lucky) decision. The town, crowned by its castle, turned out to be a fabulous slice of 'old' Spain and the riding really took me by surprise. I'd been expecting to find some decent roads, but what we found was nothing short of outstanding: miles of twisty, quiet tarmac with spectacular views. That makes this a real gem of a destination.

Route

- Leave Morella on the CV14 to Cinctorres and Zorita. This becomes the A225.
- In Mas de las Matas, turn right on the A226 to Calanda and Zaragoza.
- In Calanda, turn left on the N211 / N420 to Alcorisa and Teruel.
- After 8 miles, coming into Alcorisa, turn left on the A225 to Mas de las Matas.
- Cross Mas de las Matas and take the A226 to Castellote – which fleetingly becomes the CV121, before reverting to the A226 designation.

- In Cantavieja, turn left at the small roundabout (past the petrol station) on the A227 to La Iglesuela del Cid. Stay on it for more than 35 miles, as it becomes the CV15.
- Don't miss the left turn – coming into Els Rosildos – for the CV155 to La Serra d'en Galceran.
- In Benlloch, turn left on the CV156.
- Turn left on the CV10 to San Mateu.
- At San Mateu, go straight over the roundabout on the CV132 to Morella.
- After 3 miles, join the N232 to return to Morella.

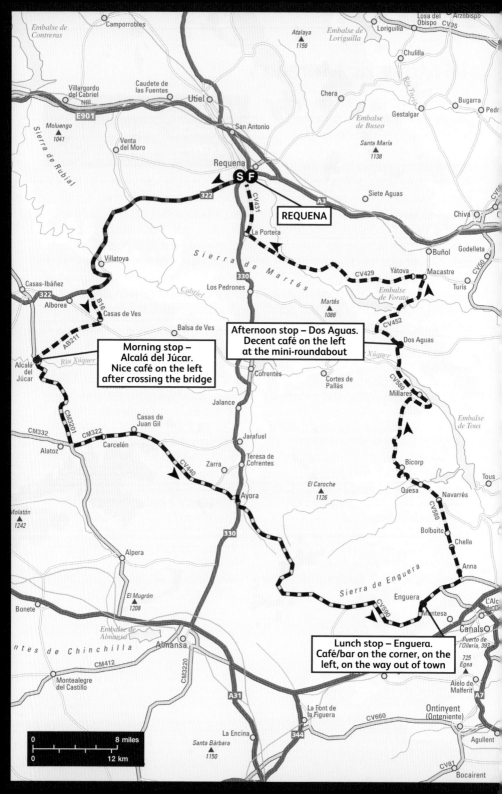

REQUENA

Morning stop –
Alcalá del Júcar.
Nice café on the left
after crossing the bridge

Afternoon stop – Dos Aguas.
Decent café on the left
at the mini-roundabout

Lunch stop – Enguera.
Café/bar on the corner, on the
left, on the way out of town

19 Requena and Dos Aquas

The run to the sun for the traditional final round of the Grand Prix season in Valencia is all well and good – but it's even better if you take a day to ride your bike when you're down there, not just watch the pros riding theirs. This route has more of a MotoGP connection than just the area: I asked Triumph test rider David Lopez to recommend a road and he suggested the CV580 through Dos Aguas... as recommended to him by Spanish GP star Hector Barbera, who was born in the village. It was an inspired tip – it's an absolutely amazing road.

FROM	Requena
DISTANCE	180 miles
ALLOW	5½ hours

This route also takes in another of my favourite bits of crazy Spanish tarmac: the serpentine CM3201 that twists its way down and then up the cliffs on either side of Alcalá del Júcar. The rest of the route is flowing, smooth tarmac, much of it as good as any track. It's a winning way to wrap up a trip to Valencia, even when there's no racing on.

Route

- Leave Requena on the N332 to Albacete.
- Don't miss the left turn 24 miles later for the B16 to Casas de Ves.
- In Casas de Ves, turn right then (after about 500 m) left on the AB211 to Zulmea.
- In Alcalá del Júcar, turn left on the CM3201.
- At the crossroads by the Repsol (after the really long straight), turn left on the CM322 to Carcelén. This becomes the CV440.
- In Ayora, turn right on the N330 then left on the CV590 to Enguera.
- Don't miss the left turn 2 miles outside Enguera to stay on the CV590 to Anna.
- Turn left at the roundabout on the CV580 to Anna. Stick with the CV580 for 35 miles.
- In Dos Aguas, turn left at the mini-roundabout to go through the village, still on the CV580.

- At the roundabout, go straight over on the CV425 to Macastre.
- Take the bypass round Macastre then, at the roundabout with the coach sculpture, turn left into the village and then turn right on the CV429 to Yátova.
- Turn right in La Portera and join the N330 towards Requena.
- Take the next right for the CV431 to return to Requena.

Valencia

The city of Valencia is fabulous, with beaches, a great old town and a charming port. The futuristic City of Arts & Sciences area is a must-see.

Cheste

The GP circuit is actually outside Valencia in the small town of Cheste. For race information and tickets, see www.circuitricardotormo.com

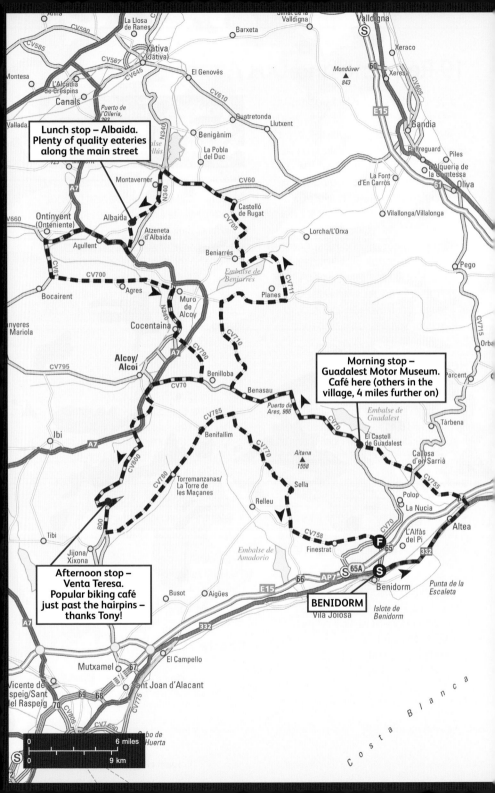

Lunch stop – Albaida.
Plenty of quality eateries
along the main street

Morning stop –
Guadalest Motor Museum.
Café here (others in the
village, 4 miles further on)

Afternoon stop –
Venta Teresa.
Popular biking café
just past the hairpins –
thanks Tony!

BENIDORM

20 Beyond Benidorm

Patriotic Spanish car maker SEAT named one of its models after Altea, the prettiest port on the Costa Blanca, and it's well worth a visit – as is the motor museum in the hills above it. There are miles of amazing biking roads here, many of them shown to me by my friend Tony Lang. This route strings together as many of the twistiest ones as I can manage – it'd be the highlight of any holiday.

FROM	Benidorm
DISTANCE	165 miles
ALLOW	5½ hours

Route

- From Benidorm, take the N332 to Altea.
- Leave Altea on the N332 and take the exit for the AP7 motorway to Alicante.
- After half a mile, turn right on the CV755 to Callosa d'en Sarrià and Altea la Vella. This will take you past the motor museum.
- Go straight across the roundabout in Benimantell on the CV70 to Alcoi. Stay on this road for 13 miles.
- Don't miss the right turn, 2 miles after Benasau, for the CV710 to Gorga.
- Go straight over the roundabout in Planes then, just before leaving the village, turn left on the CV711 to Beniarrés.
- In Beniarrés, turn right on the CV705 to Castelló de Rugat.
- Turn left in Castelló de Rugat and pick up the CV60 to Alfarrasí and Montaverner.
- After 3 miles, take the exit for the CV677 to Bèlgida. This becomes the CV60 again when it crosses the N340.
- Go through Albaida following the signs for Cocentaina and the motorway.
- Join the A7 towards Ontinyent and Xàtiva.
- Leave the motorway after 2½ miles at Jct 418 and take the CV81 to Ontinyent.
- Don't miss the left turn, after the CV81 emerges from the canyon, for the CV700 to Alfafara and Pego.
- Coming into Muro del Alcoy, turn right on the N340 to Alcoi.
- After 3 miles, take the exit for Cocentaina and pick up the CV790 to Benilloba.
- At the CV70, turn right towards Alcoi.
- At the N340, turn left towards Jijona.
- At the A7 junction, go straight over both roundabouts on the CV800 to Jijona.
- At the Jijona roundabout, turn left on the CV780 to La Torre de les Maçanes.
- At the CV785, turn right to Penàguila.
- Don't miss the left turn in Penàguila for the CV781 to Alcoleja and Benasau.
- At the CV770, go straight to Alcoleja.
- After 14 miles, turn left (2 miles after Sella) on the CV758 to Finestrat.
- At the CV70 T-junction, turn right to return to Benidorm.

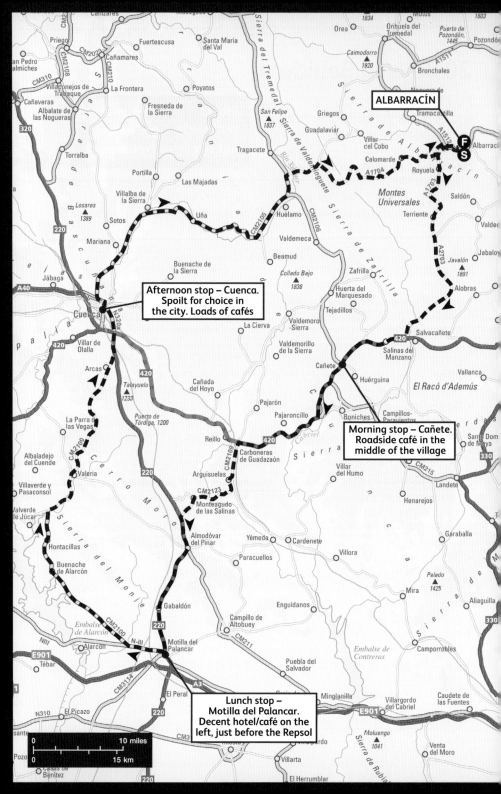

ALBARRACÍN

Afternoon stop – Cuenca.
Spoilt for choice in
the city. Loads of cafés

Morning stop – Cañete.
Roadside café in the
middle of the village

Lunch stop –
Motilla del Palancar.
Decent hotel/café on the
left, just before the Repsol

0   10 miles
0   15 km

21 Cuenca and Albarracín

I'd already discovered the small city of Cuenca, with its quirky hanging houses, when my friend Spanish Mark (not Algarve Mark) tipped me off about Albarracín. 'That's real Spain...' he told me. And it is – though, frankly, the landscape is eerily reminiscent of the American West, with red rocks rising through the scrub-pine forest of the hills and the occasional long,

FROM	Albarracín
DISTANCE	210 miles
ALLOW	6 hours

straight road across the plains. It's taken me several goes to produce this route that really makes the best of all the amazing riding to be found around here.

Route
- Leave Albarracín through the tunnel on the main A1512 towards Torres and Orihuela.
- After 4 miles, turn left on the A1703 to Royuela. It later becomes the A2703.
- At the N420, turn right to Salinas del Manzano.
- After 17 miles, turn left on the CM2109 to Cardenete.
- In 4½ miles, turn right on the CM2123 to Arguisuelas.
- At the T-junction, turn left on the CM220 to Almodóvar del Pinar.
- In Motilla del Palancar, pick up the N-III to Honrubia and Madrid.
- After about 3 miles, turn right on the CM2100 to Valverde de Júcar.
- Turn right at the roundabout to stay on the CM2100 to Valeria de Abajo and Cuenca.
- At the CM220, turn left to Cuenca. Keep going straight (as the road becomes the N320a) to go into the city.
- Stick with the N320a through the heart of Cuenca, then follow the brown signs for the Cuidad Encantada to pick up the CM2105.
- Stick with this road, following signs for Villalba de la Sierra and on past the Ventano del Diablo.
- It's about 25 miles from the Ventano del Diablo to the right turn for the CUV 9161 / CM2119 to Teruel, which becomes the A1704.
- Turn left on the A1703 and then right on the A1512 to return to Albarracín.
- *For some sightseeing time in Cuenca, just stay on the N420 after Cañete: it shortens the route by around an hour and a half.*

Hanging houses
When the old town of Cuenca met the cliffs above the Júcar River, the locals kept building – and now the crazy hanging houses are a tourist attraction.

Ventano del Diablo
The Devil's Window is a bizarre rock formation left high and dry above the Rio Júcar gorge with stunning views.

Cuidad Encantada
This area of the Serrenia de Cuenca is studded with giant rocks that nature has carved into magical shapes. Pack your walking boots to enjoy it.

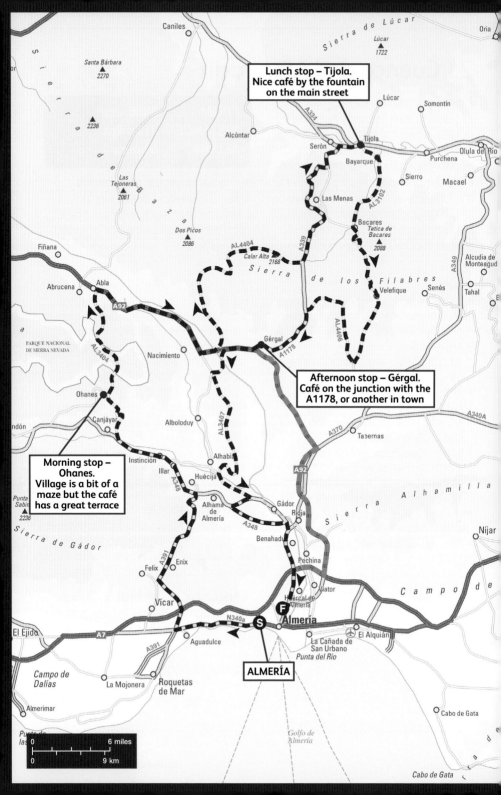

Lunch stop – Tijola.
Nice café by the fountain
on the main street

Afternoon stop – Gérgal.
Café on the junction with the
A1178, or another in town

Morning stop –
Ohanes.
Village is a bit of a
maze but the café
has a great terrace

ALMERÍA

22 Better than Stelvio

If learning about just one road makes this book worth its purchase price, that road is the AL3102 over Alto de Velefique. It might be the perfect mountain road: packed with hairpins, flowing corners and amazing views – and usually astonishingly quiet. It's heaven. But then, so is the AL3404 to Ohanes. And the run to Castro de Fibrales on the AL4406 is like the

FROM	Almería
DISTANCE	185 miles
ALLOW	5 hours

Ronda road without traffic. And the N391 that starts the ride... In fact, this route is packed with amazing roads, even if it does use a few stretches of motorway to link them.

Route

- Leave Almería on the N340a to Aguadulce.
- In El Parador de las Hortichuelas, pick up the A391 to La Envia.
- At the A348, turn left to Canjáyar.
- After 8 miles, turn right on the AL3404 to Ohanes.
- In Abla, turn right towards the A92 to Almería. You can either join the motorway for 10 miles from the edge of the village or carry on along the A1177 to Doña María and join it there for 7 miles.
- Leave the A92 at J356 and turn left to Aulago on the AL4404. The last bit of this, after the observatory, is single lane: take care.
- At the A339, turn left to Bacarés.
- At Serón, turn right and then right again on the A334 towards Huércal-Overa.

- After 3 miles, turn right to Tíjola.
- Don't miss the right turn as you come into town to stay on the AL3102 to Velefique.
- Don't miss the right turn 11 miles later for the AL4406 to Castro de Fibrales. After the village it becomes single lane.
- Turn left at the A1178 to Gérgal.
- *You can save 45 minutes by taking the A92 back to Almería from here, but for the full route take the A92 towards Granada.*
- Leave the motorway at J356 again and turn left to Las Alcubillas on the AL3410.
- Turn left on the AL3407 to Gádor. This becomes the A1075 to Almería.
- Turn left at the Huéchar roundabout on the A348 to Benahadux.
- Join the N340a to return to Almería.

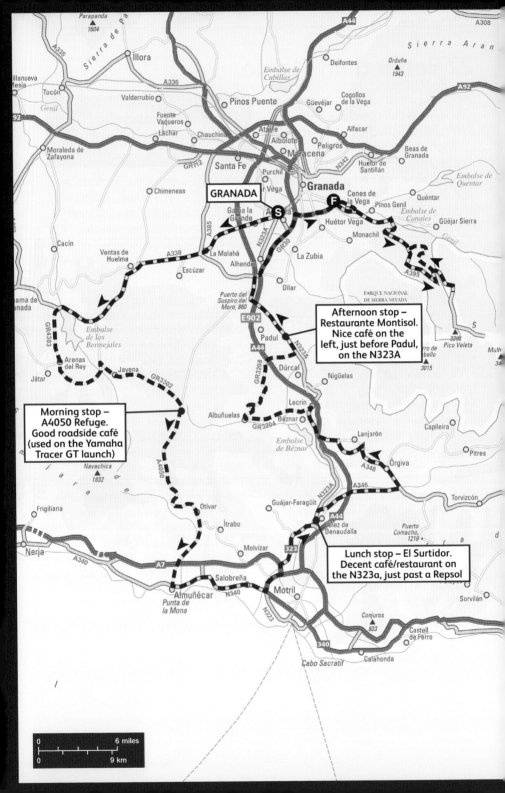

Afternoon stop –
Restaurante Montisol.
Nice café on the
left, just before Padul,
on the N323A

Morning stop –
A4050 Refuge.
Good roadside café
(used on the Yamaha
Tracer GT launch)

Lunch stop – El Surtidor.
Decent café/restaurant on
the N323a, just past a Repsol

GRANADA

Granada

0   6 miles
0   9 km

23 Sierra Nevada

The climb up the Sierra Nevada mountains outside Granada delivers some truly fabulous views – and they're even better descending on the A4205, which makes a hairpin-heavy loop halfway up the mountain. These roads are often used for testing cars, which usually set off from Motril so they go from sea level to more than 2,500 m (the road carries on, unpaved, to more than 3,000 m but

FROM	Granada
DISTANCE	180 miles
ALLOW	6½ hours

the top isn't open to the public). This loop lets you have the same experience, using great roads – warm up with a run to the coast before returning to take on the mountain.

Route

- Leave Granada on the A338 to Las Gabias. It's a bit suburban at first but picks up south of Ventas de Huelma.
- Ride past the small reservoir and take the first left: the GR4303 to Arenas del Rey.
- In Arenas del Rey, turn left on the GR3302. When the road hits a T-junction, turn left following signs for Almuñécar to stay on the GR3302.
- At the A4050 junction, turn right towards Otívar and Almuñécar. This is a long, twisty road and narrow in places.
- Coming into Almuñécar, pick up the N340 towards Motril.
- After 9 miles, join the GR14 towards Granada (also signed for the A7 to Málaga).
- Watch out: don't join the A7. At the end of the GR14, go straight ahead on the N323A towards Los Guájares and Granada.
- Don't miss the right turn (about 3 miles after the suggested lunch stop) for the A346 to Vélez Benedualla and the A44.
- At the roundabout by the dam, turn left to stay on the A346 to Órgiva.
- After 6 miles, turn left (after a short tunnel) on the A348 to Órgiva.
- Go straight across the motorway, on the N323A again.
- In Lecrín, turn left on the GR3204 to Melegís and Restebál.
- Don't miss the right fork in Restebál to stay on the GR3204 to Albuñuelas.
- Turn right at the roundabout at Albuñuelas on the GR3208 to Granada.
- Go straight over the motorway and turn left when the road meets the N323A again.
- Join the A44 then go right on the GR30.
- Take exit 16 for the ring road, following the brown signs for the Sierra Nevada.
- Get in the right-hand lane in the long tunnel, then bear right on the A395.
- Take the A395 all the way to the top of the mountain. When descending, don't miss the right turn for the A4205. It rejoins the A395 to return to Granada.

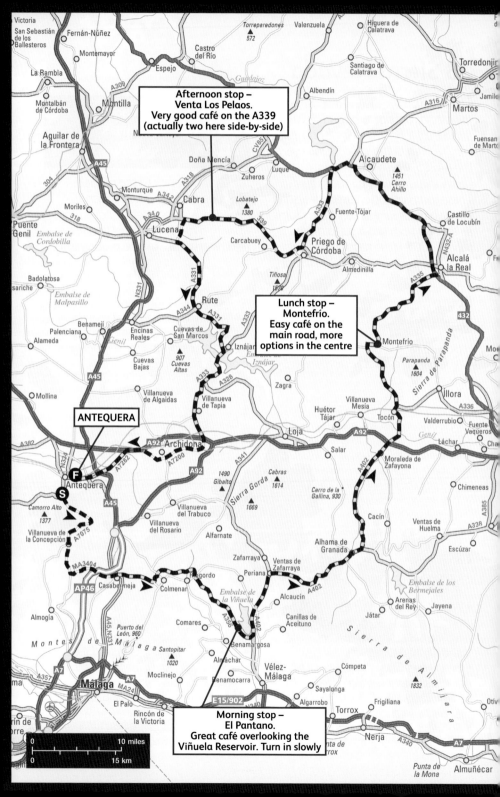

**Afternoon stop –
Venta Los Pelaos.
Very good café on the A339
(actually two here side-by-side)**

**Lunch stop –
Montefrío.
Easy café on the
main road, more
options in the centre**

ANTEQUERA

**Morning stop –
El Pantano.
Great café overlooking the
Viñuela Reservoir. Turn in slowly**

0   10 miles
0   15 km

24 Montefrío Miles

When you test bikes for any European motorcycle magazine, you inevitably end up spending a lot of time in Andalusia. The original Triumph Tiger Explorer and Honda VFR1200 were both launched (a few years apart) from the same hotel outside Iznájar, the Yamaha Tracer 900 at the Parador in Antequera and as for the number of bikes unveiled in nearby Málaga and Ronda... too many to count, but my very first launch in 2003 took in both towns. What still seems odd to me is that none of the launches I did in this area ever featured my favourite road on this route – the stunning A335 through Montefrío. At least, it

FROM	Antequera
DISTANCE	205 miles
ALLOW	6½ hours

never featured on any 'official' launch routes. But back in 2012, when I was working for RiDE, I managed to stay on for an extra day at that Explorer launch and borrow a bike. I headed out on a route essentially like this, to put more miles on the brand-new GS challenger, to get more depth into my report. It was a brilliant ride on a very good machine – and if I told you it was hard work, would you believe me? Thought not…

Route

- Leave Antequera on the A343 and keep going straight ahead as the road becomes the A7075 to Málaga and Villanueva de la Concepción.
- After 15 miles, keep going straight on the MA3404 to Casabermeja. Keep going across both motorways as the road becomes the A356 to Vélez-Málaga.
- After about 20 miles (2 miles after the coffee stop), take the exit on the right for the A402 to Periana and Alhama de Granada.
- Turn right at the first roundabout and left at the second in Alhama to stay on the A402 towards Granada and Sante Fe.
- When it meets the motorway at Moraleda de Zafayona, keep going straight ahead on the A335 to Alcalá la Real.
- Coming into Alcalá, pick up the N432 to Alcaudete and Córdoba.
- Don't miss the right turn after 17 miles for the A333 to Priego de Córdoba.
- At Priego, join the A339 to Cabra.
- After 15 miles (2½ miles from the coffee stop), take the exit for the CO6213 to Rute.
- At the A331, turn left to Rute.
- Cross the A92 on the A7200 to Archidona then join the A92 to Málaga for one junction.
- Leave the motorway at J160 and take the A7282 to return to Antequera.

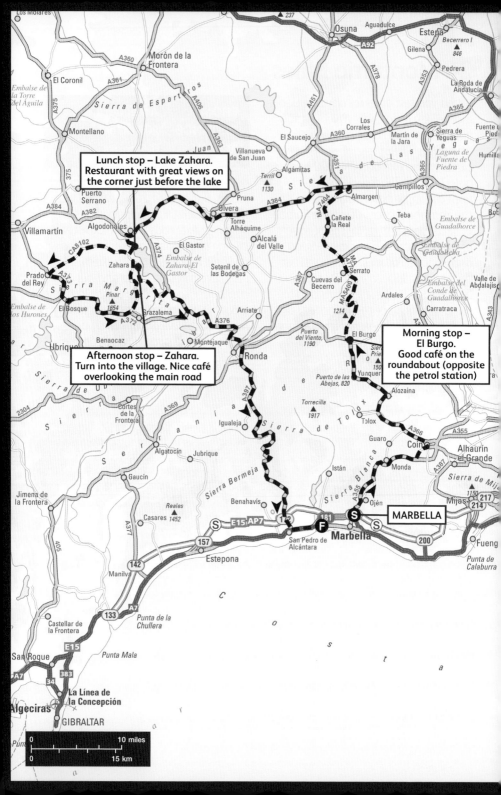

Lunch stop – Lake Zahara.
Restaurant with great views on
the corner just before the lake

Afternoon stop – Zahara.
Turn into the village. Nice café
overlooking the main road

**Morning stop –
El Burgo.**
Good café on the
roundabout (opposite
the petrol station)

MARBELLA

25 Marbella and Ronda

I rode the A397 between Ronda and San Pedro de Alcántara on my very first bike launch in 2003 (the BMW K1200GT). I didn't know it at the time, but I was to become a regular visitor, as all bike testers are. Over the years, I would ride this road on so many launches that I came to call it 'The Spanish Office'. Almost every road on this route has been used on a bike launch at some point... except

FROM	Marbella
DISTANCE	185 miles
ALLOW	5½ hours

for my favourite, shown to me by my friend Spanish Mark: the CA9104 over the Las Palomas Pass (well, I did ride it on the Triumph Tiger 800 launch, but only by sneaking off from the official route).

Route
- Leave Marbella on the A355 to Ojén.
- After 13 miles, take the slip road for Coín.
- In Coín, turn left at the roundabout on the A366 to Ronda.
- Turn left at the roundabout in Alozaina to stay on the A366 to El Burgo.
- In El Burgo, turn right and go straight over the roundabout to Serrato on the MA5400.
- Turn right at the T-junction on the edge of Serrato, towards Ronda, on the MA477.
- At the A367, turn right then immediately left to pick up the MA6401 to Cañete la Real.
- In Cañete la Real, go straight over the roundabout on the MA7404 to Almargen.
- In Almargen, turn left on the A384 to Olvera and Jerez de la Frontera.
- After 28 miles, take the exit for Algodonales and join the A2300 to Zahara de la Sierra.
- Don't miss the right turn to Zahara – and then immediately turn right again on the CA1802 to Prado del Rey.
- At the A373, turn left to El Bosque.

- In El Bosque, turn left on the A372 to Aros de la Frontera. At the bottom of the ramp, turn right to Grazalema.
- Don't miss the left turn 11 miles later for the CA9104 to Zahara de la Sierra.
- Back at the A2300 junction again, turn right to Grazalema.
- At the A374, turn right to Ronda.
- In Ronda, pick up the A397 to San Pedro de Alcántara.
- In San Pedro you have a choice: either take the AP7 (with a toll) back to Marbella or the A7 and then the more suburban N340 to get back to the start.

Fly-Ride
Not sure you have time to ride all the way to Marbella? Simple: fly to Málaga and hire a bike, enjoy riding in the sun, then fly home again.

Ronda
Ronda is deceptively large, but the compact old town is fabulous, with more to see than just its famous gorge – but you will melt walking round in bike kit...

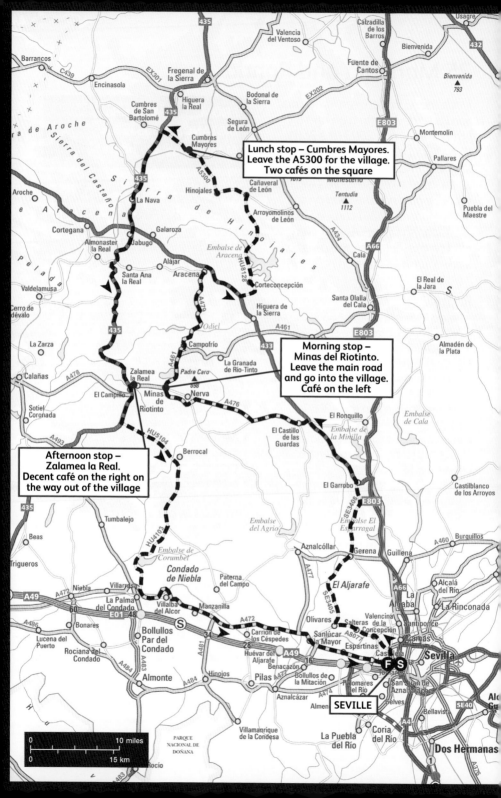

Lunch stop – Cumbres Mayores.
Leave the A5300 for the village.
Two cafés on the square

Morning stop –
Minas del Riotinto.
Leave the main road
and go into the village.
Café on the left

Afternoon stop –
Zalamea la Real.
Decent café on the right on
the way out of the village

SEVILLE

0   10 miles
0   15 km

26 Seville and Ríotinto

I'm lucky enough to have been to Seville several times. It's a fascinating city, showing the influence of both its Moorish and Christian heritage. Semana Santa, the huge Easter festival with parades of floats carried through the streets, has to be seen to be believed. But really, I keep coming back here for the riding… This day trip starts in the city and heads out to the equally man-made but far stranger landscape of the Riotinto mines. For a few miles it's like riding in an alien

FROM	**Seville**
DISTANCE	**200 miles**
ALLOW	**6 hours**

world, not beautiful, sunny rural Spain. The roads here are outstanding, with the highlight being the HU1403 from Berrocal to La Palma de Condado, which I first rode on the BMW K1300GT launch. Once you've ridden that road, you'll keep coming back here too…

Route

- Leave Seville on the A8077 to Castilleja de Guzmán.
- In Olivares, pick up the SE3405 to Gerena.
- Cross Gerena following signs for El Garrobo to pick up the SE3048.
- In El Garrobo, turn left on the N433 to Higuera de la Sierra and Portugal.
- Don't miss the right turn 9 miles later for the A476 to El Castillo de las Guardas and Minas de Ríotinto.
- From the roundabout with the train at Minas del Ríotinto, turn right on the A461 to Aracena.
- Don't miss the left turn 6 miles later for Campofrío, to stay on the A461.
- In Campofrío, take the A479 to Aracena.
- In Aracena, pick up the N433 towards Higuera de la Sierra again.
- After 2 miles, turn left on the HU8128 (HV3105) to Corteconcepción and keep going as it becomes the HV3124
- Turn left on the A5300 to Cañaveral de León.
- Turn left on the N435 to Huelva.
- A mile south of Zalamea la Real, turn left to Berrocal on the HU5104.
- After 9 miles, turn right (on a hairpin) on the HU4103 to La Palma del Condado.
- At La Palma, you have a choice: carry straight on through the town and pick up the A49 to return to Seville or turn left on the parallel A472 which will get you back to the city but takes half an hour longer.

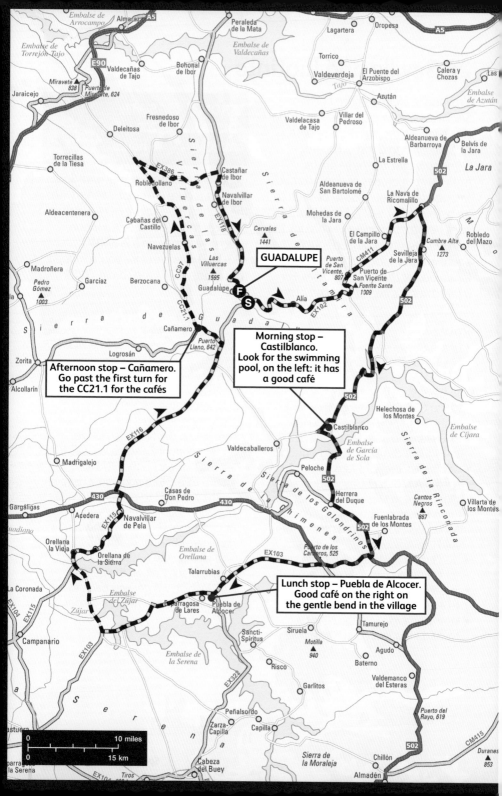

27 Guadalupe Rabbit

This route has taken a while to perfect, as there's so much great riding around Guadalupe. This full day's ride – named for its shape – packs as many of my favourite roads into a single day as possible, with everything from tight mountain corners to flowing straights. If you don't want such a long ride, the route is easily shortened (by cutting off the ears of the rabbit) though that would be a

FROM	**Guadalupe**
DISTANCE	**220 miles**
ALLOW	**6 hours**

shame, as it would mean missing the final run down the EX118. It's not only a truly brilliant road to ride but also delivers a stunning view down over Guadalupe to finish the day on a high.

Route

- Leave Guadalupe on the EX102 to Alía.
- In Puerto de San Vicente, go straight over the roundabout on the CM411 to La Nava de Ricomalillo.
- In La Nava de Ricomalillo, turn right on the N502 to Herrera del Duque.
- As the N502 becomes a dual carriageway, bear right on the N430 to Mérida.
- After 6 miles, take the first exit (J183) and pick up the EX103 to Talarrubias.
- Don't miss the right turn about a mile after the second bridge over the Serena reservoir to stay on the EX103 to Orellana la Vieja. Go left at the roundabout 5 miles later to stay on the road.
- At the lakeside roundabout, go straight on the EX115 to Orellana.
- At the N430, turn left to Mérida.
- After 2 miles, turn right on the EX116 to Obando and Guadalupe.
- At the EX102, turn left to Cañamero (or you could turn right to cut the day short and return to Guadalupe).

- In Cañamero, turn right towards Berzocana on the CC21.1.
- Go straight over the roundabout on the CC97 to Navezuelas.
- At the EX386, turn right to Robledollano.
- In Castañar de Ibor, turn right on the EX118 to return to Guadalupe.

Serena Reservoir

This huge man-made lake can look truly spectacular. A short detour from Puebla de Alcocer gives the best views – including the surreally circular roundabout island.

Orellana la Vieja

A good-sized village that hides its glory: you have to leave the main road and ride through it to get to the headland that projects into the lake.

Guadalupe Monastery

A plain-and-simple must-see...
The 14th-century Royal Monastery is a fabulous building packed to the rafters with amazing works of art. Don't rush it: allow 3 hours for a proper visit.

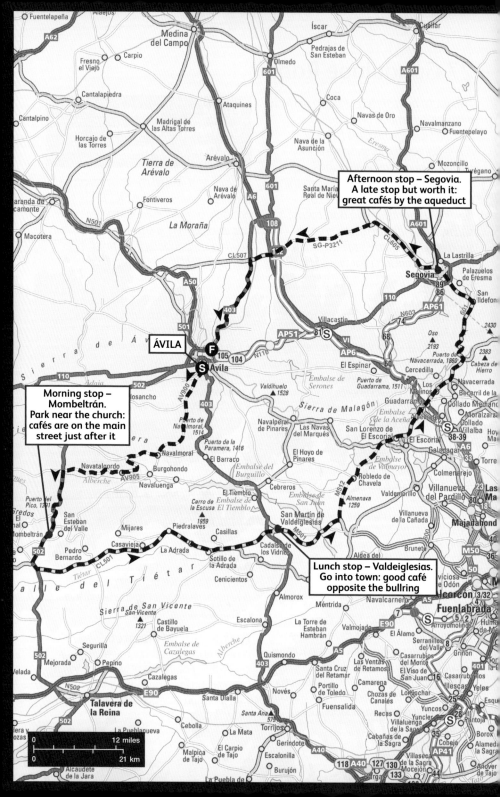

Afternoon stop – Segovia.
A late stop but worth it:
great cafés by the aqueduct

ÁVILA

**Morning stop –
Mombeltrán.**
Park near the church:
cafés are on the main
street just after it

Lunch stop – Valdeiglesias.
Go into town: good café
opposite the bullring

28 Ávila and El Escorial

This is a full day's ride linking some of Spain's most fascinating historical sites – starting from the fabulously preserved small city of Ávila. Initially it heads out through the mountains, delivering fabulous views and amazing corners, but after crossing the Pico Pass it swings back towards Madrid, ticking off one cultural highlight after another. However, this is definitely a riding day, rather than a day for stopping and doing a lot of sightseeing. You could instead use it

FROM	Ávila
DISTANCE	220 miles
ALLOW	6 hours

to decide where you'd like to spend a bit of time off the bike and then come back on a more direct route (perhaps on the motorways) to give you enough time out of the saddle to explore and do the tourist thing at the places that take your fancy.

Route

- Leave Ávila on the AV900 to Navalmoral.
- At the crossroads in Navalmoral, turn right on the AV905 to El Barco de Ávila.
- At the N502, turn left towards Arenas de San Pedro. This takes you over Pico Pass.
- Go through Ramacastañas and turn left to Lanzahíta on the CL501 (which eventually becomes the M501).
- Follow the M501 straight over the N403 and round Pelayos de la Presa.
- Don't miss the left turn 4 miles later for the M512 to Robledo.
- At the top of Cruz Verde Pass go straight over the roundabout on the M505 to Madrid.
- After 2 miles, turn left for the back road into El Escorial.
- Follow the one-way system in El Escorial to pick up the M600 to Guadarrama.
- Go straight across the motorway on the M614 to Navacerrada.

- On the ouskirts of Navacerrada town, pick up the M601 to Segovia, over the Navacerrada Pass.
- Turn left in San Ildefonso to stay on the M601a into Segovia. Cross town following the signs for the centro historicó.
- Leave Segovia on the CL607 to Arévalo.
- Turn right on the CL605 to Santa Maria.
- Don't miss the left turn after 8½ miles for the SG-P3211 to Etreros and Marazuela.
- Ignore both the motorway and the N-VI and keep going straight on the CL507.
- At the N403, turn left to return to Ávila.

San Lorenzo de El Escorial

It looks like Hogwarts, but in fact it's a monastery. Better still, the Royal Monastery of San Lorenzo de El Escorial is now a huge and fascinating museum.

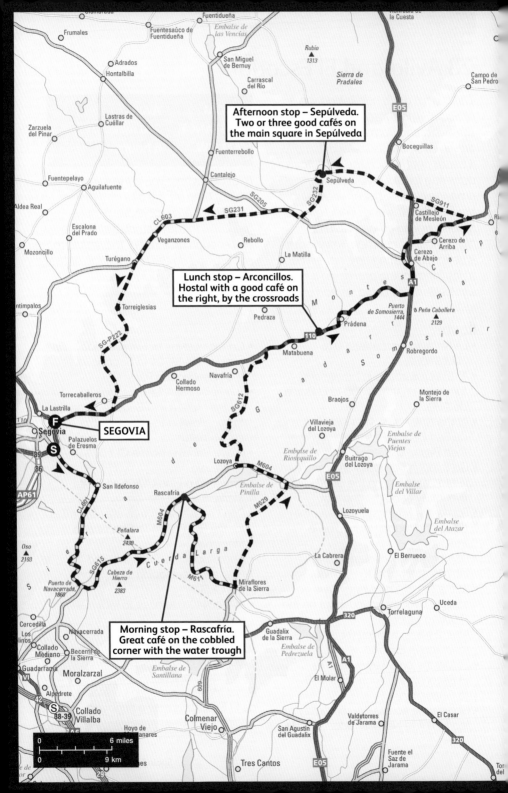

Afternoon stop – Sepúlveda.
Two or three good cafés on the main square in Sepúlveda

Lunch stop – Arconcillos.
Hostal with a good café on the right, by the crossroads

SEGOVIA

Morning stop – Rascafría.
Great café on the cobbled corner with the water trough

29 Super Segovia

The beautiful small Spanish city of Segovia really is the gift that keeps on giving, which is why I keep returning to it whenever possible. It's a wonderful, almost contradictory place: bustling with life but still laid-back; packed with history but with all mod cons. For quality time off the bike, you can explore the old town, do some people-watching from a café by the Roman aqueduct, you can visit the spectacular cathedral or take a tour of the fairytale Alcazar. But this is a

FROM	Segovia
DISTANCE	160 miles
ALLOW	5 hours

biking book and Segovia's also surrounded by amazing roads. This route criss-crosses the sierra that separates it from Madrid then heads across the plains to the lovely historic town of Sepúlveda. If it's not too contradictory, I'd say it's a relaxed but action-packed route.

Route

- Leave Segovia on the CL601 to San Ildefonso and Madrid.
- At the Navecerrada Pass ski area, turn left on the SG615 to Rascafría (also signed for the Cotos ski area).
- Don't miss the right turn in Rascafría for the M611 to Miraflores de la Sierra.
- In Miraflores de la Sierra, turn left on the M629 to Canencia.
- At the M604, turn left to Lozoya.
- Go straight in Lozoya (a right turn as the road goes left) on the M637 to Navafría. It becomes the SG612.
- At the N110 junction, turn right to Matabuena and Soria.
- Join the A1 motorway towards Burgos for two junctions.
- Leave the motorway at J103 to continue on the N110 towards Soria.

- After 5½ miles, turn left on the SG911 to Castillejo de Mesleón and Sepúlveda. This becomes the SG234.
- Don't miss the left turn for the SG232 to Sepúlveda, a quarter of a mile after a 90° right-hander.
- When it meets the SG205 after Sepúlveda, turn right to Cantalejo.
- After a bit more than a mile, turn left on the SG231 to Segovia and Turégano. When it meets a roundabout, keep going straight as it becomes the CL603.
- Go straight through Turégano on the SG-P222 to Torreiglesias and Torrecaballeros.
- In Torrecaballeros, turn right on the N110 to return to Segovia.

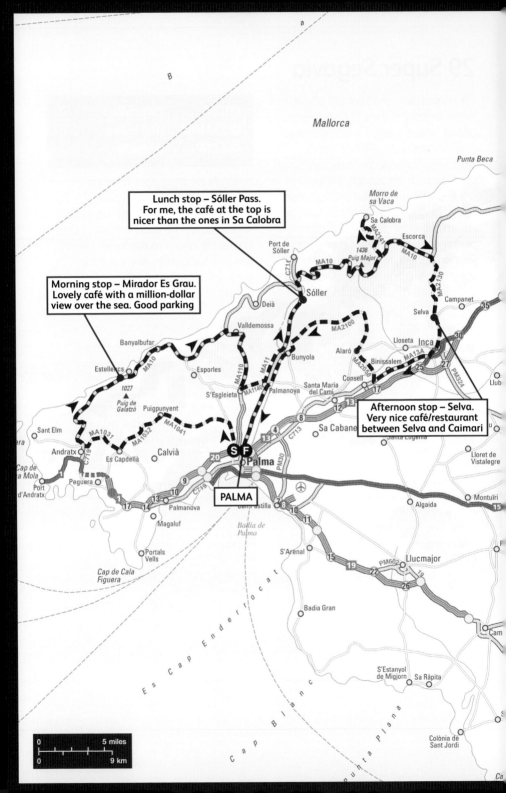

30 Palma Twin-loop

I must have done more bike launches on Mallorca than on any other island. I've enjoyed the roads of its mountainous northwest coast on everything from the Honda Crossrunner to the BMW S1000R to a 1953 Vincent Rapide C (that one wasn't a bike launch). You can get a ferry to Mallorca from Barcelona or Valencia with your bike, or you can fly in and hire one. However you get here, it is worth the effort for the amazing

FROM	Palma
DISTANCE	165 miles
ALLOW	5 hours

roads – Coll dels Reis, on the way to Sa Calobra, has a looping 270° turn and hairpins to make many an Alp jealous. You will probably be sharing that road (and many others) with quite a few cyclists, so keep a bit in hand.

Route

- Leave Palma on the MA1040 towards Secar de la Real.
- In Secar, turn left at the lights on the MA1042 to Puigpunyent, then join the MA1041, still signed for Puigpunyent.
- Turn left at the crossroads in Puigpunyent on the MA1032 to Galilea and Es Capdellà.
- In Es Capdellà, turn right on the MA1031 to Andratx.
- At the roundabout in Andratx, turn right on the MA10 to Estellencs and Sóller.
- Don't miss the left turn, 4 miles after Banyalbufar, to stay on the MA10 to Sóller.
- Go into Valldemossa as the road becomes the MA1130 and then the MA110 to Palma.
- In S'Esgleieta, turn left on the MA1140 to Palmanyola and Sóller.
- In Palmanyola, turn left at the roundabout on the MA11 to Sóller.
- After 3½ miles, turn left on the MA11A to Sóller (the 13 km route over Sóller Pass).

- Rejoin the MA11 to Sóller and take it around the town towards Port de Sóller.
- Don't miss the right turn to rejoin the MA10 towards Pollença and Sa Calobra.
- Don't miss the left turn half a mile after the tunnel for the MA2141 to Sa Calobra.
- Backtrack from Sa Calobra and turn left on the MA10 to Pollença and Inca.
- Keep going straight as the road becomes the MA2130 to Caimari and Inca.
- Don't get on the MA13 motorway at Inca: take the parallel MA13A towards Binissalem.
- Turn right on the MA2050 to Alaró.
- From Alaró, take the MA2100 to Orient.
- Cross Bunyola staying on the MA2100 and rejoin the MA11 to return to Palma.

France, Belgium & Luxembourg

D80, Cap Corse, Corsica (route 58, pages 142–3)

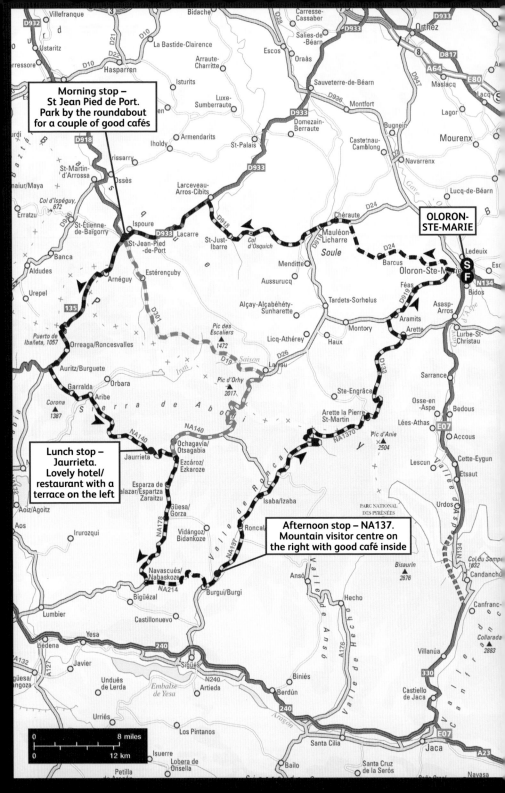

Morning stop –
St Jean Pied de Port.
Park by the roundabout
for a couple of good cafés

**OLORON-
STE-MARIE**

Lunch stop –
Jaurrieta.
Lovely hotel/
restaurant with a
terrace on the left

Afternoon stop – NA137.
Mountain visitor centre on
the right with good café inside

0   8 miles
0   12 km

31 Oloron and On and On

This route in the western Pyrenees takes in one of my absolute favourite passes, the Col de la Pierre St-Martin – one of those rare roads with a complete 360° turn on it. This is actually two routes in one. You can decide over coffee in St Jean Pied-de-Port whether to take the more laid-back run straight into Spain, on the broad (but still hairpin-heavy) N135 or whether to stay on the French side

FROM	Oloron-Ste-Marie
DISTANCE	165 miles
ALLOW	5 hours

of the mountains for longer, taking the beautiful but more demanding single-track D301 to cross the border at the Larrau Pass, which adds about half an hour to the day's ride. Both options are brilliant.

Route
- Leave Oloron-Ste-Marie on the D24 to Esquiule and Mauléon-Licharre.
- Bear right in Barcus to stay on the D24.
- Cross Mauléon-Licharre and pick up the D918 to St Jean-Pied-de-Port, which goes over Col d'Osquich.
- At the D933, turn left to St Jean.
- In St Jean, turn right at the roundabout and then take the right fork to continue on the D933 towards Pamplona and Arnéguy.
- Turn right at the roundabout in Arnéguy, to Spain, where the road becomes the N135.
- Don't miss the left turn, 15 miles from the border (about a mile after Auritz-Burguete) for the NA140 to Garralda and Isaba.
- In Ezkaroze, turn right on the NA178 to Oronz and Navascués.
- Don't miss the left turn in Navascués for the NA214 to Burgui and Isaba.
- Turn left at the roundabout on the edge of Burgui on the N137 to Isaba and France. This becomes the D132 when it crosses the border at Arette la Pierre Saint-Martin.

- In Arette, turn left on the D918 to Lanne-en-Barétous and Mauléon.
- When the D918 reaches a T-junction, turn right to Aramits and follow the road back in to Oloron.

Want something wilder?
- Go straight across the roundabout in St Jean on the D301 to Estérençuby.
- After 7 miles, take the left-hand fork to stay on the D301 to Iraty – now a single-track road.
- Don't miss the right turn, 12 miles later, for the D19 to Larrau and Iraty over Col d'Orgambidesca.
- In Larrau, turn right on the D26 to Spain over the Port de Larrau.
- At the NA140 junction, go straight (technically a right turn) to Auritz-Burguete.
- Rejoin the core route at Ezkaroze.

32 Cols of the Tour

This route strings together four of the most famous passes in France: Aspin, Tourmalet, Soulor and Aubisque. They regularly feature in the Tour de France (Tourmalet's the only pass that has been in every one) so they're popular – especially with cyclists. Always check when the Tour is visiting here: don't do this route within a week either side of it. The route starts in Bagnères-de-Luchon as I find the passes flow best from east to west. You can shorten the day by using the A64 motorway on the return run from Lourdes, but the route follows the much more fun D938.

FROM	Bagnères-de-Luchon
DISTANCE	**205 miles**
ALLOW	**6 hours**

Route

- Leave Bagnères on the D618 to Arreau over Col de Peyresourde.
- Don't miss the left turn after 13 miles for Estarvielle (D25). This will take you round the lake and over Col de Val Louron-Azet.
- Turn right at the mini-roundabout in Saint-Lary-Soulan on the D929.

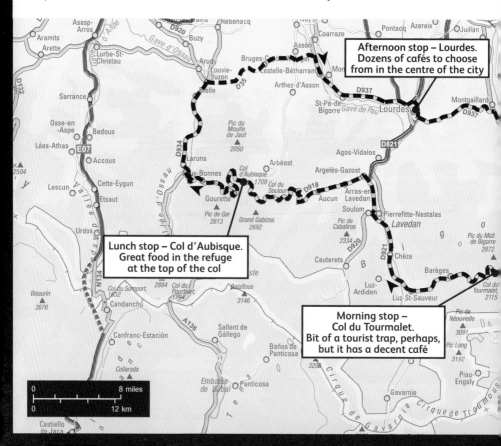

Afternoon stop – Lourdes. Dozens of cafés to choose from in the centre of the city

Lunch stop – Col d'Aubisque. Great food in the refuge at the top of the col

Morning stop – Col du Tourmalet. Bit of a tourist trap, perhaps, but it has a decent café

- In Arreau, turn left onto the D918. This goes over Col d'Aspin.
- In St Marie de Campan, turn left to stay on the D918 over Col du Tourmalet.
- In Luz-St-Saveur, turn right on the D921 to Argelès-Gazost.
- In Argelès-Gazost, pick up the D918 over Col de Soulor and Col d'Aubisque.
- In Eaux-Bonnes, turn right on the D934 to Laruns and Pau.
- Coming into Louvie-Juzon, turn right after the bridge, on the D35 to Pau.
- At the D937, turn right to Lourdes.
- Cross Lourdes and continue on the D937 towards Bagnères-de-Bigorre.
- At the D935, turn right to Bagnères.

- In Bagnères-de-Bigorre, pick up the D938 to Capvern. Don't get on the A64 – stick with the D938 all the way.
- In Montréjeau, turn right on the D825 towards Lérida.
- At the N125, turn right towards Lérida.
- In Chaum, turn right on the D125 to return to Bagnères de Luchon.

Want more?
- For a longer ride, carry on from Chaum on the N125, becoming the N230, over the border to Spain.
- From Bossòt, take the N141 over Col du Portillon to return to France and Bagnères-de-Luchon. This adds 30–40 minutes to the day.

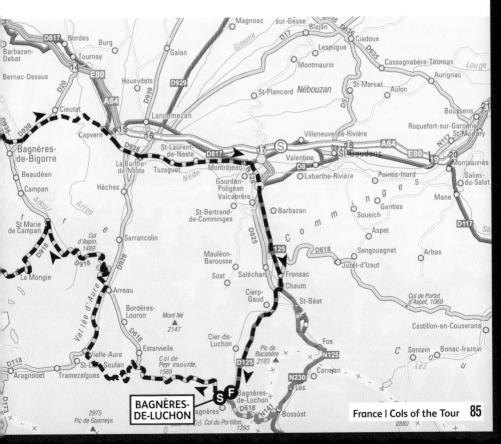

33 Cathar Castle Country

There's more to the mountains than the passes. The eastern end of the Pyrenees is stuffed with magnificent castles – many built by the Cathars. This relaxed route passes close to three of the most impressive (Peyrepertuse, Puilaurens and Quéribus) as well as Château d'Usson. Of course, it does also take

FROM	Ax-les-Thermes
DISTANCE	170 miles
ALLOW	4½ hours

in stunning mountain passes and one unforgettable gorge. This route mostly sticks to the broader, smoother roads to make it suitable for pillions.

Route

- From Ax, take the N20 towards Andorra.
- After 10 miles, bear right following signs for 'Barcelone par le Col' on the N320.

- Don't miss the left turn 4 miles later to stay on the N320 to Bourg-Madame.
- In Bourg-Madame, turn left on the N116 to Perpignan.

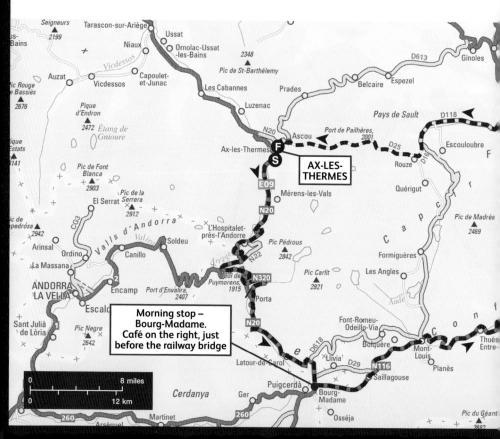

- Stick with the N116 for 50 miles. It becomes a dual carriageway as it bypasses Ille-sur-Têt: 7½ miles later, take the exit for Millas and the D916.
- In the centre of Millas, turn right beside the church on the D612 to Estagel. Turn left at the roundabout to stay on this road.
- In Estagel, turn left on the D117 to Foix.
- Don't miss the right turn in Maury for the D19 to Cucugnan (which becomes the D123). These are smaller roads.
- Turn left in Cucugnan on the D14 to Rouffiac-des-Corbières and Château de Peyrepertuse – an even smaller road.

- Turn left in Cubières-sur-Cinoble on the D10 to the Gorges de Galamus.
- In St Paul de Fenouillet, turn right to rejoin the D117 heading for Foix.
- Turn left on the D118 to Axat at the roundabout 14 miles from St Paul (4 miles from Lapradelle-Puilaurens).
- After 13 miles, by Chateau d'Usson, turn right on the D16 to Rouze.
- Leaving Rouze, turn right on the D116 to Mijanès – which becomes the D25. Stay on this road all the way back to Ax-les-Thermes.

Château de Peyrepertuse
So many magnificent castles to visit. If you have time to see only one, my tip would be Peyrepertuse. See: www.peyrepertuse.com.

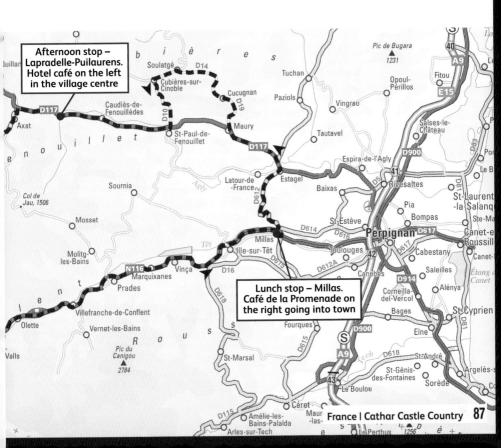

Afternoon stop – Lapradelle-Puilaurens. Hotel café on the left in the village centre

Lunch stop – Millas. Café de la Promenade on the right going into town

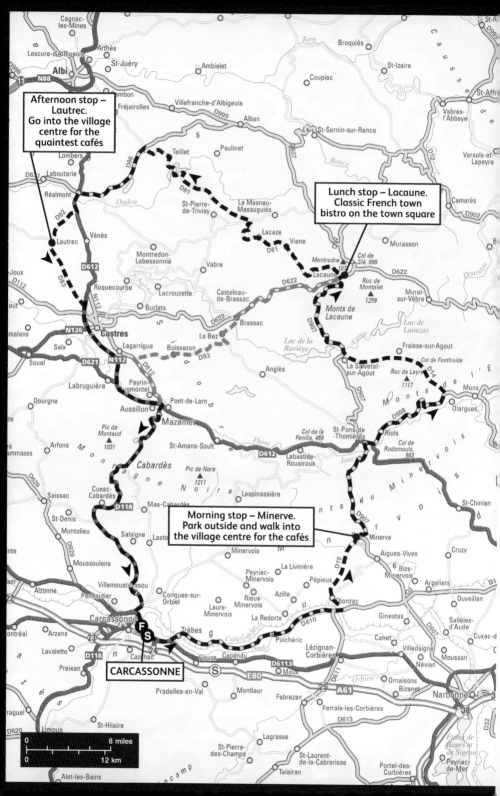

Afternoon stop – Lautrec.
Go into the village centre for the quaintest cafés

Lunch stop – Lacaune.
Classic French town bistro on the town square

Morning stop – Minerve.
Park outside and walk into the village centre for the cafés

CARCASSONNE

34 Carcassonne

I love the medieval citadel of Carcassonne – it's well worth exploring, even if it is a bit of a tourist hotspot. So this route heads out to beautiful Minerve, which is just as charming and historic but half as busy. The route also visits Olargues and Lautrec, officially two of the most beautiful villages in France – but if you

FROM	Carcassonne
DISTANCE	185 miles
ALLOW	5 hours

spend too much time in Minerve, you can cut the route short from Lacaune, missing out the extended run to Lautrec but saving an hour.

Route

- Leave Carcassonne on the D6113, signed for Narbonne – but don't head for the motorway. Keep going straight on the D6113 to Trèbes.
- In Trèbes, turn left on the D610 to Marseillette.
- Don't miss the left turn 17 miles later for the D52E to Olonzac. Turn left to go into the village, following signs for Minerve to pick up the D10.
- From Minerve, continue on the D10 towards St-Pons-de-Thomières.
- At the D907 T-junction, turn left to Rieussec and St-Pons-de-Thomières.
- In St-Pons-de-Thomières, turn right on the D612 to Béziers.
- One mile later, turn left on the D908 to Riols and Olargues.
- After visiting Olargues, backtrack on the D908 for half a mile and turn right on the D14 to Fraisse-sur-Agout and St-Vincent-d'Olargues, over Col du Fontfroide.
- In La Salvetat-sur-Agout, rejoin the D907 towards Lacaune.

- *Short of time? Turn left at the lights in Lacaune on the D622 to Brassac and Castres. After Brassac, turn left on the D93 to Mazamet and pick up the D612 into Mazamet to rejoin the core route on the D118.*
- In Lacaune, turn right at the traffic lights, then left by the church to pick up the D81 to Viane and Gijounet. Stick with the D81 for 35 twisty miles.
- At the crossroads 3 miles after Teillet, turn left on the D86 to Réalmont.
- In Réalmont, turn left on the D621 towards Castres.
- A mile outside Réalmont, turn right on the D92 to Lautrec.
- From Lautrec, take the D83 to Vielmur-sur-Agout and Castres.
- Join the D1012 to bypass Castres, heading towards Toulouse and Mazamet. This road then becomes the N112.
- Cross Mazamet following the signs for Aussillon and then Carcassonne to pick up the D118. Take this road all the way back to Carcassonne.

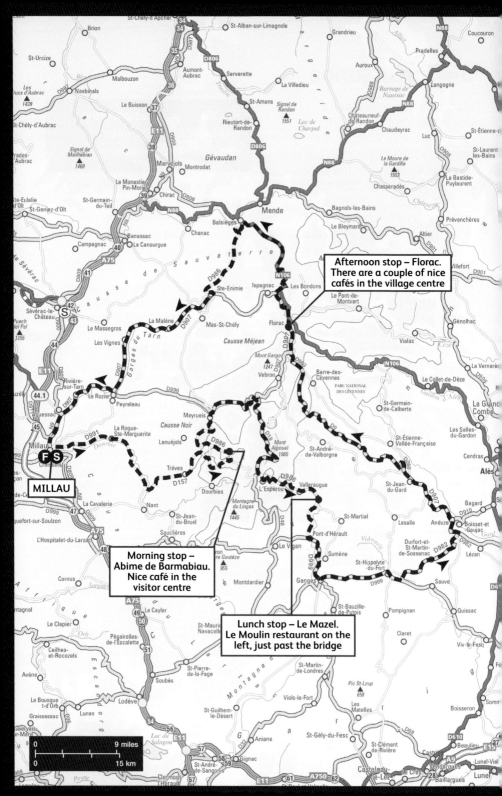

Afternoon stop – Florac.
There are a couple of nice
cafés in the village centre

MILLAU

Morning stop –
Abime de Barmabiau.
Nice café in the
visitor centre

Lunch stop – Le Mazel.
Le Moulin restaurant on the
left, just past the bridge

35 More than a Bridge

There's much more to see near Millau than just the world's tallest bridge. The Millau Viaduct spans the broad valley of the River Tarn to the west of the town. To the east, the river has cut a network of spectacular, twisting gorges – all lined with brilliant roads. Better still, the gorges are next to the steep and densely wooded slopes of the Cévennes – a real hidden gem of a biking area. Whichever way you go,

FROM	**Millau**
DISTANCE	**220 miles**
ALLOW	**6 hours**

there are great roads around Millau… but I suggest going this way to enjoy the almost-Alpine riding on Mont Aigoual and the magnificent Corniche des Cévennes.

Route

- Leave Millau on the D991 to Massebiau.
- Don't miss the left turn 16 miles later for the D145 to Trèves. This becomes the D157.
- Don't miss the right turn (over a bridge) 5 miles after Trèves to stay on the D157.
- In St-Sauveur-Camprieu, turn left at the roundabout on the D986 to Meyrueis.
- Go right/straight on at the roundabout in Meyrueis on the D996.
- Don't miss the right turn (at a crossroads) 6½ miles later for the D18 to Cabrillac.
- At the ski station – on a one-way system – pick up the D296 to L'Espérou.
- At the war memorial, turn left on the D986 and at the mini-roundabout in L'Espérou turn left to stay on this road.
- In Ganges, turn left on the D999 to St-Hippolyte-du-Fort.
- In St-Hippolyte pick up the D982 to Alès.
- In Anduze, go straight, following the river, on the D907 to St-Jean-du-Gard.
- Don't miss the right turn after St-Jean-du-Gard for the N260 signed for Florac. This becomes the D9: the Corniche des Cévennes.
- Keep going straight as the road becomes first the D938 and then the D907 to Florac.
- Cross the bridge at Florac head and turn left on the N106 to Mende.
- In Balsièges, turn left on the D986 to Ispagnac.
- In St-Enimie, turn right on the D907 to follow the Tarn Gorge to return to Millau.

The Millau Viaduct

Best viewed from the valley rather than the A75 motorway that crosses it, but the visitor centre is in the services on the motorway. Check the expo by the D996, below the bridge.

Abime de Bramabiau

Want some respite from the summer heat? Why not venture into this cool cave and take the walk to the spectacular underground waterfall? www.abime-de-bramabiau.com

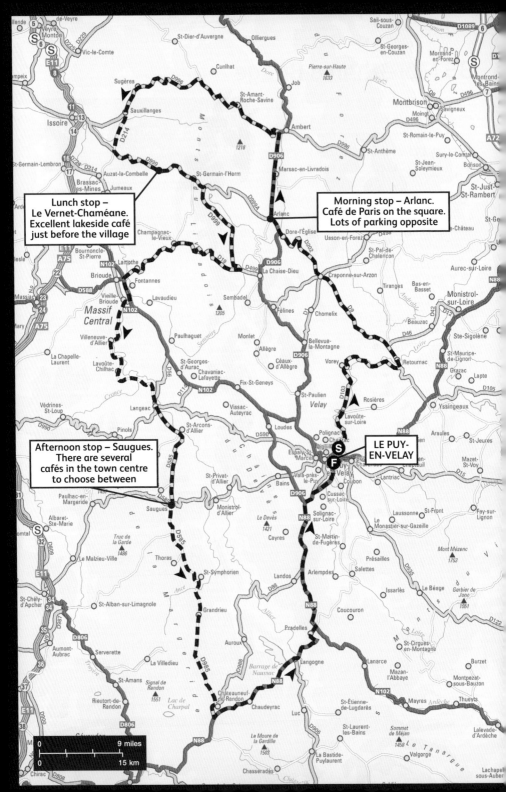

**Lunch stop –
Le Vernet-Chaméane.
Excellent lakeside café
just before the village**

**Morning stop – Arlanc.
Café de Paris on the square.
Lots of parking opposite**

**Afternoon stop – Saugues.
There are several
cafés in the town centre
to choose between**

**LE PUY-
EN-VELAY**

36 The Ducati Loop

This full day's ride through the rolling hills of the Auvergne grew out of discovering a pair of roads through the Livradois Forest: the D996 and D999. I never did get to ride either a Ducati 996 or 999 on them, but I always imagined how rewarding they'd be, with the agility to carve through the corners and the power to shrink the straights. The route got longer when my friend Paul introduced me to the D585 south of

FROM	Le Puy-en-Velay
DISTANCE	235 miles
ALLOW	6½ hours

Brioude – another of those casually brilliant bits of tarmacked French road builders sometimes leave in quiet areas. Better still, it links with the excellent N88. I'd like to see how a Ducati handles those two roads, too... maybe the new Multistrada V4.

Route

- Leave Le Puy-en-Velay on the D103 to Lavoûte sur Loire. Stick with it as it becomes the D9 in Retournac.
- Don't miss the left turn half a mile out of town to stay on the D9 to Roche-en-Régnier.
- Cross Craponne-sur-Arzon on the D9, which then becomes the D202.
- In Dore-l'Église, turn right on the D906 to Arlanc and Ambert.
- Leaving Ambert, don't miss the left turn for the D996 to Issoire.
- Don't miss the left turn 7 miles from St-Amant-Roche-Savine to stay on the D996.
- There's another easily missed left turn a mile outside Sugères to stay on the D996.

- In Sauxillanges, go straight as the D996 goes right (down a narrow lane between houses) on the D214 to St-Jean-en-Val.
- At the D999 turn left towards St-Germain-l'Herm.
- At the D19 turn left to Brioude.
- In Brioude, join the N108 towards Le Puy for one junction.
- Take the D912 into Vieille-Brioude, cross the river and turn left on the D585 to Villeneuve-d'Allier. Eventually this becomes the D985.
- At the D988 T-junction, turn right to Châteauneuf-de-Randon.
- Turn left on the N88 to return to Le Puy.

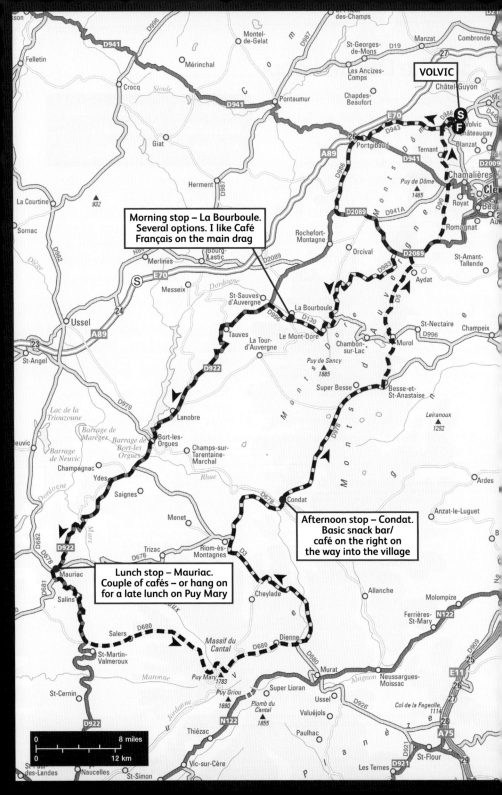

37 The Volcano Route

My friend Tony has shown me many great roads over the years, starting with one of my favourites: the D680 over Puy Mary. That's one of the dormant volcanoes that gives the Auvergne its amazing landscape and awesome roads. This route from Volvic (home of the mineral water)

FROM	Volvic
DISTANCE	210 miles
ALLOW	6 hours

heads down to Puy Mary, packing as much of the region's mountain-riding goodness into one day as possible.

Route

- Leave Volvic on the D986 to Pontgibaud.
- At the D941 roundabout, turn right towards Limoges and the A89.
- Don't miss the left turn after one mile for the D943 to Pontgibaud.
- In Pontgibaud, turn left on the D986 to La Miouze and Gelles.
- Turn left on the D2089 to Nébouzat.
- After 8 miles turn right on the D983 to Col du Guéry.
- Take the D996 through Le Mont Dore and La Bourboule and Le Mont-Dore, towards the A89.
- In St-Sauves-d'Auvergne, turn left on the D922 to Bort-les-Orgues. Stick with this road all the way through Mauriac, towards Aurillac.
- Don't miss the left turn about 9 miles outside Mauriac for the D680 to Salers.
- At Col du Pas de Peyrol, at the top of Puy Mary, go straight on the D680 to Murat.
- At the D3 turn left to Riom-ès-Montagnes.
- In Riom, pick up the D678 to Clermont-Ferrand and stick with it to Égliseneuve d'Entraigues, where it becomes the D978.
- In Besse-et-St-Anastaise, pick up the D5 back towards Le Mont-Dore.
- In Murol turn left, then left on the D996 – and at the roundabout turn right to get back on the D5 to Clermont-Ferrand and Aydat.
- Turn left at the D213, then right at the D2089 towards Clermont-Ferrand.
- After 3 miles, turn left on the D52 to St-Genès-Champanelle. It becomes the D90.
- 2 miles later, turn right on the D90. Turn left then right in La Font de l'Abre to stay on it, and stick with the D90 through Orcines, Ternant and Chanat-la-Mouteyre.
- At the D943, turn left then turn right on the D986 to return to Volvic.

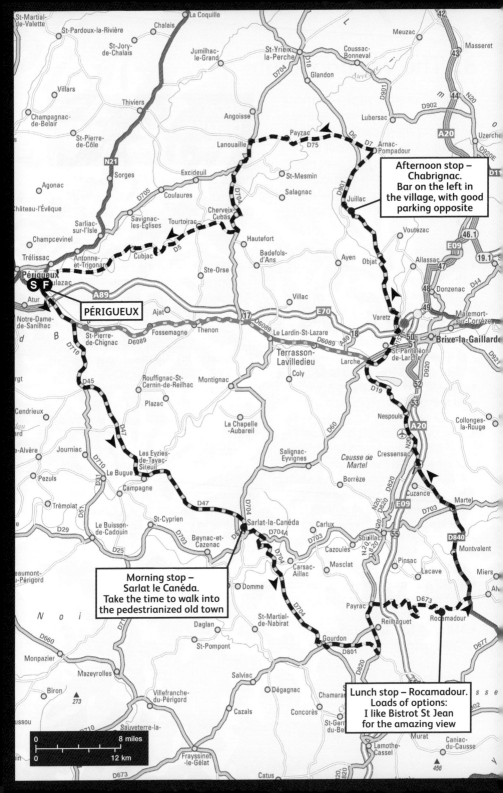

Afternoon stop –
Chabrignac.
Bar on the left in
the village, with good
parking opposite

PÉRIGUEUX

Morning stop –
Sarlat le Canéda.
Take the time to walk into
the pedestrianized old town

Lunch stop – Rocamadour.
Loads of options:
I like Bistrot St Jean
for the amazing view

38 Dordogne Day

This is a riding day... which almost seems a shame as there's so much to see in this area. Based in Périgueux, the capital of the foodie Périgord region, the route runs out to another place introduced to me by my friend Tony: Rocamadour. The roads and scenery would be memorable enough

FROM	Périgueux
DISTANCE	190 miles
ALLOW	6 hours

even before getting there – but visiting Rocamadour just makes this a truly unforgettable day on the bike.

Route

- Leave Périgueux on the N221 towards the A89, Bordeaux and Sarlat-la-Canéda.
- Don't get on the motorway: keep going straight and at the roundabout after the level crossing, take the D710 to Sarlat.
- After 8½ miles turn left on the D45. Keep going as it becomes the D47 to Sarlat.
- Go left at the first roundabout and right at the second to go into the centre of Sarlat.
- From Sarlat, continue along the D704 towards Cahors and the A20.
- In Gourdon, turn left on the D801.
- At the D820, turn left to Brive-la-Gaillarde.
- Don't miss the right turn in Payrac for the D673 to Calès and Rocamadour.
- Leave Rocamadour on the D673 to Gramat (also signed for the A20).
- At the D840, turn left to Brive and the A20. Go past the motorway on the D840.
- In Nespouls, turn left by the garage on the D19 to Noailles.
- Go straight through Larche on the D19 and straight across the D6089 – unless you spent a long time at Rocamadour, in which case, turn left for the fast way to Périgueux.
- Turn right on the D152 to St-Pantaléon-de-Larche.
- At the D901, turn left to Varetz and Objat.
- In Arnac-Pompadour, turn sharp left on the D7 to Ségur-le-Château (if you reach the castle and the square, you've overshot the turn). This road then becomes the D75.
- Don't miss the left turn in Payzac for the D75 to La Chapelle.
- In Lanouaille, turn left on the D704 towards the A89 and Périgueux.
- In Cherveix-Cubas, turn right on the D5 to Périgueux and take it all the way back.

Rocamadour

You can happily spend a day here (I have) climbing through the extraordinary village and church carved into a cliff. Best not do it in bike kit in summer, though. An extended coffee stop with a short walk should let you soak up the flavour of this amazing place.

Sarlat le Canéda

With the greatest concentration of medieval buildings in France, the centre of Sarlat is like a film set: a fabulous place for a wander (or a coffee stop).

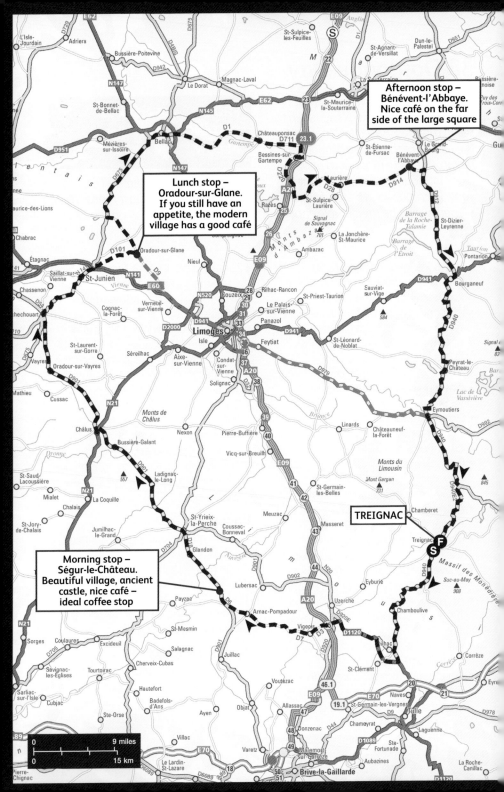

Afternoon stop –
Bénévent-l'Abbaye.
Nice café on the far
side of the large square

Lunch stop –
Oradour-sur-Glane.
If you still have an
appetite, the modern
village has a good café

Morning stop –
Ségur-le-Château.
Beautiful village, ancient
castle, nice café –
ideal coffee stop

TREIGNAC

39 Oradour-sur-Glane

Oradour-sur-Glane is a sombre place – a war memorial, preserved as it was left after the SS massacred the populace. It's a stark contrast with the beauty of the surrounding roads, which make you glad to be alive. This long route passes through several lovely villages, like Mortemart and

FROM	Treignac
DISTANCE	220 miles
ALLOW	6 hours

Ségur-le-Château, but it's a long ride, so can be shortened by 90 minutes if you want to spend longer at Oradour.

Route

- Leave Treignac on the D940 to Seilhac.
- At the D1120 roundabout, turn right towards the A20 for Limoges and Vigeois.
- At the motorway roundabout, turn right towards Uzerche then take the first left for the D3 to Vigeois.
- Climbing up the hill out of Vigeois, bear right (around the hairpin) as the road becomes the D7 to Troche and Pompadour.
- Turn left in Arnac-Pompadour, ride past the chateau, and look for the right-hand fork to stay on the D7 to Beyssenac.
- Don't miss the right turn 4 miles later for the (single-track) D6E to Ségur-le-Château. This becomes the D6, then the D18.
- In St-Yrieix-la-Perche, pick up the D901 towards Rochechouart.
- At the D675 junction turn right to Rochechouart and Limoges.
- Cross St-Junien and join the N141 towards Limoges for one junction, leaving to take the D101 towards Oradour-sur-Glane.
- Leave Oradour on the D3 towards Bellac and keep going straight as it becomes the D9.

- At the D675 crossroads turn right to Bellac and Mortemart.
- Cross Bellac following the signs for the A20 and Guéret, until you get to the major N147 roundabout: go straight across on the D1 to Bessines-sur-Gartempe. This becomes the D711 after Châteauponsac.
- At the D220 roundabout, turn right towards the A20 to Limoges – but don't join the motorway. Stay on the D220 across Bessines-sur-Gartempe.
- Don't miss the left turn after 6 miles (3½ miles outside Bessines) for the D28 to Laurière.
- Turn left in Laurière on the D914 to La Souterraine and Bénévent-l'Abbaye.
- At the D912 crossroads, turn right to Bourganeuf.
- In Bourganeuf, turn right on the D941. Half a mile later, turn left on the D940 to Tulle and Peyrat-le-Château.
- Turn right in Eymoutiers to stay on the D940. After 11 miles, turn right to stay on the D940 back to Treignac.

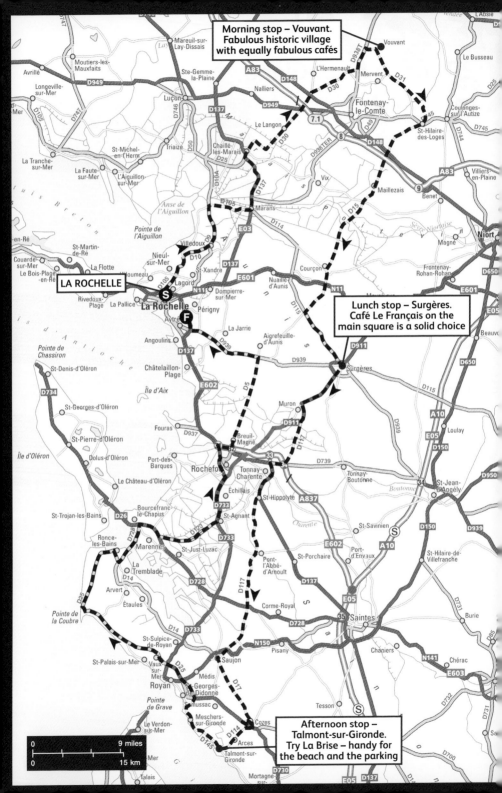

Morning stop – Vouvant.
Fabulous historic village
with equally fabulous cafés

Lunch stop – Surgères.
Café Le Français on the
main square is a solid choice

**Afternoon stop –
Talmont-sur-Gironde.**
Try La Brise – handy for
the beach and the parking

40 La Rochelle, Ma Belle…

What the west coast of France lacks in mountains, it makes up for with history and character. This long but laid-back route from the lovely city of La Rochelle heads up to the medieval gem of Vouvant, then down to Talmont-sur-Gironde for a seaside snack. In between, there's miles of quiet, gently flowing riding to

FROM	La Rochelle
DISTANCE	215 miles
ALLOW	6½ hours

enjoy – though it's easily shortened by heading straight to Rochefort after lunch.

Route

- Leave La Rochelle on the D104 to Marsilly, which becomes the D105 and then the D10.
- At Villedoux, join the D9 to La Roche-sur-Yon. After 4 miles turn right on the D105.
- In Marans, turn left on the D137.
- Don't miss the right turn in Chaillé-les-Marais for the D30 to Le Langon. Stick with the D30 and through l'Hermenault.
- Turn left on the D23, then turn right to stay on the D30 to Bourseguin.
- After Bourseguin, go straight ahead to join the D938T to La Châtaigneraie.
- After 2½ miles, turn right on the D31 to Vouvant. Stay on the D31 until it becomes the D15, which then becomes the D116.
- At the D115, turn left to Surgères.
- In Surgères, join the D911 to Rochefort.
- At the Muron roundabout, turn left on the D117 to Lussant and Tonnay-Charente.
- Turn right on the D739 to go under the motorway, then at the next roundabout turn left on the D137 to Saintes.

- At St-Hippolyte, rejoin the D117 and take it all the way to Saujon.
- In Saujon, pick up the D17 to Cozes.
- From Cozes, take the D114 to Talmont-sur-Gironde.
- From Talmont-sur-Gironde, take the D145 to Royan and join the D25.
- Keep going on the D25 to ride along the Côté Sauvage – the wild coast.
- Take the D728 to Marennes and pick up the D123 towards Rochefort.
- Take the D733 to Rochefort and around the edge of the city, towards the A837.
- Cross the motorway on the D214 to Breuil-Magné.
- At the D5 T-junction, turn left towards Aigrefeuille-d'Aunis.
- At the D939, turn left to La Rochelle.

Rochefort

Plenty to see in the historic port city of Rochefort – especially the old royal dockyards and the Arsenal, which houses the French National Naval Museum.

41 Loire Châteaux Run

This is a relaxed one-day route with a bit of from-the-saddle 'Look at that one' while passing the châteaux on the banks of the Loire – or it could be a two-day trip (stopping overnight in Tours) with time to get off the bike and explore some of them. There are lots of castles to visit, from Château d'Angers at the start, to Château de Saumur, Montsoreau, the Royal Fortress of Chinon and Château d'Ussé – famously the inspiration for Charles Perrault's Sleeping Beauty.

FROM	Angers
TO	Orléans
DISTANCE	160 miles
ALLOW	5½ hours

There's Villandry, Chenonceau (built out across the River Cher – it has to be seen to be believed), Cheverny, Villesavin in Bracieux and of course the huge Château de Chambord, so impressive it was a Bond-villain lair in Moonraker.

Route

- Leave Angers on the D160 to Les Ponts-de-Cé, crossing the Loire.
- Follow the signs for the A87 to Poitiers to pick up the D748.
- Don't get on the motorway: cross it and pick up the D751 to Juigné-sur-Loire.
- In Saumur, join the D947 to Fontevraud l'Abbaye.

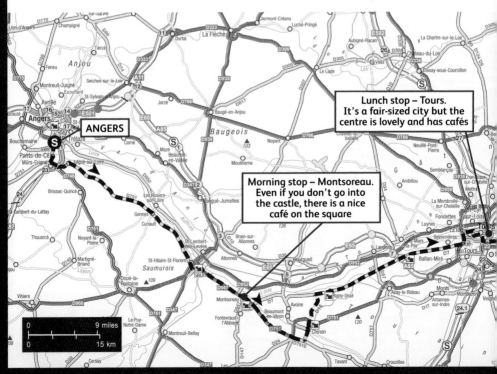

Lunch stop – Tours.
It's a fair-sized city but the centre is lovely and has cafés

Morning stop – Montsoreau.
Even if you don't go into the castle, there is a nice café on the square

ANGERS

- Turn left in Montsoreau to stay beside the river on the D751A to Candes-St-Martin, past the château (now an art gallery).
- At the D751, turn left to Chinon.
- Go straight over the roundabout on the D751E to Châtelleraut.
- At the next roundabout, turn left on the D749 to the town centre and Chinon.
- Cross the river, turn left, then bear right on the D751E towards Château Chinon.
- Don't miss the left turn for the D16 to Huisme and Rigny-Ussé.
- At the D7, turn right to Rigny-Ussé, past Château d'Ussé. Take this road past Château de Villandry, all the way to Tours.
- Leave Tours on the D140 to Vierzon.

- At La Croix-en-Touraine, go straight across the D31, turn left through the village, then turn right on the D40 to Chenonceaux (the château is on the right, after the garage).
- In Montrichard, pick up the D764 to Pontlevoy and Blois.
- In Sambin, turn right on the D52 to Cour-Cheverny.
- From Cour-Cheverny, take the D102 to Tour-en-Sologne.
- Cross Bracieux and pick up the D112 to Chambord. Follow the road (now the D33) past the château and turn right on the D122.
- From Chambord, take the D112 (go right from the car parks) to Muides-sur-Loire.
- From Muides, take the D951 to Orléans.

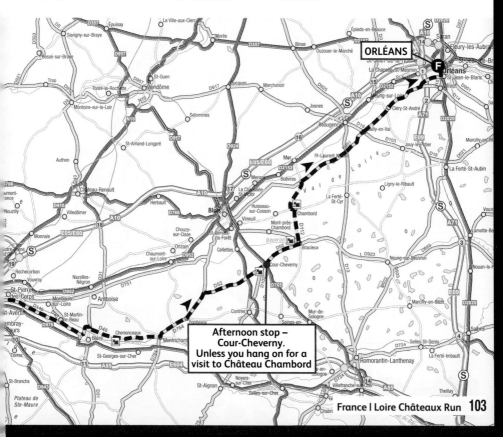

Afternoon stop – Cour-Cheverny. Unless you hang on for a visit to Château Chambord

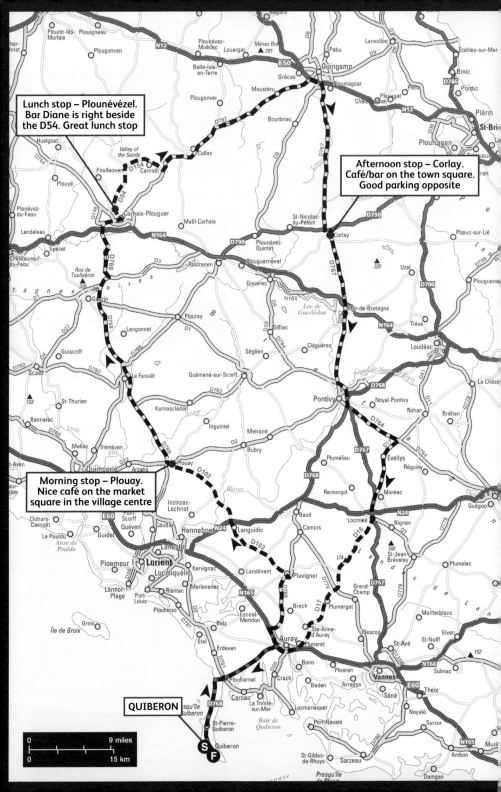

**Lunch stop – Plounévézel.
Bar Diane is right beside
the D54. Great lunch stop**

**Afternoon stop – Corlay.
Café/bar on the town square.
Good parking opposite**

**Morning stop – Plouay.
Nice café on the market
square in the village centre**

QUIBERON

42 Quiberon Balloon

Northern France is a great destination for a first European trip or a relaxed two-up tour, especially for a novice pillion. There's a lot of lovely laid-back riding around the far west of Brittany and lots to see – from the ancient megaliths of Carnac to the modern megalithic statues of the Valley of the Saints. This full day's ride loops out

FROM	**Quiberon**
DISTANCE	**205 miles**
ALLOW	**6 hours**

from the peninsula resort of Quiberon on lovely, flowing, quiet roads to the Valley of the Saints.

Route

- Leave Quiberon on the D768 and stick with it through Plouharnel to Auray.
- In Auray, join the N165 to Lorient.
- Take the first exit (J34) to Pontivy, picking up the D768 again.
- In Pluvigner, pick up the D102 to Languidic and stay on it all the way to Plouay.
- Cross Plouay and join the D769 towards Morlaix. Keep going straight when it becomes the D264.
- Cross Carhaix-Plouger to pick up the D54 to Plounevezel.
- Don't miss the right turn after 6 miles for the D154 to Carnoët.
- After 2 miles, turn right following the brown sign for the Valley of the Saints.
- After your visit, continue along the minor road and turn right on the D97 to Carnoët.
- At the D787, turn left to Callac.
- After 20 miles, bear left towards St-Brieuc and join the N12 to bypass Guingamp.
- Take the first exit for the D767 to La Chesnay.
- In Le Haut-Corlay, turn left on the D790.
- In Corlay, turn right through the village centre, staying on the D767 to Pontivy.
- After 16 miles, turn left on the D764 to Pontivy Nord (signed for other directions).
- Join the D768 to Vannes and Lorient.
- After 2 miles take the exit for the D764 to Vannes. Turn right at the bottom of the slip road and turn left at the next roundabout to stay on the D764.
- In another 6 miles, turn right at the roundabout on the D17 to Locminé.
- Turn left at the roundabout in Évellys to stay on the D17.
- Turn left at the D767 to Locminé.
- In Locminé, pick up the D16 to Plumelin.
- Don't miss the left turn when the road forks (in the woods) for the D17 to Brandivy.
- At the roundabout, go straight over on the D17bis to Auray.
- Join the N165 to Lorient.
- After 2½ miles, take the exit (J33) to pick up the D768 to return to Quiberon.

43 Normandy Beaches

Normandy is a lovely place for a short break – especially if you're interested in history. This relaxed ride works well as a one-day whistlestop tour or split over two days, which allows a decent amount of time for visiting the many museums and memorials dedicated to the D-Day landings.

FROM	Caen
DISTANCE	180 miles
ALLOW	6 hours

Route

- Leave Caen on the D9 to Caumont.
- Don't miss the right turn after 6½ miles for the D13 to Balleroy.
- Turn left on the D572 to St-Lô.
- In St-Lô, join the N174 towards Cherbourg and Carentan.
- Leave at J7 on the D900 to Périers.
- After 2½ miles, turn right on the D29 to Les Champs-de-Losque.
- Turn right on the D971 to Carentan.
- Join the N13 towards Cherbourg.

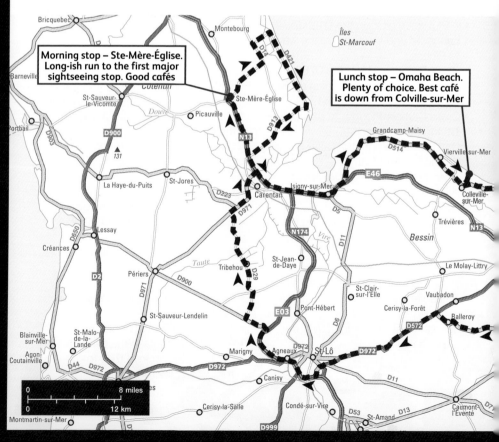

Morning stop – Ste-Mère-Église. Long-ish run to the first major sightseeing stop. Good cafés

Lunch stop – Omaha Beach. Plenty of choice. Best café is down from Colville-sur-Mer

- After 6½ miles, take the exit for the D67 into Ste-Mère-Église.
- Leave Ste-Mère on the D15 to Ravenoville.
- Turn left at the D14.
- After 2 miles, turn right on the D69.
- Turn right on the D421 at the seafront, to Ravenoville-Plage.
- At the T-junction, turn left on the D15.
- Take the D913 to Ste-Marie-du-Mont and Carentan.
- Join the N13 towards Caen.
- After 10 miles, take the exit for the D124 to Osmanville and La Pointe du Hoc. This becomes the D514.
- Follow the D514 along the coast. This goes past all the D-Day landing sites (don't miss the left turn in Colleville-sur-Mere for Omaha Beach and the American Cemetery). Take the D514 all the way to Courseulles-sur-Mer and the Juno Beach Centre.

- Get back on the D514 but at the T-junction in Courseulles, turn right on the D12 towards Caen, then turn left at the roundabout on the D79 to Caen.
- At the next roundabout, turn left on the D35 to Tailleville and Ouistreham (car ferry).
- In Colleville-Montgomery, bear left on the D35A to Ouistreham.
- Turn left at the D514 signed for Courseulles and the car ferry.
- Leave Ouistreham on the D84 to Caen.
- Take the exit for Bénouville.
- About 4½ miles from Pegasus Bridge, turn right in Merville, past the battery.
- At the end of the road, turn right on the D233 and take it across Ranville to pick up the D223 to Colombelles and Caen.
- Turn right on the D226 back to Caen.

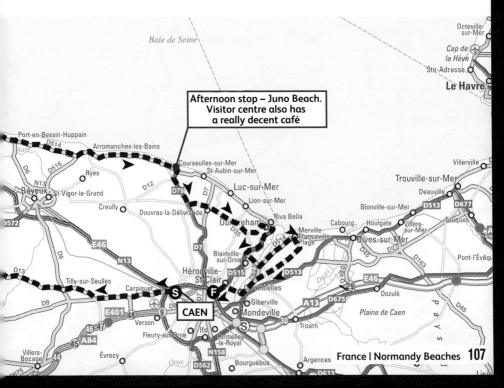

Afternoon stop – Juno Beach. Visitor centre also has a really decent café

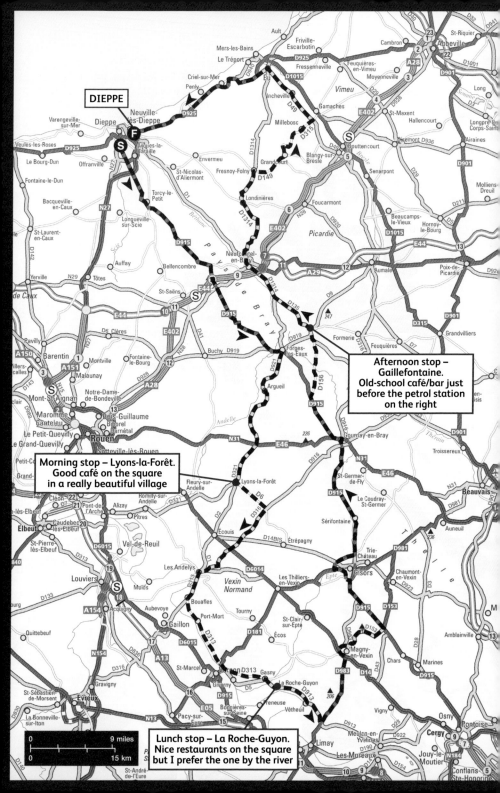

DIEPPE

Afternoon stop –
Gaillefontaine.
Old-school café/bar just
before the petrol station
on the right

Morning stop – Lyons-la-Forêt.
Good café on the square
in a really beautiful village

Lunch stop – La Roche-Guyon.
Nice restaurants on the square
but I prefer the one by the river

0   9 miles

0   15 km

44 Vexin Booster

There's more to Normandy than the D-Day beaches. This route from Dieppe goes through beautiful Lyons-la-Forêt to La Roche-Guyon on the banks of the River Seine – a popular meet for bikers from nearby Paris. Then it heads back through the Vexin region, for the best headline of the Covid era... An overnight ferry

FROM	Dieppe
DISTANCE	215 miles
ALLOW	6½ hours

from Newhaven to Dieppe (and back again) lets it work as a day trip, but I'd stay in Dieppe or do it over two days, staying in La Roche-Guyon.

Route

- Leave Dieppe on the D915 past the airport, towards the A28 and A29 motorways. Stick with it for about 30 miles.
- Go into the centre of Forges-les-Eaux on the D919 and pick up the D921 to Argueil and Lyons-la-Forêt. This becomes the D931.
- From Lyons-la-Forêt, take the D6 towards La Neuve-Grange and Étrépagny.
- At the D316 crossroads in La Neuve-Grange, turn right to Puchay and Les Andelys.
- In Les Andelys, turn left on the D313 towards the A13, Évreux and Louviers. Go straight over the roundabout by the suspension bridge to stay on the D313 towards the A13 and Vernon.
- Go left at the next roundabout on the D313 to Port-Mort and Vernon.
- In Vernon, turn left at the roundabout after the castle to stay on the D313 to Gasny and take it all the way to La Roche-Guyon, where it becomes the D913.
- In Vétheuil, turn left to stay on the D913 to Magny-en-Vexin and Fontenay-St-Père.

- At the D983 roundabout, turn left to Beauvais and Magny-en-Vexin.
- Go across Magny and take the D86 to Beauvais and Serans. This becomes the D153.
- At the D915 roundabout, turn left to Dieppe and Gisors – stick with it round Gisors, following the signs for Dieppe.
- At Gournay-en-Bray, turn left on the N31 then right to stay on the D915 to Dieppe.
- Don't miss the right turn 5 miles later for the D156 to Ménerval and Gaillefontaine.
- At the D135 T-junction, turn left to Gaillefontaine.
- At the D1314 T-junction, turn right to Neufchâtel-en-Bray.
- In Fresnoy-Folny, turn right on the D149 to Les Ifs.
- In Grandcourt, go straight ahead on the D14 to Guerville.
- Go straight aross the roundabout on the D216 to Millebosc.
- In Millebosc, turn right on the D315 to Incheville.
- At the D49, turn left to Incheville and Eu.
- In Eu, join the D925 to Dieppe.

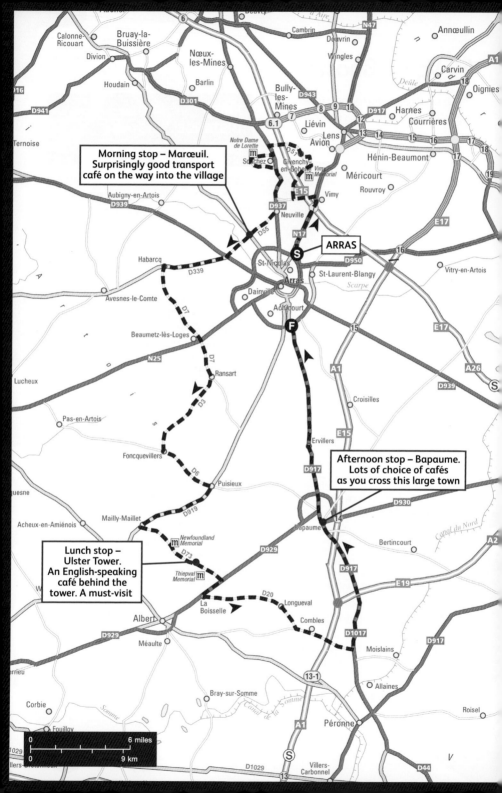

Morning stop – Marœuil.
Surprisingly good transport
café on the way into the village

ARRAS

Afternoon stop – Bapaume.
Lots of choice of cafés
as you cross this large town

Lunch stop –
Ulster Tower.
An English-speaking
café behind the
tower. A must-visit

0   6 miles

0   9 km

45 Somme Memorials

This is a relatively short route, but there's so much to see – stopping at even a few of the war memorials and cemeteries (and I've marked some key ones but there are many more) will make this a full day, especially as there are more memorial sites to see in Arras itself. It's good riding in

FROM	Arras
DISTANCE	95 miles
ALLOW	3½ hours

the relaxed, great-for-pillions sense: lovely countryside, decent roads and (usually) very little traffic.

Route

- Leave Arras on the D917 towards the A26 and Lens. This then becomes the N17.
- Go straight over the roundabout after the motorway on the D917 to Thélus.
- Take the first left for the D49 to Neuville-St-Vaast.
- Turn right in Neuville on the D55 to Givenchy-en-Gohelle. This will take you past the Vimy Ridge memorial and visitor centre.
- At Givenchy, turn left on the D51 to Angres and Notre Dame de Lorette.
- At the D937, turn left to Arras and Notre Dame de Lorette.
- In Souchez, turn right at the memorial to enter the huge Notre Dame de Lorette French national cemetery.
- Loop round to return to Souchez and continue on the D937 to Arras.
- In Neuville, turn right on the D55 to Marœuil. This becomes the D339 on the far side of Marœuil.
- Don't miss the left turn in Habarcq for the D7 to Montenescourt.

- At the crossroads in Ransart, turn right on the D3 to Monchy-au-Bois.
- In Foncquevillers, turn left on the D6 to Gommecourt.
- In Puisieux, turn right on the D919 to Bapaume and Miraumont.
- At Mailly-Maillet, turn left on the D73 to Hamel. Turn right in Auchonvillers to stay on it past the Newfoundland Memorial.
- In Hamel, turn left on the D50 for 300 m, then turn right on the D73 to Thiepval, past the Ulster Tower.
- From Thiepval, take the D73 to Pozières and turn left on the D929 to Amiens.
- In La Boisselle, turn left on the D20 to Contalmaison. To visit the Lochnagar Crater, follow the signs for 'La Grande Mine'.
- Continue along the D20. To visit the South African memorial, follow the signs from Longueval.
- At the D1017, turn left towards the A1 and Rancourt, past the French cemetery. This becomes the D917.
- Stay on the D917 all the way through Bapaume, back to Arras.

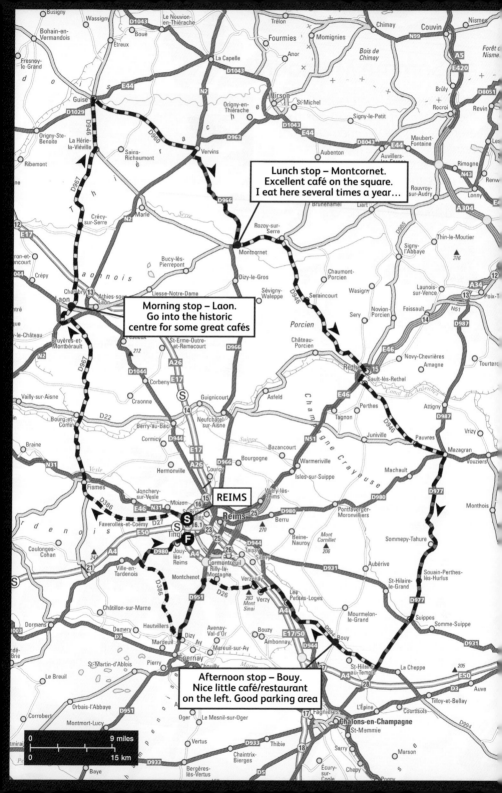

Lunch stop – Montcornet.
Excellent café on the square.
I eat here several times a year…

Morning stop – Laon.
Go into the historic
centre for some great cafés

REIMS

Afternoon stop – Bouy.
Nice little café/restaurant
on the left. Good parking area

| 0 | | | 9 miles |
| 0 | | | 15 km |

46 Champagne – All Round

Reims is a truly great city and makes a good first-night stop (or last night) on a longer European tour – but why rush off? There's so much enjoyable riding to be had in the Champagne region, especially in the Montagne de Reims – the vine-draped hills between the eponymous city and Épernay, where Dom Pérignon discovered

FROM	Reims
DISTANCE	210 miles
ALLOW	6 hours

bubbles make booze better. This is where the grapes for the famously fizzy beverage are grown and the riding is intoxicatingly good. Cheers!

Route

- Leave Reims on the N31 towards Soissons and the A4 and A26.
- Turn left at the first roundabout after going over the A26 on the D27 to Gueux, past the old Reims GP buildings.
- In Faverolles-et-Coëmy, turn right, then right again on the D386 to Savigny-sur-Ardres.
- Go straight through Fismes, picking up the D967 to Longueval and Laon.
- At the D22, turn left then first right to stay on the D967 to Laon.
- Leave Laon on the D967 towards Crécy-sur-Serre and Guise.
- In La Hérie-la-Viéville, turn left on the D946 to Valenciennes and Guise.
- In Guise, turn right on the D1029 then turn right on the D960 to Vervins.
- In Vervins, turn right at the roundabout, go under the railway bridge and turn left on the D966 to Reims and Montcornet.
- In Montcornet, turn left on the main square on the D946 to Rozoy-sur-Serre.
- Don't miss the right turn, coming into Rozoy-sur-Serre, to stay on the D946 to Fraillicourt and Château-Porcien.
- Go into Rethel, cross the river and look for the left turn to stay on the D946 towards Vouziers and Châlons en-Champagne.
- After 13 miles, turn right (second exit) at the roundabout on the D977 to Châlons-en-Champagne and Suippes.
- Turn right in Suippes to stay on the D977 towards the A4 and Reims.
- After 6½ miles, turn right at the roundabout on the D944 to Reims.
- Turn right at the T-junction after Livry-Louvercy to stay on the D944.
- Don't miss the left turn 4 miles later for the D34 to Verzy.
- In Verzy, turn right on the D26, signed for 'Autres directions'.
- Don't miss the left turn in Verzenay to stay on the D26, the Route du Champagne.
- In Montchenot, turn left on the D951 to Épernay and Dizy.
- In Dizy, turn left at the roundabout, then left at the lights on the D386 to Hautvillers.
- At the D980, turn right to Reims.

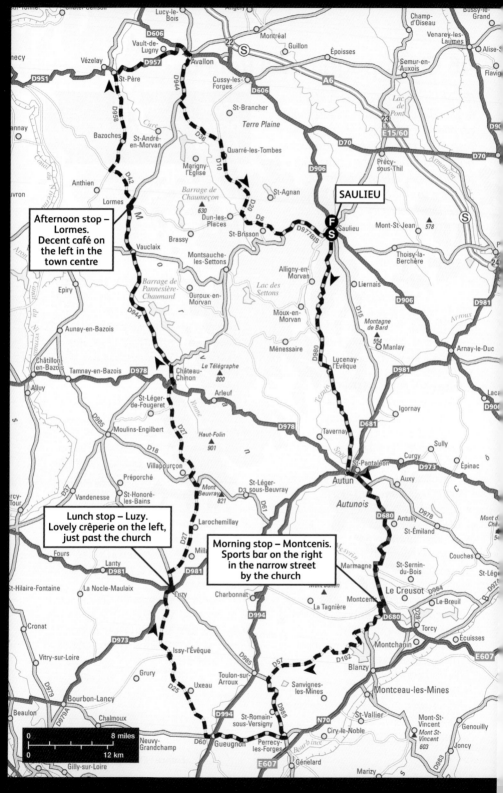

SAULIEU

Afternoon stop – Lormes. Decent café on the left in the town centre

Lunch stop – Luzy. Lovely crêperie on the left, just past the church

Morning stop – Montcenis. Sports bar on the right in the narrow street by the church

0 — 8 miles
0 — 12 km

47 Morvan: A Feeling

I admit I'd never heard of the Morvan until it was recommended by my friend François, a road tester for a French motorcycle magazine. What a great tip: it's a small corner of Burgundy packed with woods and fields and the kind of curvy roads to make any lover of high-quality British B-roads beam with joy. Over the years

FROM	Saulieu
DISTANCE	185 miles
ALLOW	5½ hours

I've stayed in Autun and Avallon too, but my current favourite route is from the quieter, quainter village of Saulieu. It's a brilliant day out.

Route

- Leave Saulieu on the D980 to Lucenay l'Évêque and Autun.
- In Autun, pick up the D680 to Le Creusot.
- After 15 miles, turn right on the D980 to Montcenis. Turn left at the roundabout through Moncenis, to Montceau-les-Mines.
- Don't miss the right turn 8 miles later for the D102 to Gueugnon (which becomes the D57).
- After 10 miles, take another easily missed left turn for the D958 to Perrecy-les-Forges.
- At the roundabout in Perrecy, turn right on the D60 to Gueungnon.
- Go through Gueungnon and turn right on the D25 to Issy l'Évêque.
- Turn right on the D973 to Autun.
- In Luzy, pick up the D985 to St-Honoré and Château-Chinon.
- Don't miss the right turn about a mile later for the D27 to Château-Chinon.

- Look out: really easy-to-miss right turn 11 miles later to stay on the D27.
- In Château-Chinon, turn left to go into the town centre, then go straight ahead at the hairpin on the D944 towards Montsauche-les-Settons.
- Leaving Lormes, turn left on the D42 to Poques-Lormes and Vézelay.
- After 5 miles, turn right on the D958 to Bazoches and Vézelay.
- In St-Père, turn right on the D957 to Pontaubert and Avallon.
- In Avallon town centre, pick up the D944 back towards Lormes and Château-Chinon.
- A mile outside Avallon, turn left on the D36 which becomes the D10 to Quarré-les-Tombes.
- Turn left at the D6 to Saulieu.
- Turn left at the D977 to return to Saulieu.

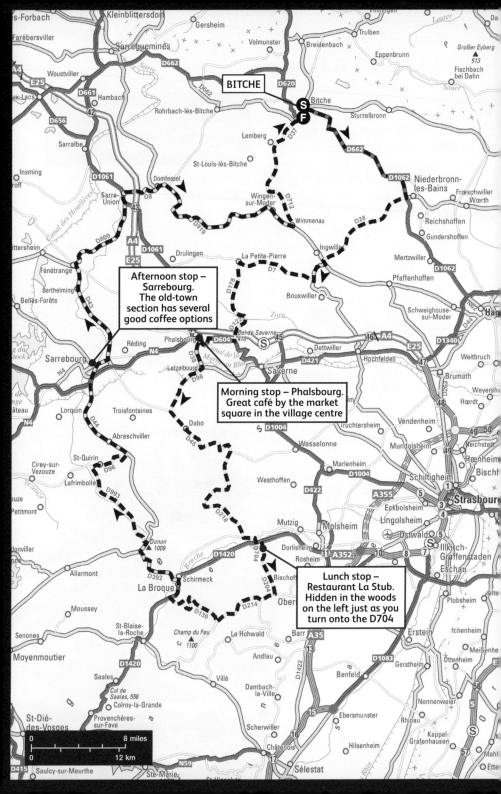

BITCHE

Afternoon stop – Sarrebourg. The old-town section has several good coffee options

Morning stop – Phalsbourg. Great café by the market square in the village centre

Lunch stop – Restaurant La Stub. Hidden in the woods on the left just as you turn onto the D704

48 Dabo and Donon

Bitche is another town that can make a good first night on a longer tour, if you're happy to pile on the miles. It also makes a great destination, with a huge Vauban citadel and miles of epic roads through the heavily forested hills of the northern Vosges. This route strings them all together, taking in the dead-end side road that spirals up the Rocher du Dabo (Rock of Dabo) for an amazing view before

FROM	Bitche
DISTANCE	190 miles
ALLOW	6 hours

heading to the Second World War Struthof concentration camp (the only one built on French soil) and back over the Col du Donon. It's mile after mile of twisty, wooded roads linking picture-postcard villages.

Route

- Leave Bitche on the D662 to Haguenau. This becomes the D1062.
- At Niederbronn-les-Bains, take the exit for the D28 to Ingwiller.
- Cross Ingwiller and pick up the D56 to Weinbourg, which becomes the D113.
- At the D7, turn right to La Petite-Pierre.
- In La Petite-Pierre, turn left on the D178 to Saverne and Phalsbourg.
- At the D122, turn left, then take the first right on the D133 to Phalsbourg.
- From Phalsbourg, take the D38 to Dabo.
- In Lutzelbourg, turn right on the D98 to Dabo, which becomes the D45.
- Don't miss the right turn half a mile(ish) outside Dabo to reach the Rocher du Dabo.
- Do another 6½ miles on the D45 then turn right on the D218 to Wangenbourg.
- At the D392, turn left to Strasbourg.
- Don't miss the right turn 2 miles later for the D704 to Mollkirch.
- Go through Mollkirch and take the D617 to Klingenthal, then the D217 and the D204 – always following signs for Klingenthal.
- In Klingenthal, turn right on the D420 to St-Odile and after a mile turn right on the D214 to La Rothlach and Le Champ du Feu.
- After 6½ miles, turn right on the D130 to Le Struthof and Schirmeck.
- Cross Schirmeck and take the D392 to Wackenbach and Col du Donon.
- After 5 miles, turn right on the D993 to Sarrebourg, over Col du Donon.
- Cross the pass and take the D193A to St-Quirin, which then becomes the D96.
- At the D44, turn left to Sarrebourg.
- Cross Sarrebourg and pick up the D43 to Fénétrange. Turn right in Berthelming to stay on the road, which becomes the D8.
- Cross Sarre-Union on the D8 to Bitche.
- In Domfessel, go straight over the roundabout on the D919 to Diemeringen.
- In Wimmenau, turn left on the D712 to Bitche. This becomes the D37.
- At the D662, turn right to Bitche.

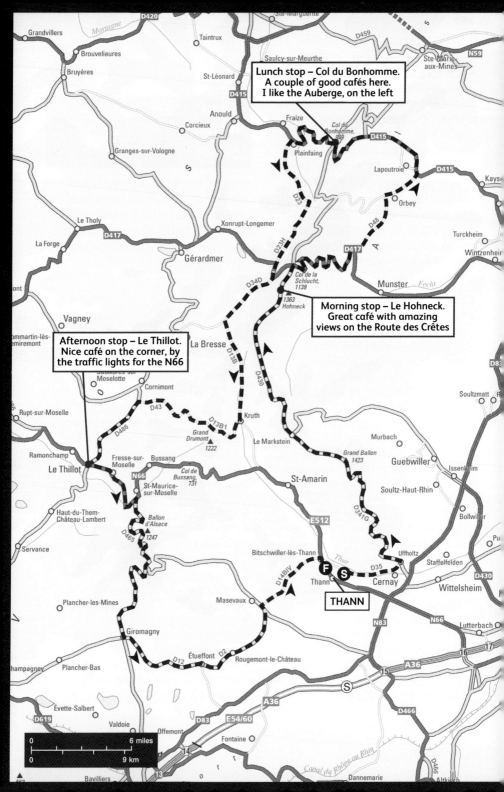

Lunch stop – Col du Bonhomme.
A couple of good cafés here.
I like the Auberge, on the left

Morning stop – Le Hohneck.
Great café with amazing
views on the Route des Crêtes

Afternoon stop – Le Thillot.
Nice café on the corner, by
the traffic lights for the N66

THANN

49 Thann. Heaven.

For a long time, the Vosges seemed to be a bit of a well-kept secret, but that secret is definitely out now. These mountains on France's eastern border, facing the Black Forest from the other side of the Rhine, are a popular biking destination and are often busy at the weekend. It's easy to understand why: the riding and

FROM	Thann
DISTANCE	150 miles
ALLOW	4½ hours

scenery are simply divine. This route links the Route des Crêtes, running along the spine of the mountains, with the best passes that cross them.

Route

- Leave Thann on the D35 to Cernay.
- Turn left by the town hall, following the signs for Uffholtz and the Route des Crêtes.
- In Uffholtz, turn left on the D431 to Le Grand Ballon. This is the start of the Route des Crêtes. It changes number at Le Markstein, becoming the D430.
- At the D471, turn right to Colmar. Follow it round to the right at Col de la Schlucht, taking the col rather than Route des Crêtes.
- After 7 miles, turn left on the D48 to Orbey and Col du Wettstein.
- Turn right on the D48II to Orbey.
- From Orbey, take the D48 to Lapoutroie.
- At the roundabout, turn left on the D415 to Saint-Dié, over Col du Bonhomme.
- Turn left at the lights in Painfaing on the D23 to Le Valtin.

- Half a mile outside Le Valtin, turn left on the D23H to La Schlucht.
- Go straight across the D417 staggered crossroads on the D34D to La Bresse.
- Don't miss the left turn 6 miles later for the D34 to Wildenstein.
- In Kruth, turn right by the church on the D13B1 to Col d'Oderen, which becomes the D43 in Ventron.
- At the D486, turn left to Le Ménil.
- In Le Thillot, turn left at the lights on the N66 to Mulhouse.
- In St-Maurice-sur-Moselle, turn right on the D465 to Giromagny.
- In Giromagny, turn left, then left again on the D12 to Vescemont and then Rougegoutte.
- In Étueffont, pick up the D2 to Masevaux.
- In Masevaux, take the D14BIV to Col du Hundsruck and Thann.
- Turn left on the N66 to Thann.

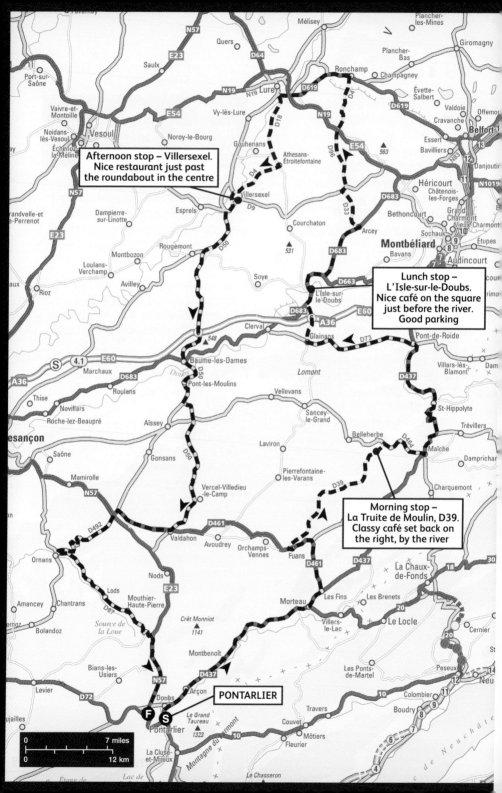

Afternoon stop – Villersexel.
Nice restaurant just past
the roundabout in the centre

Lunch stop –
L'Isle-sur-le-Doubs.
Nice café on the square
just before the river.
Good parking

Morning stop –
La Truite de Moulin, D39.
Classy café set back on
the right, by the river

PONTARLIER

50 Doubs Explorer

The great riding in the Doubs was another discovery that came to me via a tip from my friend François, a road tester for a French motorcycle magazine. This area does still feel like a bit of a secret: a stunning area of hills and gorges packed with some amazingly twisty tarmac, but without loads of tourists. This good day in the saddle more-or-less retraces my first foray into the region – fine-tuned

FROM	Pontarlier
DISTANCE	190 miles
ALLOW	5½ hours

following further visits. Though I've only marked the usual three stops, it's worth also taking some time in the pretty village of Lods, before tackling the Gorges du Nouailles on the final leg back to Pontarlier.

Route

- Leave Pontarlier on the D437 to Montbéliard and Morteau.
- In Les Fins, turn left on the D461 to Orchamps-Vennes and Besançon. Turn left when it hits a T-junction to stay on the D461.
- In Fuans, turn right on the D39 to Guyans-Vennes. Stay on it for 15 miles – when it becomes the D464 to Maîche.
- In Maîche, rejoin the D437 to Montbéliard.
- Cross the river in Pont-de-Roide and turn left on the D73 to Clerval and Vermondans.
- In Glainans, turn right by the church on the D31 to the A36 and L'Isle-sur-le-Doubs.
- Cross the A36 and turn right on the D683 to Montbéliard and L'Isle-sur-le-Doubs.
- Bear right after crossing the river in L'Isle-sur-le-Doubs then, just over half a mile later, turn left to stay on the D683 towards Belfort and Héricourt.
- Turn left in Arcey on the D33 to Villers-sur-Saulnot. This becomes the D96.

- Go straight in Clairegoutte as the road becomes the D4 to Ronchamp.
- Turn left at the T-junction in Ronchamp, on the D619 to Lure.
- Pick up the D486 to Montbéliard on the outskirts of Lure, then turn left by the big supermarket on the D18 to Le Val-de-Gouhenans and Vouhenans.
- Bear right in Athesans-Étroitefontaine, joining the D4 to Senargent.
- Cross Villersexel and join the D9 towards the A36 and Vesoul – but take the first exit to pick up the D486 to Baume-les-Dames (still signed for the A36). This becomes the D50.
- In Valdahon, rejoin the D461 towards Besançon. Turn left at the roundabout to stay on it – then go straight over the N57 on the D492 to Saules and Ornans.
- In Ornans, turn left on the D67 to Mongesoye and Pontarlier.
- At the N57 T-junction, turn right to return to Pontarlier.

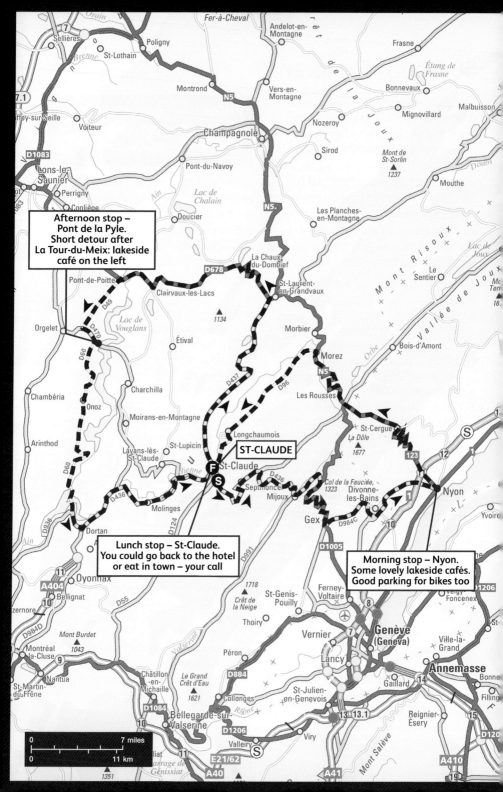

Afternoon stop – Pont de la Pyle. Short detour after La Tour-du-Meix: lakeside café on the left

Lunch stop – St-Claude. You could go back to the hotel or eat in town – your call

Morning stop – Nyon. Some lovely lakeside cafés. Good parking for bikes too

ST-CLAUDE

0 ___ 7 miles
0 ___ 11 km

51 St-Claude Butterfly

If the Vosges has been discovered, the Jura still has that slightly secret quality to it. With so many people hurrying past to 'the Alps', the section of mountains that make the border between France and Switzerland, north of Lake Geneva, tend to be relatively quiet. It's a shame to miss the riding here because the roads and scenery are simply stunning. I love it around here. I have friends and family in Switzerland, so have

FROM	St-Claude
DISTANCE	**155 miles**
ALLOW	**5 hours**

been visiting for years. I even spent my 21st birthday in Nyon – the morning coffee stop on this relaxed route. This ride takes in some of my favourite roads and is ideal for those who haven't ridden in the mountains before and for pillion couples.

Route

- Leave St-Claude on the D436 to Genève and Gex. This becomes the D936.
- Turn left in Mijoux to stay on the D936 over Col de la Faucille.
- In Gex, turn left on the D984C to Divonne-les-Bains.
- Go around Divonne following signs for Nyon to stay on the D984C to Switzerland.
- In Nyon, follow signs for the hospital and then the centre of town to pick up highway 1 along the lake, towards the ferry.
- Retrace your steps along the lake front to Nyon hospital, turn right and take route 123 to St-Cergue (passing over the motorway).
- Turn left in St-Cergue to La Cure.
- In La Cure, pick up the N5 to La Dôle.
- In Morez, turn left on the D25 to the town centre. Pick up the D69 to St-Claude.
- Leave St-Claude on the D437 to St-Laurent-en-Grandvaux.
- In St-Laurent, turn left on the D678 to Lons-le-Saunier.
- In Pont-de-Poitte, turn left on the D49 to Largillay-Marsonnay.
- At the D470, turn left to Moraine.
- After a mile (just after La Tour-du-Meix), turn right on the D60 to Onoz.
- Turn left on the D3 to Onoz. After Onoz this becomes the D60 to Cernon… and then the D60E to Chancia and Oyonnax.
- At the D936, turn left to Dortan. Turn left at the lights in Dortan to stay on the road, towards Lons-le-Saunier.
- Turn left at the roundabout on the D436 to Lons and St-Claude. Stay on this road all the way back to St-Claude.

The Gorges de l'Abîme

Swap the bike boots for walking boots and explore this gorgeous gorge in St-Claude, complete with waterfalls and well-maintained walkways.

Grottes de Baume

Just outside Lons-le-Saunier (about an hour from St Claude) is a system of amazing caves. Well worth a visit. www.baumelesmessieurs.fr

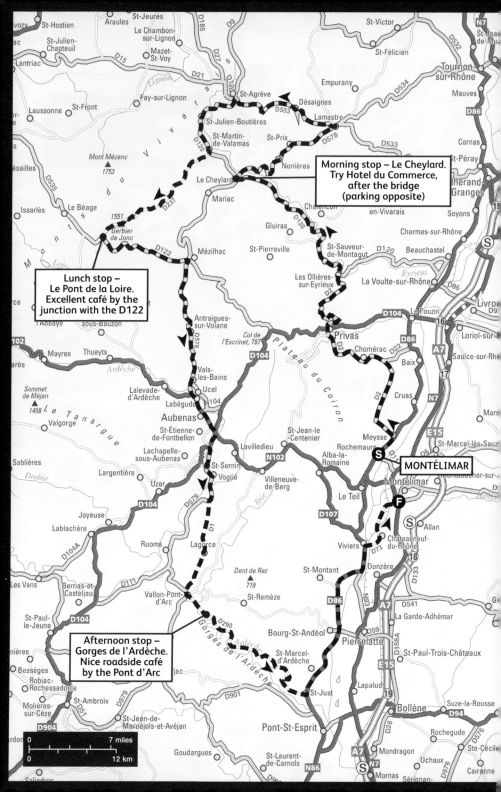

Morning stop – Le Cheylard.
Try Hotel du Commerce,
after the bridge
(parking opposite)

Lunch stop –
Le Pont de la Loire.
Excellent café by the
junction with the D122

Afternoon stop –
Gorges de l'Ardèche.
Nice roadside café
by the Pont d'Arc

MONTÉLIMAR

0   7 miles
0   12 km

52 Ardèche Dash

I love the Ardèche – it's a region with miles of quiet but crazily twisty roads that could have been built for bikers, all strewn over rugged wooded hills. The famous road is the D290 along the spectacular Gorges de l'Ardèche, but there's so much good riding here. This route is based around

FROM	Montélimar
DISTANCE	195 miles
ALLOW	5½ hours

Montélimar (home of nougat) but it's also worth visiting super-quaint Vogüé outside Aubenas.

Route

- Leave Montélimar on the D86 to Privas.
- In Meysse, turn left on the D2 to Privas.
- In Privas, turn right (towards the motorway) then turn left to stay on the D2 to Le Cheylard.
- In Les Ollières-sur-Eyrieux, turn left on the D120 to Le Cheylard.
- In Le Cheylard, turn right over the bridge on the D578 to Lamastre.
- Turn left in Lamastre on the D533 to Désaignes and St-Agrève.
- At the roundabout in St-Agrève, turn left on the D120 to St-Martin-de-Valamas.
- Go straight on at the hairpin in St-Martin (a right turn) on the D237 to Mt Gerbier de Jonc and St-Martial.
- Don't miss the hard left turn (doubling back on yourself) in the middle of St-Martial to stay on the D237.

- At the D122 T-junction, turn left to Sagnes-et-Goudoulet.
- Turn right by the auberge on Col de Mézilhac on the D578.
- In Labégude, join the N102 to Aubenas.
- At the huge roundabout in Aubenas turn right on the D104 to Alès, then after a mile and a half turn left (at a smaller roundabout) on the D579 signed for the Gorges de l'Ardèche and Vallon-Pont-d'Arc.
- Go past super-cute Vogüé and look for the left turn for the D1 to Lagorce.
- Cross Vallon-Pont-d'Arc and pick up the D290 to St-Martin-d'Ardèche.
- At the St-Just roundabout, turn left on the D86 to Aubenas.
- In Viviers, turn right on the D861, which becomes the D73 when it crosses the river – and stay on it back to Montélimar.

Europe's 15 highest paved roads

1. Ötztal Glacier Road, Austria (2,830 m), dead end (route 75, pages 184–5)
2. Col de la Bonette, France (2,802 m), summit loop (route 53, pages 132–3)
3. Col de l'Iseran, France (2,770 m), pass (route 53, pages 130–1)
4. Stelvio Pass, Italy (2,757 m), pass (route 84, pages 204–5)
5. Kaunertal Glacier Road, Austria (2,750 m), dead end (route 75, pages 184–5)
6. Col Agnel, Italy/France (2,744 m), pass, Europe's highest border point
7. Col du Galibier, France (2,645 m), pass (route 53, pages 130–1)
8. Colle del Nivolet, Italy (2,641 m), dead end
9. Gavia Pass, Italy (2,621 m), pass
10. Großglockner High Alpine Road, Austria (2,571 m), dead end (route 76, pages 186–7)
11. Sierra Nevada, Spain (2,565 m), dead end (route 23, pages 64–5)
12. Umbrail Pass, Switzerland/Italy (2,501 m), pass
13. Colle dei Morti, Italy (2,481 m), pass
14. Nufenen Pass, Switzerland (2,478 m), pass (route 82, pages 200–1)
15. Grand St Bernard Pass, Switzerland/Italy (2,469 m), pass (route 54, pages 134–5)

D4, Col de la Bonette (route 53, pages 128–9)

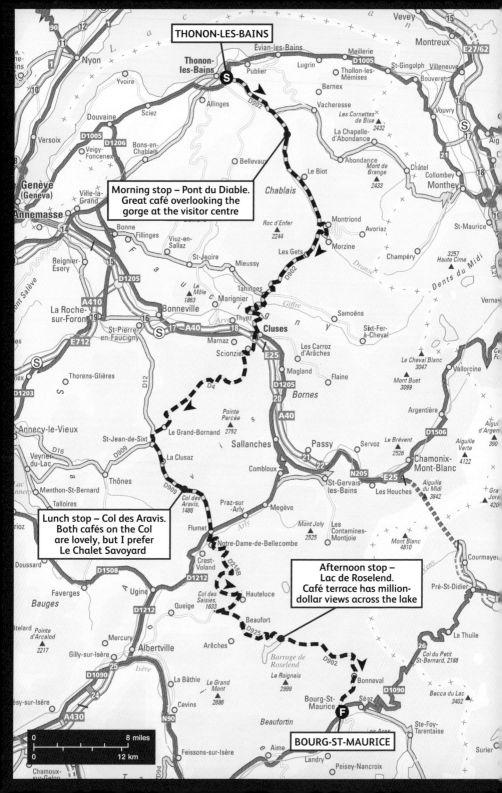

THONON-LES-BAINS

Morning stop – Pont du Diable. Great café overlooking the gorge at the visitor centre

Lunch stop – Col des Aravis. Both cafés on the Col are lovely, but I prefer Le Chalet Savoyard

Afternoon stop – Lac de Roselend. Café terrace has million-dollar views across the lake

BOURG-ST-MAURICE

53 Route des Grandes Alpes (day one)

If you've never ridden in the high mountains before, France's Route des Grandes Alpes is the perfect introduction. Running from Thonon-les-Bains on the shore of Lake Geneva to Menton on the Mediterranean coast, it's more than 400 miles of amazing riding that crosses seventeen brilliant passes. It was created by the French Touring Club and completed in 1937, when the last road was opened, over Col de l'Iseran. I've ridden the full length of the route several times and it's most enjoyable when not rushed.

FROM	**Thonon-les-Bains**
TO	**Bourg-St-Maurice**
DISTANCE	115 miles
ALLOW	3½ hours

I prefer to take not-quite-three days, picking it up mid-morning on day one (which is the route presented here). The highest passes are closed by snow until June, the Tour de France visits in July, and August is always busy, so my top tip for the best time to ride this route is September.

Route

- From Thonon-les-Bains, take the D902 towards Féternes and Morzine-Avoriaz.
- In Morzine, turn right to stay on the D902 to Cluses (signed for the A40).
- Turn left at the roundabout in Taninges to stay on the D902 to Cluses.
- In Cluses, follow signs for Annecy and Geneva until you cross the river. At the next roundabout, turn left on the D4 to Scionzier. It gets a little narrow as it passes through the villages, but broadens out as it climbs. This takes you over Col de la Colombière.
- In St-Jean-de-Sixt, turn left at the roundabout on the D909 to La Clusaz. This will take you over Col des Aravis.
- In Flumet turn left on the D1212 towards Chamonix, then after about 300 m turn right (over the old bridge) on the D218B to Notre-Dame-de-Bellecombe.
- Turn right at the T-junction to continue to Les Saisies and Beaufortain on the D218B.
- At the D925 junction, turn left to Beaufort. This will take you over Cormet de Roselend – where it becomes the D902 – and all the way to Bourg-St-Maurice.

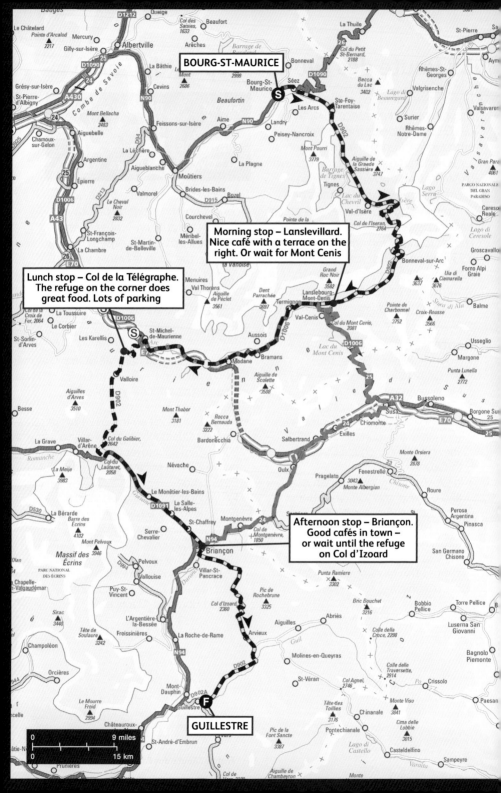

BOURG-ST-MAURICE

Morning stop – Lanslevillard.
Nice café with a terrace on the
right. Or wait for Mont Cenis

Lunch stop – Col de la Télégraphe.
The refuge on the corner does
great food. Lots of parking

Afternoon stop – Briançon.
Good cafés in town –
or wait until the refuge
on Col d'Izoard

GUILLESTRE

53 Route des Grandes Alpes (day two)

There are so many amazing roads on this day's ride – and it starts with one of the best. While not the highest road in Europe, at 2,770 m Col de l'Iseran is the highest pass. It's a wild ride: steep and twisty, bumpy in places, occasionally with meltwater running across it from the snow beside the road, even in summer. The authentic Route des Grandes Alpes takes in Col du Télégraphe and Col du Galibier, joining Col du Lautaret to descend to Briançon. A popular alternative is to cross into Italy over the spectacular Col du Mont-Cenis, in the footsteps of Hannibal and his elephants, then take the SS24 from

FROM	Bourg-St-Maurice
TO	Guillestre
DISTANCE	170 miles
ALLOW	5 hours

Susa, over Col de Montgenèvre. I love both routes – and even on the classic route it's worth taking a short detour to see the lake at Mont-Cenis. Whichever version you do, this day also includes my all-time favourite pass: Col d'Izoard. The top section of crazy scree slopes and rocky spikes is called the Casse Desert and it's strangely beautiful – and the pass is fantastic to ride.

Route

- Leave Bourg-St-Maurice on the D1090 to Séez and Tignes.
- In Séez, turn right on the D902 to St-Foy-Tarrentaise and Val d'Isère. This will take you over Col de l'Iseran.
- After the roundabout in Lanslebourg-Mont-Cenis, turn left on the D1006 to Susa. This takes you onto Mont-Cenis. After admiring the lake, backtrack to Lanslebourg and continue along the D1006 to Modane.

- In St-Michel-de-Maurienne, turn left at the lights on the D902 to Valloire. This takes you over Col du Télégraphe and Col du Galibier.
- At Col du Lautaret, turn left on the D1091 to Briançon.
- Cross Briançon and pick up the D902 to Cervières and Col d'Izoard.
- At the T-junction after Arvieux, turn right on the D902 to Guillestre. This will take you through the Gorges du Guil.

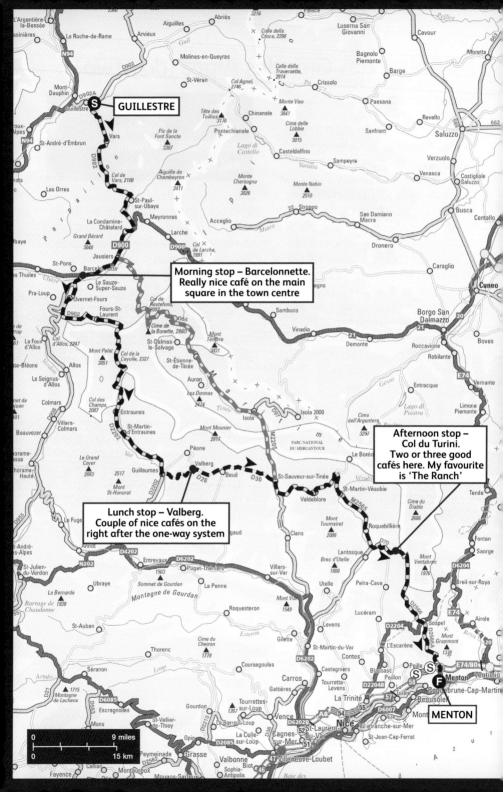

GUILLESTRE

Morning stop – Barcelonnette.
Really nice café on the main
square in the town centre

Afternoon stop –
Col du Turini.
Two or three good
cafés here. My favourite
is 'The Ranch'

Lunch stop – Valberg.
Couple of nice cafés on the
right after the one-way system

MENTON

0   9 miles
0   15 km

53 Route des Grandes Alpes (day three)

More epic riding in the high Alps, starting with the brilliant and often undervalued Col de Vars. Some riders then ditch the classic route to take Col de la Bonette and go up to the 2,802 m summit that's France's highest road (the highest non-dead-end paved road in Europe). The traditional route goes to Barcelonnette and over Col de la Cayolle, Col de Valberg and the always-bumpy Col

FROM	Guillestre
TO	Menton
DISTANCE	170 miles
ALLOW	5 hours

de la Couillole. Then it heads to St-Martin-Vésbuie and on to the Col de Turini, made famous by the Monte Carlo Rally, before the final run down to Menton over Col du Castillion.

Route

- From Guillestre, take the D902 to Vars, which takes you over Col de Vars
- At the D900, turn right to Condamine.
- For the La Bonette alternative, turn left in Jausiers on the C4 signed for Nice, and rejoin the main route at St-Saveur-sur-Tinée.
- For the full Route des Grandes Alpes, take the D900 to Barcelonnette and pick up the D902 to Pra-Loup.
- As you leave Barcelonnette, turn left to stay on the D902 to Uvernet-Fours. This takes you over Col de la Cayolle.
- In Guillaumes, turn left on the D28 to Valberg – over Col de Valberg.
- In Beuil, turn left on the D30 to St-Sauveur-sur-Tinée, over Col de la Couillole.

- At the M2205, turn right towards St-Sauveur and Nioo.
- Don't miss the ultra-sharp right turn (doubling back on yourself) 2½ miles later for the M2565 to Colmaine and Rimplas.
- Go straight across the mini-roundabout in Roquebillière on the M2565 to Belvédère.
- After 2 miles, turn left on the D70 to La Bollène-Vésbuie.
- Turn left at Col de Turini on the D2566 to Moulinet and Sospel.
- In Sospel turn left and then – about 200 m later – turn right to stay on the D2566 to Menton. At the roundabout, turn left to go over Col du Castillon to Menton (if you go right, it's a less dramatic ride to Menton).

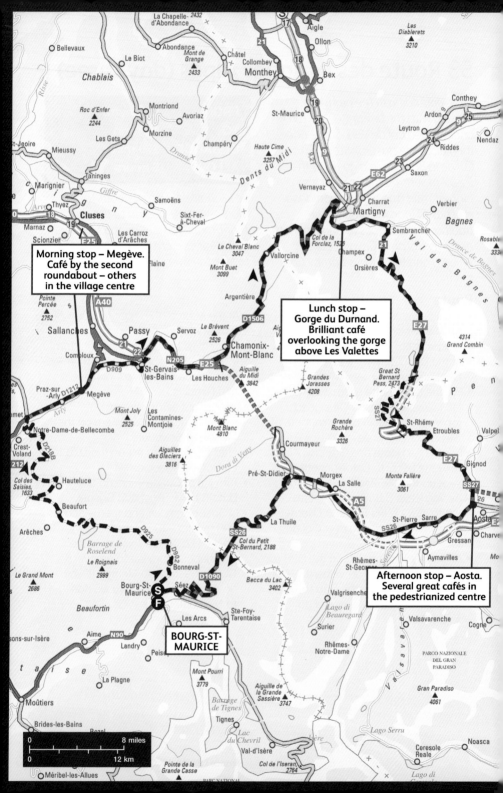

Morning stop – Megève.
Café by the second
roundabout – others
in the village centre

**Lunch stop –
Gorge du Durnand.
Brilliant café
overlooking the gorge
above Les Valettes**

**Afternoon stop – Aosta.
Several great cafés in
the pedestrianized centre**

**BOURG-ST-
MAURICE**

0 ———— 8 miles
0 ———— 12 km

54 The St Bernards Loop

This full day's ride is another that was introduced to me by my friend John Cundiff of Alpine TT (though it wasn't quite such a long day when the French speed limit was 90 kph, rather than 80...). It's one of the more famous routes in the Alps, taking you through three countries. It can be ridden clockwise or anticlockwise, but I think it's best leaving Bourg-St-Maurice and starting with the magical Cormet de Roselend, before shuttling quickly

FROM	**Bourg-St-Maurice**
DISTANCE	**200 miles**
ALLOW	**6 hours**

to Chamonix, at the foot of Mont Blanc (using the only really major road on the route). Then you circle the mountain, hopping to Switzerland, to Italy, then back to France, using the Grand St Bernard and Petit St Bernard Passes.

Route

- Leave Bourg-St-Maurice on the D902 to Beaufort and Cormet de Roselend.
- Don't miss the right turn 1 mile after Beaufort for the D218 to Hauteluce.
- In Flumet, turn right on the D1212 to Chamonix and Mont Blanc.
- About 1½ miles after Megève, turn right at the roundabout on the D909 to Chamonix. Keep following signs for Chamonix.
- Join the A40 to Chamonix-Mont-Blanc.
- After 10 miles, go left at the roundabout to Chamonix: don't go straight ahead on the main road to the Mont Blanc tunnel.
- Cross Chamonix and pick up the D1506 to Martigny.
- At the roundabout in Martigny, turn right on route 21 towards Aosta and Verbier.
- After 2 miles, turn right to Les Valettes, then after 400 m turn right to Champex.
- In Orsières, rejoin Swiss route 21 towards Aosta and Grand St Bernard.

- Don't miss the turn 11 miles later – in a tunnel – to take the Col. It's not well-signed: just a small blue arrow saying 'col'.
- In Italy, join the SS27 to Aosta.
- In Aosta, turn right by the hospital on the SS26 towards Courmayeur and Petit St Bernard. Don't get on the motorway: stick with the SS26 for 19 miles.
- In Pré-St-Didier, turn left to France (Francia) and Piccolo St Bernard on the SS26. This becomes the D1090 when it crosses into France. Stick with it all the way back to Bourg-St-Maurice.

Mont Blanc

The route orbits Europe's highest mountain. The closest you can get to the top is taking the Aiguille du Midi cable car from Chamonix.

St Bernards

The famous breed of rescue dog not only comes from here but also can often be seen being trained around the Grand St Bernard refuge.

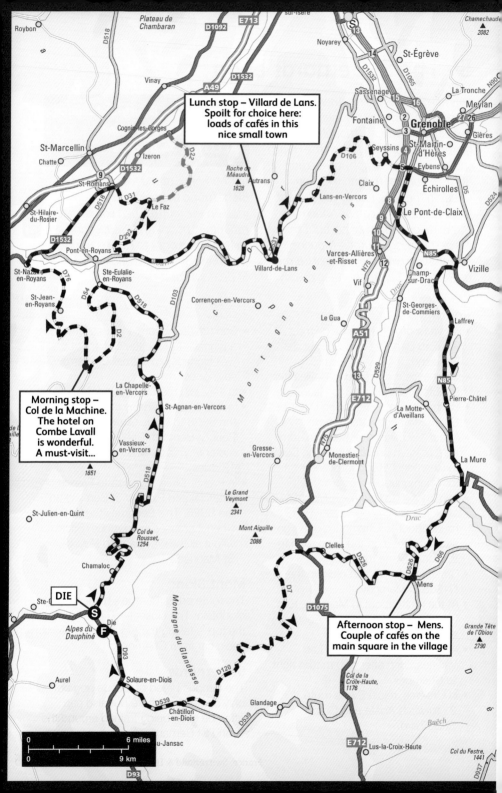

Lunch stop – Villard de Lans.
Spoilt for choice here:
loads of cafés in this
nice small town

Morning stop –
Col de la Machine.
The hotel on
Combe Lavall
is wonderful.
A must-visit...

DIE

Afternoon stop – Mens.
Couple of cafés on the
main square in the village

55 Vercors Balconies

In September 2020, as Europe enjoyed a few free weeks between lockdowns, I grabbed the keys for my Honda CrossTourer and came to the Vercors to ride the balcony roads carved out of the cliffs. The most famous is Col de la Machine, but there are loads in the Vercors. This route has high passes, nerve-testing balcony roads and flowing valley runs – plus a couple of miles of

FROM	Die
DISTANCE	190 miles
ALLOW	6 hours

Route Napoleon. It passes so close to Grenoble that it needs a Crit'Air sticker for the bike. For a longer ride, carry on from St-Romans to Cognin-les-Gorges and take the D22 through the Gorges du Nan to Le Faz.

Route
- Leave Die on the D518 to Chamaloc.
- Turn right after the tunnel at the top of Col de Rousset to stay on the D518.
- Leaving Les Barraques en Vercors, turn left at the roundabout (through another tunnel).
- In Ste-Eulalie-en-Royans, turn left on the D54 to St-Laurent-en-Royans.
- Turn left by the church in St-Laurent on the D2 to Lente.
- At the D76, turn right to St-Jean-en-Royans and Combe Laval.
- Turn left in St-Jean to stay on the D76.
- In St-Nazaire-en-Royans, turn right on the D1532 to Grenoble.
- Don't miss the right turn 6½ miles later for the D31 to St-Pierre-de-Chérennes.
- In Le Faz, turn right to Presle on the D292.
- Turn left on the D531 to Villard-de-Lans.
- In Lans-en-Vercors, turn right at the roundabout towards Grenoble on the D106.
- Cross Seyssins following signs for the A480 and Grenoble.
- Join the A480 towards Gap for 2 miles.
- From J8, take the N85 towards Gap.
- At the first hairpin after La Mure, turn right on the D526 to St-Jean-d'Hérans.
- Turn right on the D1057, then left on the D7 to Col de Menée (it becomes the D120).
- In Châtillon-en-Diois, turn right on the D539 to St-Roman.
- In Solaure-en-Diois, turn right on the D93 to return to Die.

Caves
For a cool sightseeing trip on a hot day, try visiting the spectacular Caves of Chorance or the Cave of Thaïs. www.visites-nature-vercors.com

Resistance
The Vercors was a centre for the Resistance in the Second World War. There's a good museum dedicated to it in Vassieux-en-Vercors.

Grenoble
A fabulous little city with lots to see (including more museums). Be sure to include a trip to the bastille in Les Bulles – the bauble-shaped cable car.

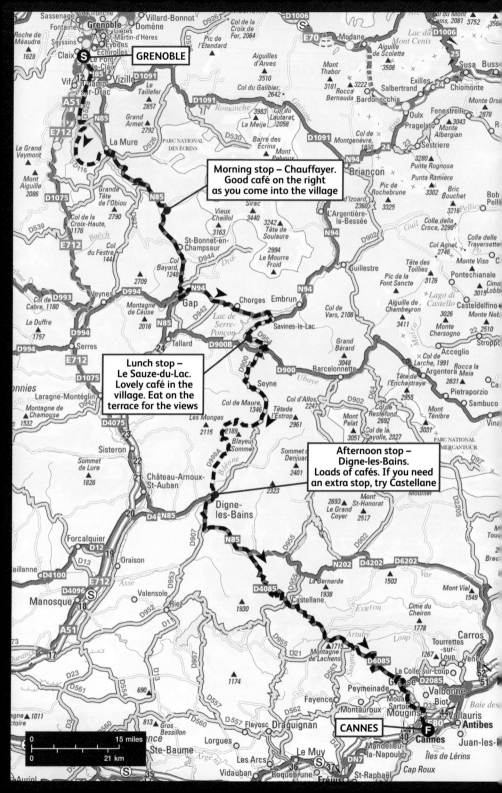

GRENOBLE

Morning stop – Chauffayer.
Good café on the right
as you come into the village

Lunch stop –
Le Sauze-du-Lac.
Lovely café in the
village. Eat on the
terrace for the views

Afternoon stop –
Digne-les-Bains.
Loads of cafés. If you need
an extra stop, try Castellane

CANNES

56 Route Napoleon

There's no doubt that this is one of the most famous routes in Europe – not just for bikers but also for history buffs. Route Napoleon traces the path the exiled emperor took when returning from Elba in 1815 to resume his rule. The diminutive imperialist landed in Golfe-Juan, between Antibes and Cannes, but the popular modern route broadly follows the N85 from Grenoble to the Riviera town, famed for its film festival. My version of the route doesn't slavishly follow the N85 – because why would you need a route guide for that? Besides, it's essentially merged with the A51

FROM	Grenoble
TO	Cannes
DISTANCE	225 miles
ALLOW	6 hours

motorway between the towns of Gap and Digne. No point wasting time on that when there's brilliant mountain riding to be had. Obviously, Napoleon started at the coast and headed inland, but I'd expect the majority of British tourists will be going the other way. I'd recommend not staying on the Riviera, but slightly inland – in Grasse or even Castellane.

Route

- From J8 of the A480 motorway, take the N85 towards Gap and Vizille.
- Go straight over the first roundabout, then take the first exit for the D529 to Champs-sur-Drac and follow it to La Mure.
- Don't miss the right turn just after Monteynard for the D116B to La Motte-St-Martin. It gets quite narrow in the village.
- In St-Martin, turn right on the D116 to Marceau (back on a two-lane road).
- At the roundabout in La Mure, turn right to bypass the village and join the N85 to Gap.

- In Gap, turn right at the roundabout on the N94 to Briançon.
- In Savines-le-Lac, turn right after the bridge on the D954 to Le Sauze-du-Lac.
- Turn right on the D900 to Gap.
- Don't miss the left turn, after 3 miles, for the D900 to St-Vincent-les-Forts.
- After 18 miles, turn right on the D900A to Vedrache – a bit narrow, but leads to the awesome Clues de Barles.
- In Digne-les-Bains, pick up the N85 and follow Route Napoleon (as it changes number to the D4085 and then the D6085) all the way to Cannes.

57 Gorge Yourself

Just like Southern Spain, the French Riviera has long been a popular place for bike launches so I've been coming here for years. It was here that I first tested the model of Kawasaki Z1000SX, that I later took across America and Australia, trying it on some of the roads on this route. This full day's ride is built around two amazing gorges: the Gorges du Verdon, often referred to as France's Grand Canyon; and the nearby Gorges du Loup. In between it uses bits of Route

FROM	Grasse
DISTANCE	180 miles
ALLOW	5 hours

Napoleon, the lovely Col de Vence and the stunning D2. It's easily extended by adding the D23, Route des Crêtes (see map) or shortened by returning to Grasse on Route Napoleon from Le Logis du Pin. It can also be adapted to run from Castellane, using that town as a base for this route and route 56.

Route

- Leave Grasse on the N85 / D6085 (Route Napoleon) towards Digne.
- After 25 miles, turn left at the roundabout on the D21 to Draguignan.
- Don't miss the right turn 10 miles later for the D955 to Trigance.
- After 6 miles, turn left to go into Trigance on the D90.

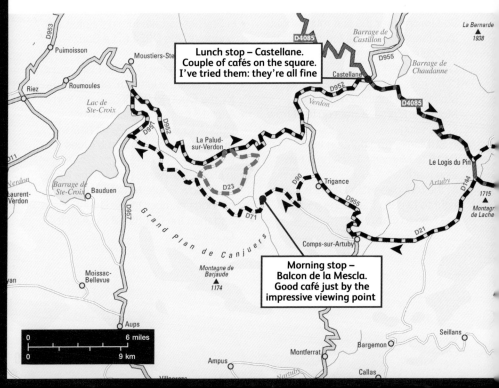

Lunch stop – Castellane.
Couple of cafés on the square.
I've tried them: they're all fine

Morning stop –
Balcon de la Mescla.
Good café just by the
impressive viewing point

- At the D71, turn right to Aiguines. This runs along the southern lip of the Gorges du Verdon, including the Corniche Sublime.
- At the D957, turn right to Moustiers.
- In Moustiers, turn right at the roundabout on the D952 to Castellane. This will take you on the north side of the Gorges du Verdon, through La Palud-sur-Verdon.
- In Castellane, go straight over the roundabout on the D4085 towards Grasse.
- Turn left at the roundabout in Le Logis du Pin on the D2211 to St-Auban.
- After 1½ miles, turn right on the D2 to Valderoure. Stay on it all the way over Col de Vence.
- In Vence, turn right towards Grasse (and the motorway to Nice) on the D2210.

- Don't miss the right turn in Pont de Loup for the D6 to Thorenc, which takes you into the Gorges du Loup.
- Keep going straight to Courmes as the road becomes the D3.
- At the D2 roundabout, take the last exit for the D603 to Cipières. This brings you back down the other side of the gorge.
- Turn right on the D3 towards Gourdon.
- At the roundabout in Châteauneuf, turn right on the D2085 to return to Grasse.

Want more?

Pass through La Palud-sur-Verdon and turn right on the D23 Route des Crêtes: a spectacular loop on the edge of the gorge; it's so narrow that it's one-way in places and you have to ride it in this direction.

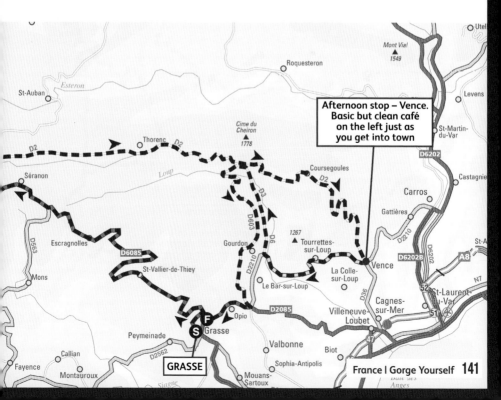

Afternoon stop – Vence. Basic but clean café on the left just as you get into town

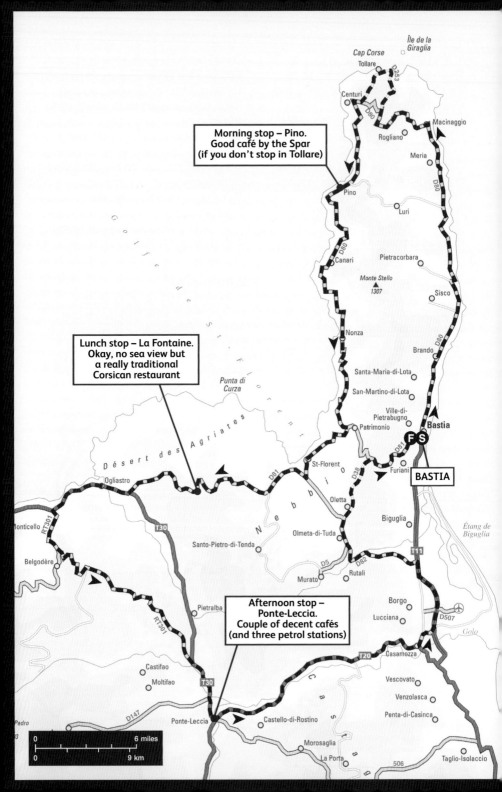

Morning stop – Pino.
Good café by the Spar
(if you don't stop in Tollare)

Lunch stop – La Fontaine.
Okay, no sea view but
a really traditional
Corsican restaurant

Afternoon stop –
Ponte-Leccia.
Couple of decent cafés
(and three petrol stations)

Île de la
Giraglia

Cap Corse

Tollare

Centuri

Macinaggio

Rogliano

Meria

D253

D80

Pino

Luri

D80

Canari

Pietracorbara

Monte Stello
1307

Sisco

D80

Nonza

Brando

Santa-Maria-di-Lota

San-Martino-di-Lota

Ville-di-
Pietrabugno

Bastia

Patrimonio

F S

St-Florent

D81

D38

Furiani

D81

BASTIA

Oletta

Biguglia

Étang de
Biguglia

Olmeta-di-Tuda

RT301

Ogliastro

Punta di
Curza

Désert des Agriates

N e b b i o

Golfe de St-Florent

Monticello

T30

Santo-Pietro-di-Tenda

D5

D82

Rutali

T11

Belgodère

Murato

Borgo

Lucciana

D507

Pietralba

RT301

Castifao

Moltifao

T30

D147

Ponte-Leccia

Castello-di-Rostino

Casamozza

T20

Vescovato

Venzolasca

Penta-di-Casinca

Golo

Padro
3

Morosaglia

La Porta

506

Taglio-Isolaccio

0   6 miles
0   9 km

58 Cap Corse

I adore Corsica. The riding is simultaneously breathtaking and bonkers. There are very few straight or flat bits of road, so there's an endless succession of great bends – but one moment you'll be on immaculate fresh tarmac and the next it'll be rough enough to rattle out your fillings. It's demanding riding, but hugely rewarding. One thing that is utterly consistent as you ride around Corsica is how spectacular the views

FROM	Bastia
DISTANCE	170 miles
ALLOW	5½ hours

are – though they're very different, depending on whether you're in the mountains or by the sea. This route from the port of Bastia has the best of both, as it loops out to the tip of Cap Corse, the peninsula at the top of the island. It's truly stunning.

Route

- Leave Bastia on the D80 to Cap Corse. Stay with this one amazing road all the way round the coast.
- Turn right in Botticella on the D253 to Tollare. It's a narrow, twisty road. Keep going as it loops back to Botticella as the D153.
- Rejoin the D80.
- Keep going on the D80 – the best stretch is coming up. In Patrimonio it becomes the D81 to St-Florent.
- Cross St-Florent and turn right on the D81 to Casta and L'Île Rousse.
- At the T30, turn right to L'Île Rousse.
- Don't miss the left turn after 5½ miles for the RT301 to Belgodère.
- When the RT301 meets the T30 again, turn right towards Corte.

- Turn left at the roundabout in Ponte Leccia on the T20 to Bastia.
- In Casamozza, turn left on the T20 to Bastia, past the airport. Keep going straight as the road becomes the T205 to Crocetta and Lucciana.
- Join the T11 to Bastia for a mile and a half.
- At the end of the dual carriagoway, turn left at the roundabout towards Rutali and St-Florent on the D82.
- In Oletta, turn right (on a left-hand hairpin) on the D38 to Poggio d'Oletta.
- At the D81, turn right to return to Bastia.

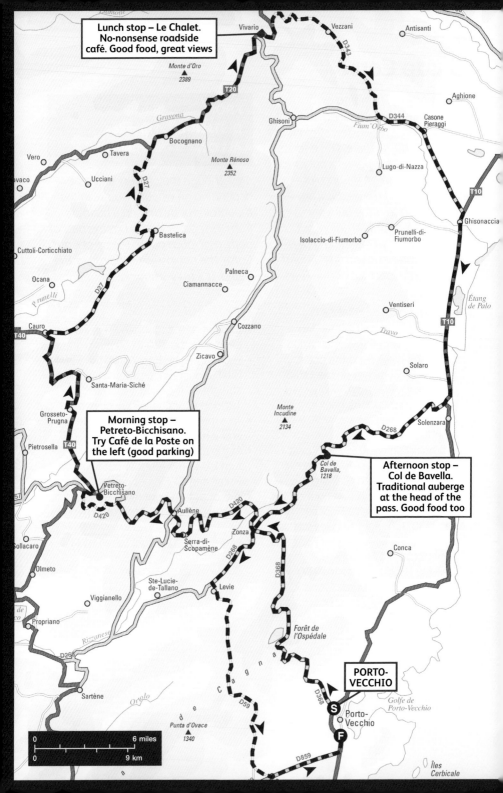

Lunch stop – Le Chalet. No-nonsense roadside café. Good food, great views

Morning stop – Petreto-Bicchisano. Try Café de la Poste on the left (good parking)

Afternoon stop – Col de Bavella. Traditional auberge at the head of the pass. Good food too

PORTO-VECCHIO

S
F
Porto-Vecchio

0   6 miles
0   9 km

Vivario
Vezzani
Antisanti
Monte d'Oro
2389
D343
T20
Aghione
Ghisoni
Fium'Orbo
D344
Casone Pieraggi
Bocognano
Vero
Tavera
D27
Ucciani
Monte Rénoso
2352
Lugo-di-Nazza
T10
Ghisonaccia
Bastelica
Isolaccio-di-Fiumorbo
Prunelli-di-Fiumorbo
Cuttoli-Corticchiato
Ocana
D27
Palneca
Ciamannacce
Ventiseri
Étang de Palo
Prunelli
Cauro
T40
Cozzano
Travo
T10
Zicavo
Solaro
Santa-Maria-Siché
Grosseto-Prugna
Monte Incudine
2134
Solenzara
D268
Pietrosella
T40
Petreto-Bicchisano
D420
Col de Bavella, 1218
D420
Aullène
D420
Zonza
Serra-di-Scopamène
D268
Conca
Ste-Lucie-de-Tallano
Levie
D368
Sollacaro
Olmeto
Viggianello
Propriano
Rizzanese
Forêt de l'Ospédale
D268
Cagna
D59
D368
Sartène
Orylo
Punta d'Ovace
1340
Golfe de Porto-Vecchio
D859
Îles Cerbicale

59 Zonza Figure-of-Eight

I must apologize, as this route contains the only two boring roads on Corsica (those straight bits on the map). I'm not apologizing much though, as the rest of the route is made up of the island's best roads. The climb into the mountains and over the sublime Col de la Tana sets the tone – and if the T40 calms things down slightly, the pace rises on the D27, which is followed by the best stretch of the island-bisecting T20.

FROM	Porto-Vecchio
DISTANCE	200 miles
ALLOW	6 hours

The D343 is a little more challenging, but then there's a breather on those flat, straight roads before the jewel in Corsica's crown: Col de Bavella. Even the final run on the D59 and D859 makes other rides look ordinary – and I make no apology for that.

Route

- Leave Porto-Vecchio on the D368 to L'Ospedale and Zonza.
- In Zonza, pick up the D420 to Ajaccio. Take it through Aullène and over Col de la Tana and Col de St-Eustache.
- In Petreto-Bicchisano, turn right on the T40 to Ajaccio.
- In Cauro, turn right on the D27 to Bastelica. There are some big drops beside the road as it descends from Col de Scalella.
- At the T20, turn right towards Calvi and Bastia.
- Don't miss the sharp right turn in Vivario, doubling back on yourself, for the D343 to Muracciole.
- Turn right in Casone Pieraggi on the D343A to Ghisonaccia.
- After a mile, turn left on the D344 to Ghisonaccia – a rare flat and straight Corsican road.
- In Ghisonaccia, turn right on the T10 to Porto-Vecchio (the island's other flat and straight road).
- In Solenzara, turn right at the roundabout on the D268 to Zonza, over Col de Bavella. Stay on the D268 through Zonza, to Sartène.
- Don't miss the left turn in Levie for the D59 to Porto-Vecchio.
- At the D859, turn left to Porto-Vecchio and Sotta, then rejoin the T10 to go into Porto-Vecchio.

60 Spa Classic

*This just might be the best full day's
ride within easy reach of Calais.
The Ardennes is packed with great
roads and this route uses many
recommended by my friend Neil, who
runs the AE Aventures biking guest
house, just outside Spa (stay with him
when you go!). It's a long-ish day on*

FROM	Spa
DISTANCE	220 miles
ALLOW	6½ hours

*amazing, twisty tarmac, but is easily
shortened by taking the N833 from La
Roche, through Hotton, to Petit-Han.*

Route

- Leave Spa on the N629 and take it all the way to Eupen.
- In Eupen, pick up the N68 to St Vith.
- In Malmedy, follow the one-way system through the centre for the N62 to Waimes.

- From Waimes, take the N676 to St Vith.
- After 10 miles, turn right on the N670 towards the E42 and Malmedy.
- Go over the motorway and turn right on the N675 to Vielsalm.
- From Vielsalm, take the N68 to Clervaux.

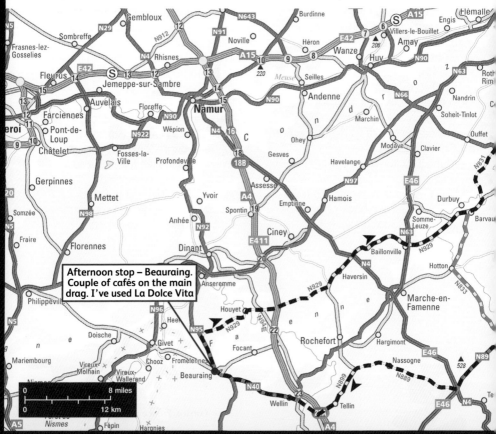

Afternoon stop – Beauraing.
Couple of cafés on the main
drag. I've used La Dolce Vita

- In Salmchâteau, go straight on at the lights on the N89 to La Roche.
- In Joubiéval, turn right on the N645 to Lierneux and Sart.
- At the N66, turn left to Huy.
- Don't miss the left turn 9 miles later for the N86 to Durbuy.
- In Bomal-sur-Ourthe, turn left on the N806 to Manhay.
- In Manhay, turn right on the N807 to Marche-en-Famenne.
- In Érezée, turn left at the roundabout on the N841 to La Roche-en-Ardenne.
- At the N89, turn right to La Roche.
- Stick with the N89 through La Roche towards St-Hubert.
- After the N89 goes under the N4, turn right on the N889 to Forrières.
- In Tellin, turn right on the N846 to Wellin.

- Join the N40 and go right at the roundabout on the N40 to Gedinne.
- From Beauraing, take the N95 to Dinant.
- After 3½ miles, turn right on the N292 to Houyet and Finnevaux. Stay with it all the way to Petit-Han, where it becomes the N983.
- Turn left in Barvaux-sur-Ourthe on the N831 to Hamoir.
- In Hamoir, turn right to go into the centre, then turn left on the N66 to Huy.
- Go straight as the road becomes the N654 to Esneux.
- Go through Comblain-au-Pont and turn right on the N633 to Aywaille.
- Turn right then left in Aywaille to stay on the N633 to Remouchamps.
- In Remouchamps, turn left on the N697.
- Turn right on the N62 to return to Spa.

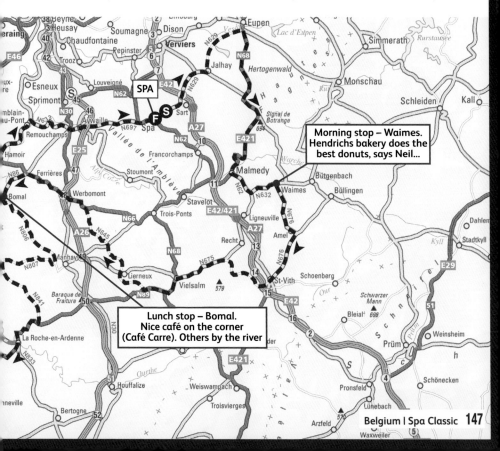

Morning stop – Waimes.
Hendrichs bakery does the best donuts, says Neil...

Lunch stop – Bomal.
Nice café on the corner (Café Carre). Others by the river

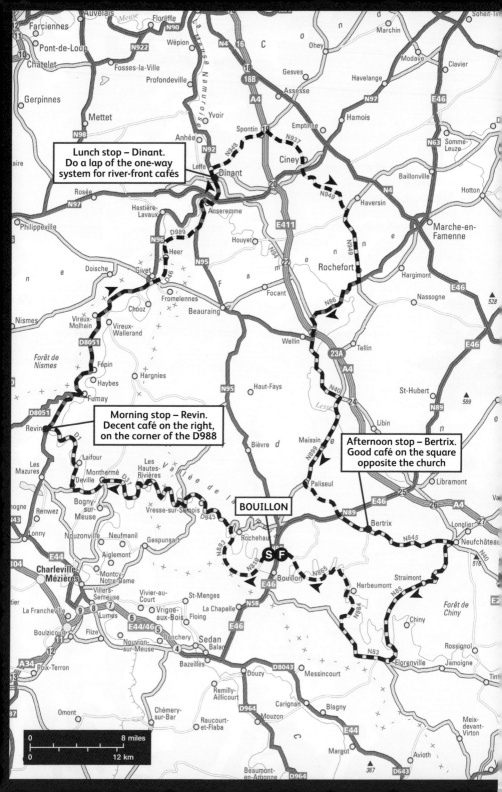

61 Bouillon Stock Route

It was my colleague Kev Raymond who introduced me to the riding on the French–Belgian border – a corner of the Ardennes I'd previously bypassed. What a mistake that had been! It's an area packed with brilliant roads and fabulous small towns. Like Reims, Bouillon makes a good first- or

FROM	Bouillon
DISTANCE	185 miles
ALLOW	5½ hours

last-night stop for a bigger trip… but with roads like this on the doorstep, it's a great destination as well.

Route

- Leave Bouillon on the N810 to Corbion.
- In Corbion, take the N893 to Rochehaut.
- From Rochehaut, take the N819 to Alle and Vresse sur Semois.
- At the N945, turn right to Dinant.
- Don't miss the left turn 2 miles later for the D943 to Vresse.
- In Vresse, turn left on the D914 to Membre and Bohan.
- Turn left in Membre then, after half a mile, turn right to stay on the D914 to Bohan and Monthermé.
- Turn left after crossing the river in Bohan to stay on the N914 to Monthermé. This becomes the D31 in France.
- Cross the river in Monthermé and turn right on the D1 to Rocroi and Revin.
- Turn right in Revin on the D988 to Fumay and Givet. This becomes the D8051 in Fumay.
- Turn right in Givet, cross the river and turn left on the D46 to Heer. This becomes the N909, then the N989 in Heer.
- Turn left on the N919 to Dinant.

- In Leffe (yes, where the beer comes from), turn right on the D948 to Spontin.
- Turn right on the N937 to Ciney.
- In Ciney, turn right on the N97 then turn left on the N949 to Rochefort.
- Turn right in Rochefort on the N86 to Arlon and Wellin.
- Turn left on the N94 and then left on the N40 to Arlon and St-Hubert.
- After 7 miles, turn right on the N899 to Bouillon and Paliseul.
- In Paliseul, turn left on the N853 to Libramont-Chevigny and Bertrix.
- From Bertrix, take the N845 to Neufchâteau.
- In Neufchâteau, turn right on the N85 to Florenville.
- In Florenville, join the N83 to Sedan and Bouillon.
- After 5 miles, turn right on the N884 to Bertrix and Herbeumont.
- About a mile outside Herbeumont, turn left on the N865 to Bouillon. Keep going straight as it becomes the N816.
- Turn left on the N89 and then turn right on the N828 to return to Bouillon.

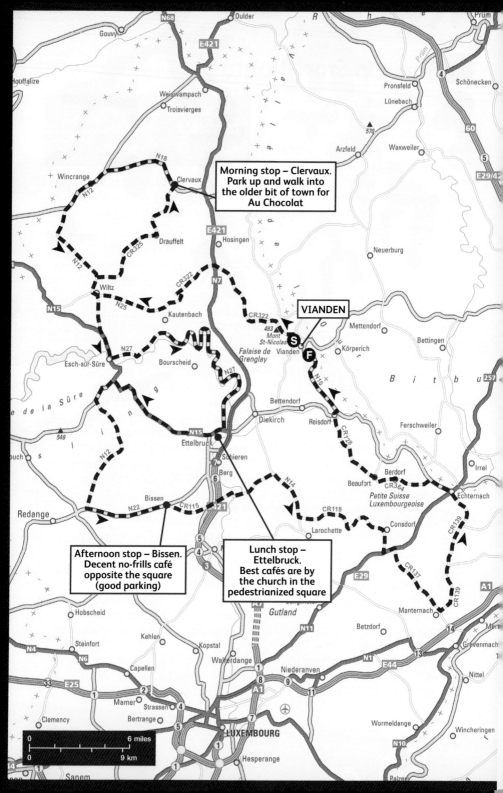

Morning stop – Clervaux.
Park up and walk into
the older bit of town for
Au Chocolat

VIANDEN

Afternoon stop – Bissen.
Decent no-frills café opposite the square
(good parking)

Lunch stop –
Ettelbruck.
Best cafés are by
the church in the
pedestrianized square

0   6 miles
0   9 km

62 Europe's Biking Secret

Luxembourg is perhaps the most surprising of biking paradises. The city that's now best known for its EU institutions is at the heart of a compact country packed with rolling hills, draped in a patchwork blanket of fields and woods, stitched together with quiet, twisty and immaculately surfaced roads. It's a small state with

FROM	Vianden
DISTANCE	155 miles
ALLOW	5 hours

a lot to offer the touring motorcyclist – like this laid-back day's ride (which is easily shortened by leaving off the Clervaux loop from Wiltz).

Route

- Leave Vianden on the N17 to Diekirch.
- At the top of the hill, turn right on the CR322 to Diekirch (past the castle).
- In Kautenbach, take the N25 to Wiltz.
- In Wiltz, turn right on the N12.
- Don't miss the right turn coming into Eperldange, for the CR325 to Clervaux.
- Turn left in Drauffelt to stay on the road.
- From Clervaux, take the N18 towards St Vith and Troisvierges.
- Turn left on the N12 to Bastogne – which takes you back to Wiltz.
- Leave Wiltz on the N12 to Goesdorf.
- Turn left on the N15 to Esch / Sure.
- Don't miss the left turn 2 miles later for the N27 to Goebelsmühle (The sign may say: G'Mühle).
- When it eventually reaches a T-junction, turn right to stay on the N27 into Ettelbruck.
- Turn right at the roundabout to go into Ettelbruck. Follow the one-way system to pick up the N15 to Feulen and Bastogne.
- Don't miss the left turn 8 miles later (on the hairpin) for the N12 to Grosbous.
- Turn left on the long straight after Reichlange, on the N22 to Everlange.
- Turn left in Useldange to stay on the road.
- In Bissen, turn right on the CR306 to Luxembourg then left on the CR115 to Cruchten and Roost.
- In Cruchten, turn right then left to stay on the CR115 to Larochette.
- At the N14, turn right to Larochette.
- In Larochette, turn left on the CR118 to Echternach.
- In Consdorf, turn right on the CR137 to Altrier and Luxembourg.
- At the CR139, turn left to Echternach.
- Turn left in Echternach and go straight over at the lights on the N10 to Diekirch.
- After a mile, turn left on the CR364 to Berdorf (through the Gorges du Loup).
- Turn right in Berdorf to stay on this road.
- In Beaufort it becomes the CR128.
- In Reisdorf, turn left on the N19 to Diekirch, cross the river and turn right on the N10 to return to Vianden.

Germany, Austria, Czechia & Slovenia

The Großglockner High Alpine Road, Austria (route 76, pages 186–7)

63 Baltic Explorer (day one)

Northern Germany has a bit of a bad rep in biking terms: my Bavarian friend Sep thought I was crazy to come here. 'The riders from the north all come down here for fun,' he told me. True, the Baltic coastline is lacking in mountains, but there are still plenty of lovely roads – especially in the Swiss Holstein region, near the Danish border. There are some amazing old towns too, packed with half-timbered

FROM	Kiel
TO	Wismar
DISTANCE	210 miles
ALLOW	5½ hours

buildings... not to mention a seaboard with sandy beaches and piers. This laid-back two-day route is an ideal two-up trip with lots to see.

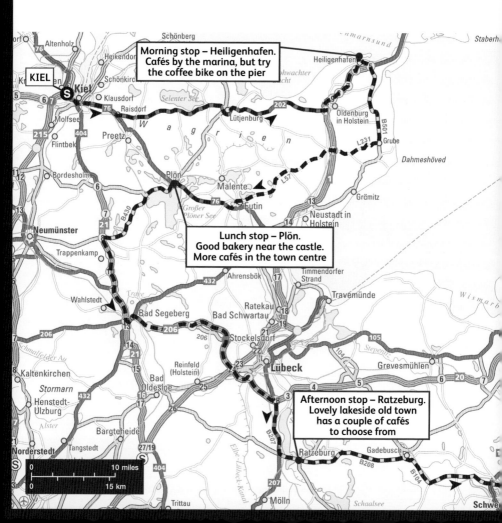

Morning stop – Heiligenhafen. Cafés by the marina, but try the coffee bike on the pier

Lunch stop – Plön. Good bakery near the castle. More cafés in the town centre

Afternoon stop – Ratzeburg. Lovely lakeside old town has a couple of cafés to choose from

Route

- Leave Kiel on the B76 towards Preetz.
- In Raisdorf, take the exit for the town centre and at the bottom of the slip road, turn right to Lütjenburg on the B202.
- At Oldenburg in Holstein, join the A1 towards Denmark.
- After 6 miles, get off the autobahn at J6 and follow the signs for Heiligenhafen centre and the beach.
- From Heiligenhafen, take the B501 to Neukirchen and Heringsdorf.

- In Grube, turn right on the L231 to Riepsdorf. At the T-junction, turn right to Kabelhorst to stay on the L231.
- Go straight over the A1 into Lensahn and take the L57 to Schönwalde am Bungsberg. Stay on the L57 all the way to Eutin.
- In Eutin, pick up the B76 to Plön.
- In Plön, turn left towards the castle and follow the B430 to Ascheberg.
- In Bornhöved, join the A1 south.
- After 11 miles, take J12 for Bad Segeberg Nord and the B206 to Lübeck. This becomes the A20.
- Leave the A20 at J2b for Lübeck Sud and take the B207 to Ratzeburg.
- At the B208, turn left into Ratzeburg.
- In Gadebusch, turn right on the B104 to Schwerin. Go straight over the B106 into Schwerin and stick with the B104 to Rampe.
- You can save half an hour by joining the A14 to Wismar (I'd do this if it's after 4.30 p.m.).
- Otherwise, take the B104 to Brüel. Cross the town to pick up the B192 to Warin.
- At the A20, join the motorway towards Lübeck for one junction.
- Go north on the A14 to Wismar.

Kiel

This is a fantastic compact city, with a charming old-town section. It wears its naval history with pride – WWII buffs should visit the U 995 Museum.
https://deutscher-marinebund.de

Plön

This fabulous town sits on the biggest lake in Schleswig-Holstein, dominated by the largest castle in the region (part of which is a museum).
www.fielmann-akademie.com

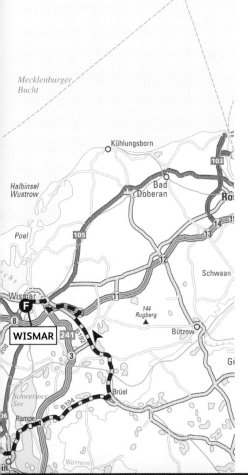

63 Baltic Explorer (day two)

There is a bit of motorway to start this day's ride, getting briskly past Rostock before heading out closer to the coast. There is the option of running out along the coast from Ribnitz: scenic, but it adds half an hour into a day that will also involve a bit of waiting for ferries. That's because from Stralsund, one of the jewels in the crown of the Hanseatic League, the route crosses the bridge onto Rügen, Germany's largest island. It's laid-back riding, linking sleepy beach towns, before taking a ferry back to the mainland. The route then heads to Heringsdorf on the isle of Usedom, the sunniest place in Germany. The pier there – once Europe's longest – is well worth visiting.

FROM	Wismar
TO	Heringsdorf
DISTANCE	220 miles
ALLOW	5½ hours

Route
- From Wismar, join the A20 to Rostock.
- At J16, head north on the A19.
- At J6 (Rostock Ost), pick up the B105 to Bentwish and Ribnitz-Damgarten.
- A choice: after 11 miles you can turn left on the L21 to Dierhagen, hugging the shore, looping round to rejoin the B105 at Löbnitz. This adds 30 minutes to the day.
- Otherwise, stay on the B105 all the way to Stralsund.

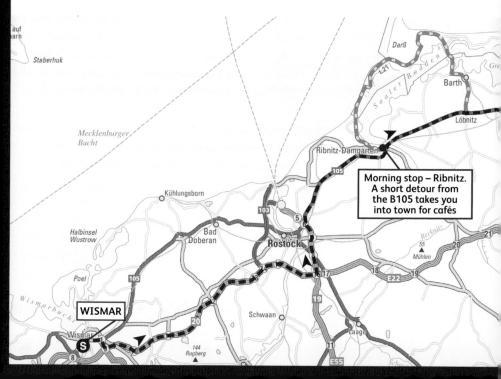

Morning stop – Ribnitz. A short detour from the B105 takes you into town for cafés

- In Stralsund, join the B96 to Rügen.
- Once you're on the island, leave the B96 at the first exit and loop round to take the L296 that runs parallel with it.
- In Samtens, turn left on the L30 to Dreschvitz.
- Don't miss the left turn 1½ miles after Gingst to stay on the L30.
- Turn right in Trent to stay on the L30.
- Take the ferry and follow the L30 through Weik, Altenkirche and Glowe.
- In Sagard, turn right on the B96 to Lietzow.
- After half a mile, turn left on the E251 to Sassnitz Port.
- Turn right at the traffic lights on the L29 to Binz.

- Turn left at the B196 then take the first right to stay on the L29, now heading to Putbus.
- In Garz, turn left, then left by the square to pick up the L30 to the ferry.
- Take the ferry and when the L30 meets the B105, turn left to Mesekenhagen. Keep going straight as it orbits Greifswald and becomes the B109.
- About 8–10 miles from Greifswald, go left on the B111 to Lühmannsdorf and Wolgast.
- Keep going straight (24 miles later) as the road becomes the L266 to Heringsdorf.

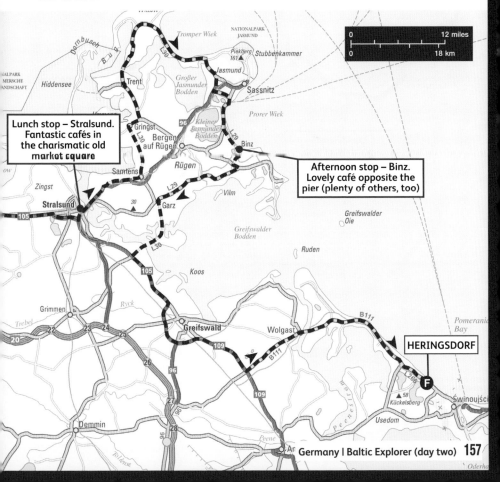

Lunch stop – Stralsund. Fantastic cafés in the charismatic old market square

Afternoon stop – Binz. Lovely café opposite the pier (plenty of others, too)

HERINGSDORF

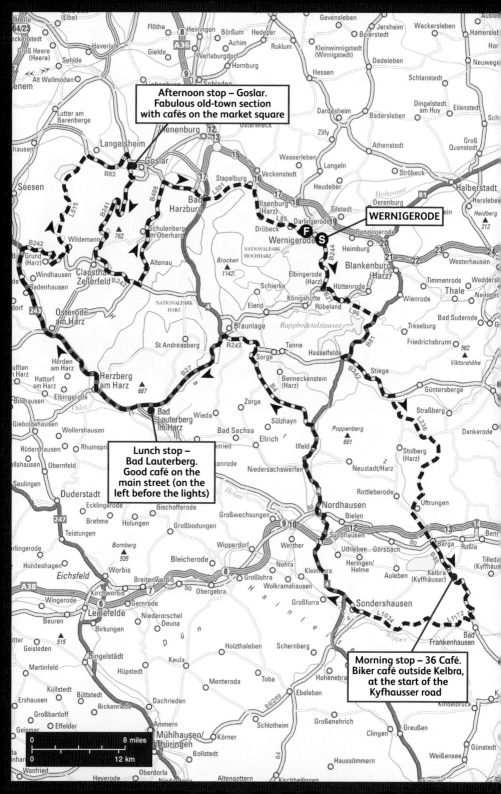

Afternoon stop – Goslar.
Fabulous old-town section
with cafés on the market square

WERNIGERODE

Lunch stop –
Bad Lauterberg.
Good café on the
main street (on the
left before the lights)

Morning stop – 36 Café.
Biker café outside Kelbra,
at the start of the
Kyfhausser road

0   8 miles
0   12 km

64 Sheer Harz Attack

I'd heard many tales of the Harz mountains, but when I first started touring, they weren't fully accessible: Europe was still divided and so was the Harz, with Wernigerode, Goslar and other eastern towns out of reach behind the Iron Curtain. My first proper visit was more than 20 years after the fall of the Berlin Wall, on a RiDE tourers test, staying at an English-run guesthouse in Bad Lauterberg. I was so impressed I've been back since

FROM	**Wernigerode**
DISTANCE	**200 miles**
ALLOW	**5½ hours**

to explore further, but the pick of the roads remains one shown to us by Greg, our host on that first trip. The B85 Kyffhauser road is a local legend, with thirty-six tight turns packed into a short, steep climb. All of the roads in the Harz are good, but that one's exceptional.

Route

- Leave Wernigerode on the B244 to Elbingerode.
- Turn left in Elbingerode on the B27 to Blankenburg and Hüttenrode.
- In Rübeland, turn right beside the station on the L96.
- At the B81, turn right to Hasselfelde.
- In Hasselfelde, go straight on by the church (a left turn as the B1 turns right) on the B242 to Stiege.
- Don't miss the right turn, 6 miles later, for the L236 to Breitenstein.
- Turn left in Rottleberode to stay on this road, which becomes the B85 after Berga.
- In Bad Frankenhausen, turn right on the L1172 to Rottleben. This becomes the L1034.
- From Sondershausen, take the B4 towards the autobahn and Nordhausen. Follow it all the way through Nordhausen and Harztor.
- At the B242, turn left to Braunlage.
- After 3 miles, take the exit for the B27 to Bad Lauterberg im Harz.
- In Herzberg am Harz, turn right on the B243 to Osterode am Harz.
- After 15 miles, take the exit for the B242 towards Bad Grund and Braunlage.
- Don't miss the left turn 6 miles later (on a right-hand bend) for the L515 to Wildemann.
- Join the B82 to Goslar (if you get into Langelsheim, you've overshot it).
- From Goslar, take the B241 to Clausthal-Zellerfeld.
- From Clausthal, take the B242 towards Braunlage again.
- After 3½ miles, turn left on the B498 to Altenau.
- Turn right at the roundabout in Oker on the L501 to Bad Harzburg. Stick with it through town and across the B4.
- As the L501 bypasses Stapelburg, turn right on the L85 to Ilsenburg and take it all the way back to Wernigerode.

Castles

Several good schlosses to visit: Wernigerode's is probably the finest, followed by the Kaiserpfalz in Goslar and ruined, romantic Regenstein.

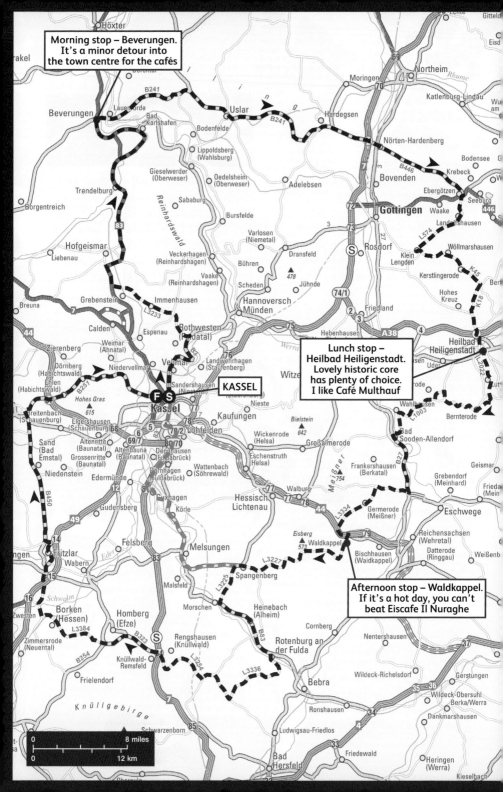

Morning stop – Beverungen.
It's a minor detour into the town centre for the cafés

Lunch stop –
Heilbad Heiligenstadt.
Lovely historic core
has plenty of choice.
I like Café Multhauf

Afternoon stop – Waldkappel.
If it's a hot day, you can't
beat Eiscafe Il Nuraghe

KASSEL

65 The Fairytale Loop

To capitalize on the legacy of the Brothers Grimm, Germany created The Fairytale Route in the 1970s. Like the Romantic Road (see route 70) it's all about linking historic towns, in this case those with a storybook connection. There are several possible ways to explore its central section,

FROM	Kassel
DISTANCE	235 miles
ALLOW	6½ hours

so this ride around Kassel strings together the roads offering the best riding for a magical day out.

Route

- Leave Kassel on the B3 to Göttingen.
- In Wilhelmshausen, turn left on the L3233 to Warburg and Immenhausen.
- In Grebenstein, join the B83 to Höxter and Hofgeismar.
- In Beverungen, turn right on the B241 to Uslar. Keep going straight when it becomes the B446 through Nörten-Hardenburg.
- At Ebergötzen, go straight across the B27 on the L523 to Landolfshausen and pick up the L574 towards Göttingen and Diemarden.
- In Klein Lengden, pick up the L569 to Duderstadt.
- After 3 miles, turn right to Wöllmarshausen on the L567, which becomes the K45.
- 4 miles after Kerstlingerode, turn right on the K18, then turn left to Heilbad Heiligenstadt.
- Turn left on the L1005 to go into Heilbad Heiligenstadt and pick up the L2022.
- Turn right in Bernterode on the L2026 to Rüstungen. Follow the road round through Wüstheuterode to pick up the L1003 to Wahlhausen and Bad Sooden-Allendorf.
- In Bad Sooden, join the B27 towards Eschwege.
- After 6 miles, take the exit for Eschwege but turn right on the L3241 to Meißner.
- Don't miss the left turn after 5 miles for the L3334 to Germerode.
- At the K33, turn left to Waldkappel.
- From Waldkappel, take the L3226 to Rotenburg an der Fulda. Keep going straight as it becomes the L3227 to Spangenburg.
- *Short of time? From Spangenburg, take the B487 and B83 to Guxhagen, then join the A7 to return to Kassel, saving 90 minutes.*
- For the full route, take the L3225 from Spangenburg to Morschen and turn left on the B83 to Rotenburg an der Fulda.
- Cross Rotenburg and take the L3336, then pick up the L3254 and L3465 to Knüllwald.
- Take the B323 to Homberg then cross the B254, taking the L3384 to Borken.
- In Borken, turn left on the L3149, then right on the L3150. Pick up the B450 to Fritzlar and take that to Istha.
- At Istha, join the B251 to return to Kassel.

66 Not the Nürburgring

There's no question that one of Germany's best biking roads is also its most intimidating: the Nürburgring Nordschleife used to hold grands prix; now it's a toll road and test track that the public can ride (on the increasingly limited public sessions... see nuerburgring.de). A lap of the Ring isn't for everyone – but nobody could fail to enjoy this route through the wooded slopes of the Eifel mountains

FROM	Nürburg
DISTANCE	170 miles
ALLOW	5½ hours

that surround it. Just remember that the local police are more than bored of riders pretending the B258 is part of the circuit, so it's well monitored... ride respectfully and cautiously if you like your licence.

Route

- Leave Nürburg on the B258 towards Blankenheim.
- At Blankenheim, turn left on the B51 for one junction, then rejoin the B258 to Schleiden.

- In Schleiden, turn left at the roundabout on the B265 to Blumenthal.

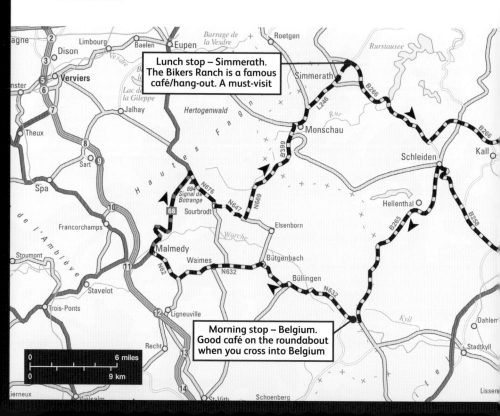

Lunch stop – Simmerath.
The Bikers Ranch is a famous café/hang-out. A must-visit

Morning stop – Belgium.
Good café on the roundabout when you cross into Belgium

- After 15 miles, on a left-hand bend, turn right (effectively going straight) to Belgium.
- Cross the border and turn right at the roundabout on the N632 to Malmedy.
- Turn left at the roundabout in Bütgenbach to stay on the N632.
- At the N62, turn right to Malmedy.
- From Malmedy, take the N68 to Eupen.
- Don't miss the right turn 8 miles later for the N676 to Sourbrodt.
- In Sourbrodt, turn left on the N647 to Elsenborn.
- Turn left on the N669 to Monschau. This crosses the border and becomes the B399.
- Turn left on the B258 to Monschau.
- Don't miss the left turn in Imgenbroich for the L246 to Simmerath.

- Leave Simmerath on the B266 to Gemünd.
- At the roundabout in Weissbrunnen, turn right on the B477 to Mechernich.
- At the fifth roundabout, turn left towards the A1 (don't get on the motorway) and take the L165 to Bad Münstereifel.
- Cross Bad Münstereifel and take the L234 to Altenahr. It becomes the L76.
- In Altenahr, take the B267 to Bad Neuenahr-Ahrweiler.
- Cross the river in Bad Neuenahr for the L84 to Rammersbach. It becomes the L83.
- In Kempenich, turn right on the B412 to return to Nürburg.

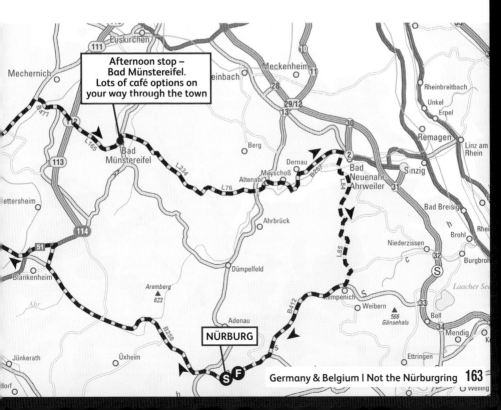

Afternoon stop – Bad Münstereifel. Lots of café options on your way through the town

67 Cochem and Burg Eltz

This short day includes an element of sightseeing and is ideal for a relaxed two-up trip. If you're staying in Cochem, you already have the imposing Reichsburg castle on your doorstep… but this route heads out to another impressive schloss, Burg Eltz. After exploring there, the route devours miles of enjoyable and usually very quiet roads as it loops back to the Moselle. If you want to pack short

FROM	Cochem
DISTANCE	145 miles
ALLOW	4½ hours

visits to both castles into one day, take the route as far as Kaisersesch, then short-cut it on the L52 and L100 to Büchel, picking up the B259 – the Panoramastraße – which will take you back to Cochem.

Route

- Leave Cochem on the B49 to Koblenz.
- In Treis-Karden, keep going straight (staying on the north bank of the Moselle) on the B416 to Koblenz.
- In Hatzenport, turn left on the L113 to Mayern and Münstermaifeld.
- In Münstermaifeld, look out for the minor road to Wierschem, following signs for Burg Eltz.

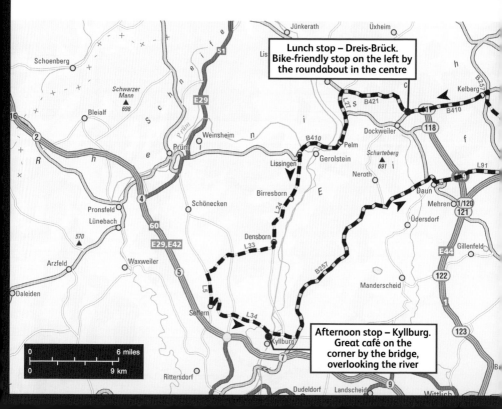

Lunch stop – Dreis-Brück.
Bike-friendly stop on the left by the roundabout in the centre

Afternoon stop – Kyllburg.
Great café on the corner by the bridge, overlooking the river

- Return to Münstermaifeld and pick up the L82 to Naunheim.
- Don't miss the left turn for the L110 to Möntenich and Pillig.
- In Pillig, turn right on the K35 to Roes, which becomes the K27.
- Go straight at the L109, cross Kaifenheim and go straight over the motorway – sticking with the L109 / L108 to Kaisersesch.
- In Kaisersesch, turn right on the L98 towards Mayern and Monreal.
- Turn left at the L96, towards Lirstal.
- In Mosbruch, go straight ahead on the L101 and then join the B257 to Kelberg.
- In Kelberg, join the B410 to Prüm.
- In Dreis-Brück, turn right on the B421 to Köln, Hillesheim and the A1.

- Cross Walsdorf and turn left at the roundabout on the L27 to Gerolstein, then rejoin the B410 towards Prüm.
- Don't miss the left turn in Lissingen for the L24 to Bitberg and Kyllburg.
- Keep going straight in Densborn as the road becomes the L33 to Bitberg.
- Go straight across the L32 but at the L5, turn left to Bitberg.
- In Seffern, turn left on the L34 to Kyllburg.
- Turn left on the B257 to Daun and take it all the way to the A1.
- Go straight over the motorway on the L91 to Ulmen.
- From Ulmen, take the B259 that goes all the way back to Cochem.

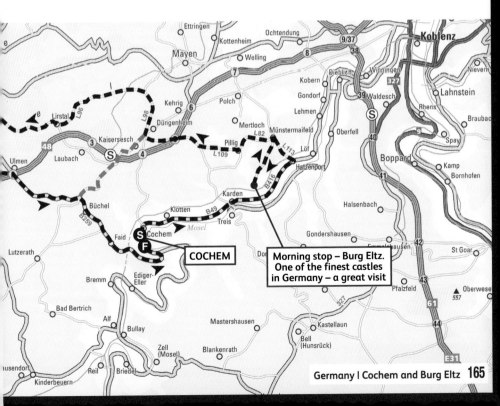

COCHEM

Morning stop – Burg Eltz. One of the finest castles in Germany – a great visit

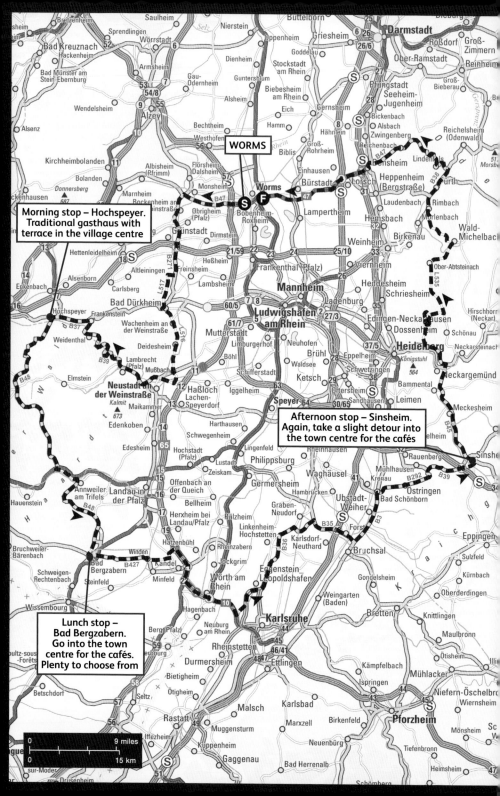

WORMS

Morning stop – Hochspeyer.
Traditional gasthaus with
terrace in the village centre

Afternoon stop – Sinsheim.
Again, take a slight detour into
the town centre for the cafés

Lunch stop –
Bad Bergzabern.
Go into the town
centre for the cafés.
Plenty to choose from

68 Wine, Pfalz and Oden

From the historic city of Worms, this day-long ride takes in a section of the German Wine Route, before heading into the Pfalzerwald (think Black Forest without the traffic). There's a bit of transit on major roads to get quickly past Karlsruhe and into another lesser-known riding heaven, the Odenwald

FROM	**Worms**
DISTANCE	**210 miles**
ALLOW	**6½ hours**

outside Heidelberg. That's three classic German rides on one brilliant day in the saddle.

Route

- Leave Worms on the B47 to Monsheim.
- At the B271, turn left to Mannheim.
- In Herxheim am Berg, turn right on the L522 to Weisenheim am Berg.
- In Weisenheim, turn left on the L517 to Leistad and Bad Dürkheim.
- Cross Bad Dürkheim and take the L516 to Forst an der Weinstraße.
- Turn right in Mußbach to stay on the L516 towards Neustadt.
- Go straight over the B38 roundabout to Neustadt an der Weinstraße.
- In Neustadt, turn right on the B39 to Frankenstein and Kaiserslautern.
- Turn left in Frankenstein on the B37 to Kaiserslautern. After 3 miles, take the exit for Hochspeyer and pick up the B48.
- Stay with the B48 for 35 miles, all the way into Bad Bergzabern.
- From Bad Bergzabern, take the B427 towards Kandel. Keep going straight at Winden on the L548 towards the A65.
- Join the motorway to Karlsruhe.
- Leave the A65 at J10 for Knielingen. Cross the town following signs for Mannheim.
- Join the B36 towards Mannheim. After 12 miles, take the exit for the B35 to Bruchsal.
- At the B3, turn left towards Heidelberg.
- At Bad Schönborn, turn right on the B292 to Östringen.
- Turn left in Angelbachtal, then turn right on the B39 towards the A6 and Sinsheim.
- Cross the A6 and go into Sinsheim, then pick up the B45 towards Heidelberg.
- Cross the river at Neckargemünd and turn left on the L534 to Ziegelhausen.
- Turn right in Ziegelhausen on the L596 to Wilhelmsfeld.
- In Wilhelmsfeld, turn right on the L536.
- After 3 miles turn left on the L535 to Weinheim.
- In Ober-Abtsteinach, turn right on the L535 then pick up the L3409.
- Turn right on the B38 to Rimbach.
- Don't miss the left turn in Krumbach to stay on the B38.
- After a mile and a half, turn left on the B47 and take it all the way back to Worms.

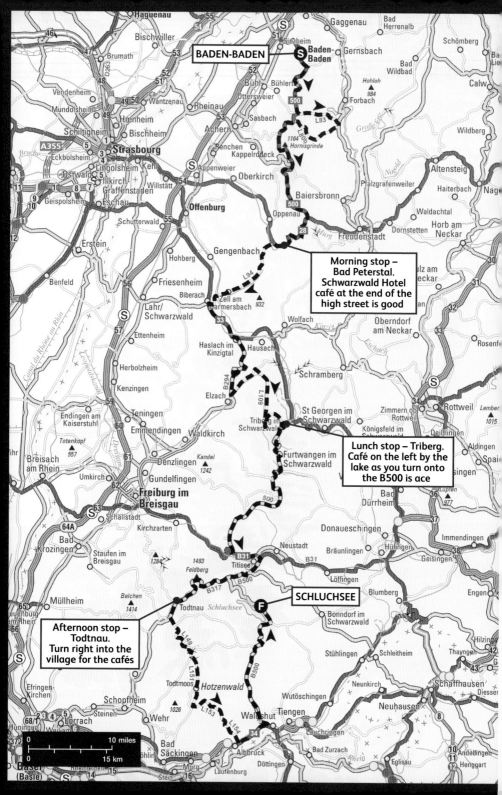

BADEN-BADEN

Morning stop –
Bad Peterstal.
Schwarzwald Hotel
café at the end of the
high street is good

Lunch stop – Triberg.
Café on the left by the
lake as you turn onto
the B500 is ace

SCHLUCHSEE

Afternoon stop –
Todtnau.
Turn right into the
village for the cafés

0   10 miles
0   15 km

69 Beyond the B500

The Black Forest is one of Europe's most popular biking areas – mostly thanks to the reputation of one road, the B500. The northern stretch from Baden-Baden to Freudenstadt, running along the crest of this low range of mountains, is the Black Forest High Road – a brilliant road now hobbled with ludicrously low speed limits. It's still worth riding for the views, but a lot of the fun has been

FROM	Baden-Baden
TO	Schluchsee
DISTANCE	185 miles
ALLOW	5 hours

smothered out of it – but it's not the only road in the Black Forest. My day-long route hops on and off the B500, riding the best bits, but adding some other often-overlooked gems.

Route

- Leave Baden-Baden on the B500.
- After about 9 miles, turn left on the L83 to Herrenweis and Talsperre.
- Don't miss the left turn 6 miles later for the L80b to Hundsbach.
- At the B500, turn left to Freudenstadt.
- At the B28 T-junction, turn right to Bad Peterstal-Griesbach.
- Don't miss the left turn in Löcherberg (about a mile past Bad Peterstal) for the L94 to Oberharmersbach.
- In Biberach, turn left on the B33 to Steinach and Villingen-Schwenningen.
- In Haslach im Kinzigtal, turn right on the B294 to Mühlenbach.
- After 8 miles, turn left (by the petrol station) on the back road to Oberprechtal. This becomes the L109 to Triberg.
- In Triberg, turn right on the B500 to Furtwangen and stick with it for 25 miles.
- At the B31, turn left to Titisee.
- Leave the B31 at the third exit, signed for the B500 / B317 and take the B317 to Todtnau and Feldberg (the Black Forest's highest peak).
- Don't miss the left turn a mile after Todtnau for the L149 to Todtmoos.
- After a mile, turn right on the L151 to Todtmoos. Turn left in the village to stay on it.
- Don't miss the left turn 6½ miles later for the L153 to Görwihl.
- At the L154, turn right to Albbruck.
- In Albbruck, take the B34 towards Waldshut-Tiengen.
- After 3 miles, turn left on the B500 to Schluchsee and Titisee. Take this all the way to the end of the route.

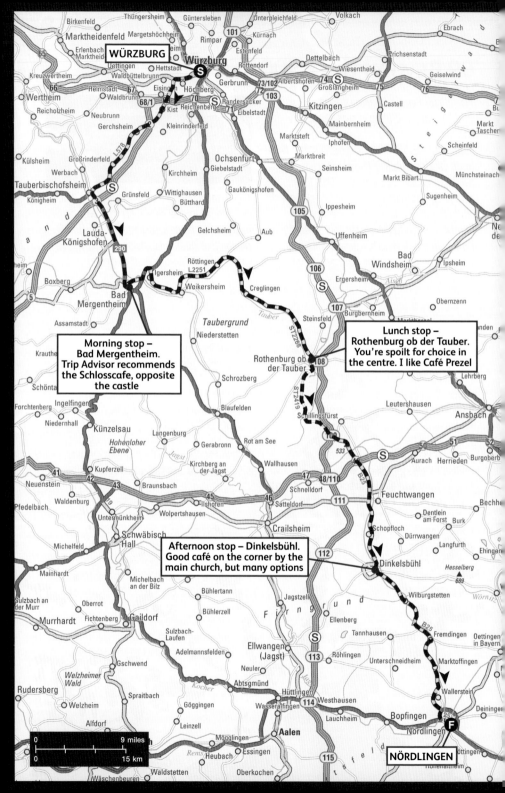

WÜRZBURG

Morning stop –
Bad Mergentheim.
Trip Advisor recommends
the Schlosscafe, opposite
the castle

Lunch stop –
Rothenburg ob der Tauber.
You're spoilt for choice in
the centre. I like Café Prezel

Afternoon stop – Dinkelsbühl.
Good café on the corner by the
main church, but many options

NÖRDLINGEN

0   9 miles

0   15 km

70 The Romantic Road (day one)

This looks like a short route... and it is. In fact, it's possible to ride the entire length of the Romantic Road in a day – but not if you want to appreciate it. The whole point of the trip is to take time off the bike admiring the olde-worlde charm of its well-preserved towns, which are packed with traditional half-timbered buildings. While the suggested stops at Bad Mergentheim, Rothenburg ob der Tauber and Dinkelsbühl are three of the highlights of the route,

FROM	Würzburg
TO	Nördlingen
DISTANCE	110 miles
ALLOW	3 hours

it is also worth taking a bit of time off the bike in Tauberbischofsheim, Lauda-Königshofen and Creglingen as well. There's a host of additional information about all the towns at www.romanticroadgermany.com to help you plan your visit.

Route

- Leave Würzburg on the B27.
- Don't miss the exit (after the one for Höchberg) to stay on the B27 to the A3.
- Go straight across the A3, through Kist, on the ST578.
- Go over the A81 and stay on the ST579 (which becomes the L578) all the way to Tauberbischofsheim.
- In Tauberbischofsheim, turn left on the B27 and keep going straight as it becomes the B290 to Lauda-Königshofen.
- From Bad Mergentheim, take the B19 to Würzburg and within a mile turn right for Igersheim and Wiekersheim on the L2251.
- Turn left at the roundabout in Wiekersheim to stay on the L2251.
- Turn right in Schäftersheim to stay on the L2251 to Röttingen, which then becomes the ST2269 and then the ST2268.
- Follow the road to Creglingen, where it briefly becomes the L2251 – and then the ST2268 to Rothenburg ob der Tauber.
- From Rothenburg, take the ST2419 to Insingen. Go straight over the A7 and A6 autobahns – after which it becomes the B25.
- Stay with the B25 all the way to the overnight stop in Nördlingen.

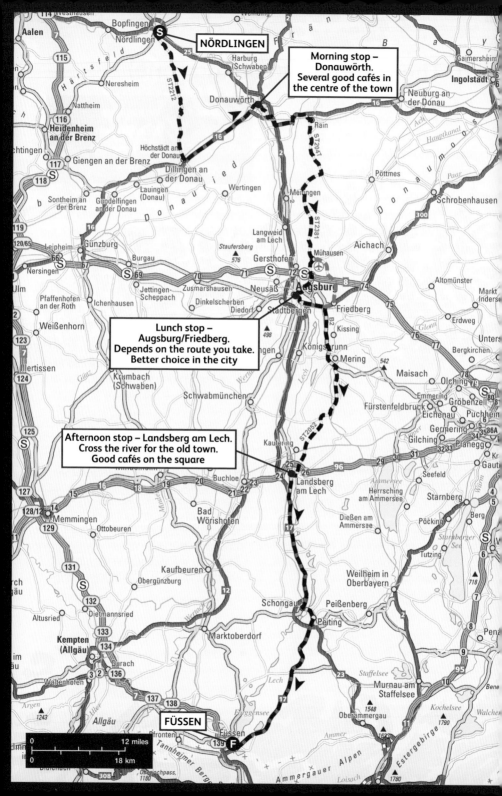

NÖRDLINGEN

Morning stop –
Donauwörth.
Several good cafés in
the centre of the town

Lunch stop –
Augsburg/Friedberg.
Depends on the route you take.
Better choice in the city

Afternoon stop – Landsberg am Lech.
Cross the river for the old town.
Good cafés on the square

FÜSSEN

| 0 | 12 miles |
| 0 | 18 km |

70 The Romantic Road (day two)

There's a big decision: will you go into Augsburg or not? If you skip past it, you could spend a couple of hours at the Neuschwanstein in the afternoon. Alternatively, you can spend the afternoon exploring the walled city and ride straight to Füssen, then spend the whole of the following day visiting both the Neuschwanstein and the older Hohenschwangau castles (take a bus and leave your bike gear in

FROM	Nördlingen
TO	Füssen
DISTANCE	120 miles
ALLOW	3½ hours

the hotel). It's all down to how many days you have for your trip. Personally, I'd go into Augsburg and enjoy a relaxed off-bike day seeing the sights at Schwangau.

Route

- Leave Nördlingen on the ST2212 to Reimlingen.
- After 10 miles, turn right to stay on the ST2212 to Höchstädt an der Donau.
- In Höchstädt, turn left on the B16 to Donauwörth.
- In Donauwörth, pick up the B16 to Rain.
- Cross Rain and take the ST2047 to Münster, which becomes the ST2381.
- Look out: in Thierhaupten, go left at the roundabout through the town centre to stay on the ST2381 to Rehling.
- In Mühausen, turn right to Augsburg and the airport on the ST2035 to go into the city. Leave Augsburg on the B300 towards Dasing and turn right on the B2.

- Alternatively, turn left at Mühausen on the back road to Derching. Cross the A8 and go to Friedberg. Turn right on the B300 and, after half a mile, turn left on the ring road. At the B2, turn left towards Kissing.
- Look out: as the B2 bypasses Mering, take the exit for the ST2052 for Merching and Egling an der Paar.
- Cross Landsberg am Lech and pick up the B17 south towards Schongau.
- Stick with the B17 all the way to Füssen – leaving only to go into Schongau and, if visiting the Neuschwanstein, Schwangau.

Castles

For information about visiting the castles, see https://en.schwangau.de.

European speed limits (km/h)

	TOWN	COUNTRY	MOTORWAY
Austria	50	100	130
Belgium	50	90	120
Czechia	50	90	130
France	50	80*	130 (110 in wet)
Germany	50	100	none (130 when busy)
Italy	50	90	130
Luxembourg	50	90	120
Portugal	50	90	120
Slovenia	50	90	130
Spain	50	100	120
Switzerland	50	80	120

* Some departments in France have returned to 90 km/h.

Many stretches of country roads will have lowered speed limits if they're in mountainous terrain, if there are a lot of junctions, or if there have been a high number of accidents on the road: 70 km/h is common; 50 km/h isn't unusual. City, town and village centres may have 30 km/h or even 20 km/h limits.

B4, Harz mountains (route 64, pages 158–9)

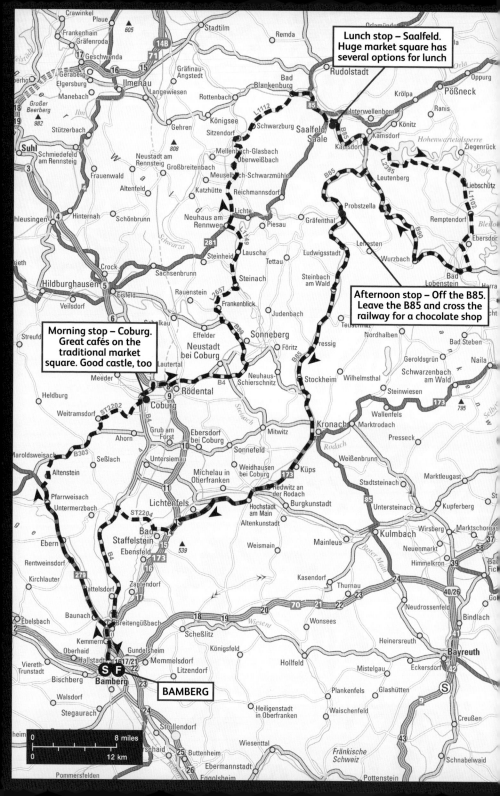

Lunch stop – Saalfeld.
Huge market square has
several options for lunch

Afternoon stop – Off the B85.
Leave the B85 and cross the
railway for a chocolate shop

Morning stop – Coburg.
Great cafés on the
traditional market
square. Good castle, too

BAMBERG

0 — 8 miles
0 — 12 km

71 Bamberg and Beyond

I confess, I hadn't heard of Bamberg until my youngest went there on a school exchange trip. Turns out, it's an absolute gem of a small city. Better still, when I visited I discovered it has some great riding on its doorstep, especially heading north into the wooded hills of Thuringia. Along the way there are more picture-

FROM	Bamberg
DISTANCE	220 miles
ALLOW	6½ hours

postcard towns and atmospheric castles, though this full day in the saddle doesn't allow too much time for stopping to see the sights.

Route

- Leave Bamberg on the ST2244 towards Breitengüßbach.
- Don't miss the left turn in Breitengüßbach for the B279 towards Fulda and Bad Neustadt an der Saale.
- Don't miss the right turn after 16 miles for the minor road to Altenstein.
- At the B303, turn right to Coburg.
- After 7 miles, turn left on the ST2022 to Weitramsdorf and follow this road all the way into Coburg.
- From Coburg, take the B4 to Neustadt bei Coburg.
- At the B89, turn left towards Sonneberg and Eisfeld.
- After 4½ miles, turn right on the L2657 to Frankenblick and Steinach.
- From Steinach, take the L1145 and then L1149 to Neuhaus am Rennweg.
- In Neuhaus, turn right on the B281 towards Saalfeld, then turn left at the roundabout on the L1145 to Schwarzatal and Unterweißbach.
- At the L1112 junction, turn right to Bad Blankenburg.

- In Bad Blankenburg, pick up the B88 to Saalfeld.
- From Saalfeld, take the B85 towards Kronach and Kulmbach.
- In Kaulsdorf, turn left at the roundabout, then right on the minor road to Hohenwarte.
- After 3½ miles turn right on the L2385 to Drognitz.
- In Liebschütz, turn right on the L1102 to Remptendorf and Bad Lobenstein.
- In Bad Lobenstein, turn right on the B90 to Saalfeld and Wurzbach. Don't miss the right turn in Wurzbach to stay on the B90.
- At the B85, turn left to Kronach.
- Go straight through Kronach as the road becomes the B303 and then the B173 to Hochstadt am Main (where it becomes the B289 for a few miles before continuing as the B173).
- Go into Bad Staffelstein and pick up the ST2204 to Itzgrund.
- At the B4, turn left to return to Bamberg. Keep going straight as it becomes the ST2244.

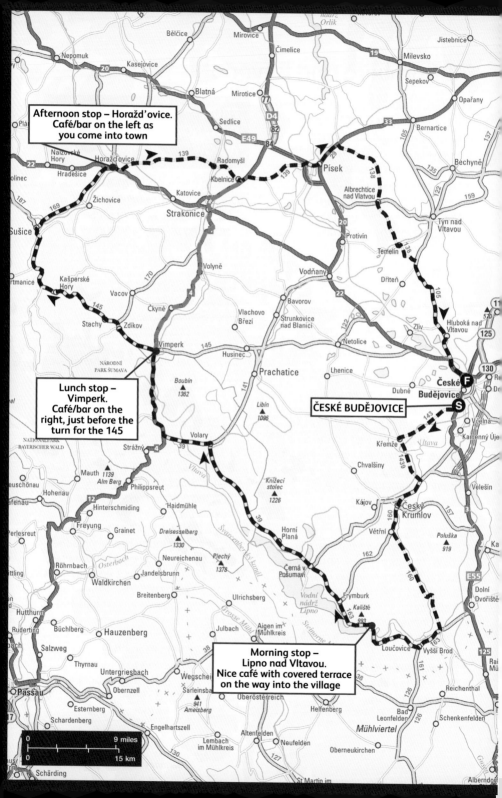

Afternoon stop – Horažďovice.
Café/bar on the left as
you come into town

Lunch stop –
Vimperk.
Café/bar on the right, just before the
turn for the 145

ČESKÉ BUDĚJOVICE

Morning stop –
Lipno nad Vltavou.
Nice café with covered terrace
on the way into the village

72 Bohemian Rhapsody

I confess that I don't know Czechia half as well as I'd like. The one reliable, memorable route I feel confident to share is this one, shown to me by my friend Robert who was a regular visitor to the international beer festival. As a brewer, he insisted it was work... The riding in Czechia is a lot like that in neighbouring Germany: lots of flowing, usually smooth roads through forests and farmland. The big

FROM	České Budějovice
DISTANCE	190 miles
ALLOW	5½ hours

difference is a fair bit less traffic. This is a fantastic country for riding and I look forward to exploring more of it... not least because there's a great beer at the end of every ride.

Route

- Leave České Budějovice on highway 3 towards Linz and Austria.
- After about 3 miles, take the exit for Včelná. Turn right on the 143 to Křemže.
- Don't miss the left turn in Křemže for the 1439 to Český Krumlov.
- Turn right on the 39 to Český Krumlov.
- In Český Krumlov, turn left on the 157 to Kaplice. Cross the river and turn right on the 160 to Větřní.
- At the163 T-junction, turn right to Lipno nad Vltavou and the ski area.
- Turn left by the church in Černá v Pošumaví on the 39 to Volary. Turn left by the green in Volary to stay on the 39 to Vimperk.
- At Highway 4, turn right to Strakonice.
- *For a shorter ride, stick on Highway 4 from Vimperk to Kbelnice, picking up the 139 to Písek. This will save 30 miles / 45 minutes.*
- For the full route, pick up the 145 in Vimperk to Kašperské Hory and U Sloupü.

- Turn left in Zdíkovec to stay on the 145.
- At the 169, turn right to Sušice.
- At Highway 22, turn right to go into Horažďovice town centre. Turn left by the church to pick up the 139 to Třebohostice.
- Don't miss the (unsignposted) right turn about 300 m after going over the railway to stay on the 139.
- In Radomyšl, turn left then right to stay on the 139 to Ošek.
- In Kbelnice, turn left and go over Highway 4 to stay on the 139 to Písek.
- Cross Písek and pick up the 29 to Tábor.
- In Záhoří, turn right by the sports field on the 138 to Albrechtice nad Vltavou.
- Turn right then left in Albrechtice to stay on the 138.
- In Temelín, turn left then right to stay on it.
- At the 105 T-junction, turn right to return to České Budějovice.

73 The DAS

The Deutsche Alpen Straße – the DAS – skips through the mountains of the Tyrol, hopping over the border from Bavaria into neighbouring Austria and back. I'd ridden the western end, from Lake Constance to Garmisch-Partenkirchen, many times on the way to the annual BMW-owners shindig in Garmisch. When I finally rode the full length of it, I kicked myself for not doing it sooner: it's great! My version might not strictly follow the 'official' route, as I've fine-tuned it slightly, dialling up the scenery and keeping to the quiet roads with the best bends. There are plenty of those, but this is the

FROM	Lindau
TO	Berchtesgaden
DISTANCE	235 miles
ALLOW	6½ hours

easy end of the Alps. It's ideal for those new to mountain riding and is a great trip for two – but this is potentially a challengingly long day with a passenger; for a more relaxed pace, maybe break it into two short days with a stopover in Garmisch. Some stretches of the road have lowered speed limits and others have noise restrictions in place – no loud exhausts!

Route

- Leave Lindau on the B12 towards Weißensberg and the motorway.
- At the B31, turn right towards the A96.

- Carry on straight past the motorway as the road becomes the B308 to Scheidegg. Stay on the B308 all the way to Immenstadt im Allgäu.

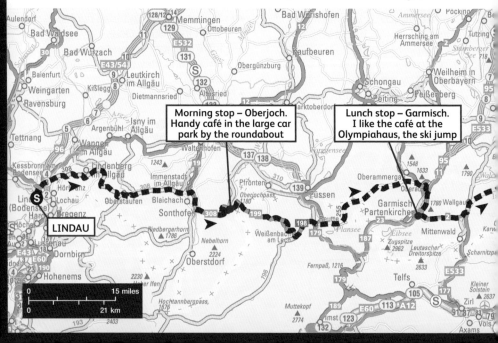

Morning stop – Oberjoch. Handy café in the large car park by the roundabout

Lunch stop – Garmisch. I like the café at the Olympiahaus, the ski jump

- Go straight through Immenstadt and take the B19 south for one junction to Sonthofen.
- Rejoin the B308 through Sonthofen to Bad Hindelang and Oberjoch.
- Turn right at the Oberjoch roundabout on the B308 to Austria, where the road becomes the B199.
- In Weißenbach am Lech, turn left on the B198 to Reutte.
- Keep going straight though Reutte to pick up the L255 to Plansee. The road becomes the ST2060 when it crosses the border.
- Turn right on the B23 to Oberau.
- In Oberau, turn right on the B2 to Garmisch-Partenkirchen. Stay on it all the way through town.
- After 14 miles on the B2, take the exit for the B11 to Kochel and Walchensee.
- Don't miss the right turn in Wallgau (past the golf course) for the back road to Vorderriß, where it becomes the B307.

- About 2 miles outside Tegernsee, on the lake shore, turn right at the roundabout on the ST2076 to Hausham.
- Turn right in Hausham on the B307 to Schliersee.
- Look out: don't miss the right turn for the minor road to Auerbach and Oberaudorf, about 7 miles after Bayrischzell (just past the Tatzelwurm waterfall).
- In Oberaudorf, turn left towards the A93, but go straight over the motorway, over the river and into Austria on the B172. Stay with it past Walchsee, back to Germany.
- In Reit im Winkl, turn right on the B305 to Weitsee. Don't miss the right turn 12 miles later to stay on the B305.
- Turn right at the T-junction to stay on the B305 and follow it to Berchtesgaden.

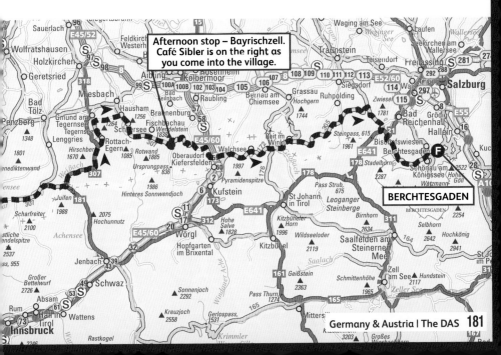

Afternoon stop – Bayrischzell. Café Sibler is on the right as you come into the village.

BERCHTESGADEN

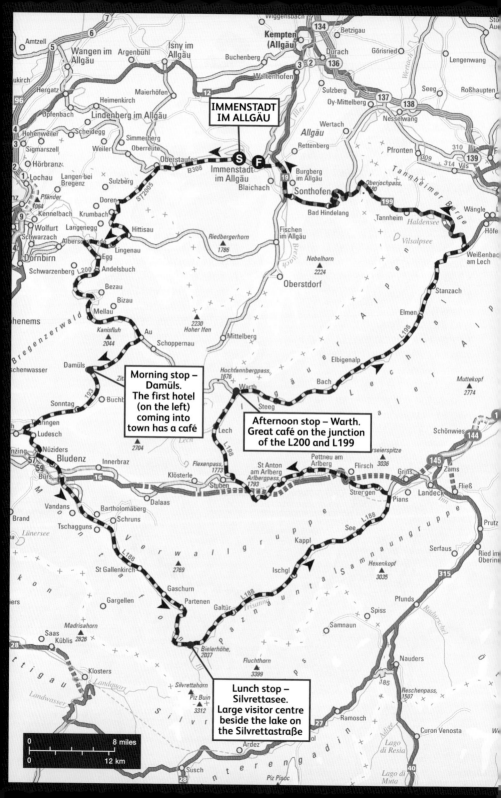

IMMENSTADT IM ALLGÄU

Morning stop – Damüls. The first hotel (on the left) coming into town has a café

Afternoon stop – Warth. Great café on the junction of the L200 and L199

Lunch stop – Silvrettasee. Large visitor centre beside the lake on the Silvrettastraße

74 Silvrettastraße

*Austria has some amazing roads –
though you do have to pay a toll for
the best of them. The Silvrettastraße
is one of these marvels of mountain
road building, with thirty-four hairpins
crammed into the 14 miles covered
by the toll. Sadly, these roads have
all had a lower speed limit imposed
– not that you'd be ripping through
the hairpins at high speed anyway.
This route, based around Immenstadt
just over the border in Bavaria, tackles
the steep section as a climb, as most*

FROM	Immenstadt im Allgäu
DISTANCE	215 miles
ALLOW	6 hours

*people seem to find hairpins easier
and more enjoyable to ride on the
ascent than the descent. However,
the route is equally good when ridden
in the opposite direction. Whichever
way you go, the views are stunning.*

Route

- Leave Immenstadt on the B308 to Lindau.
- In Oberstaufen, turn left on the ST2005 to Dornbirn. This becomes the L205 in Austria.
- At the L200, turn left to Warth and Au.
- In Au, turn right on the L193 to Sonntag and Damüls.
- Turn left at the lights in Thüringen to stay on the L193 to Bludenz and the motorway.
- Turn left on the L190 – and if you have an Austrian vignette for the motorway (a ten-day tourist one is all you need), join the A14 towards Innsbruck to bypass Bludenz. Take the motorway for 2½ miles, leaving at J61 to pick up the L188 to Montafon.
- If you don't have the vignette, take the L190 through Bludenz and keep going straight as it becomes the L188.

- Keep going on the L188, which becomes the Silvrettastraße.
- In Pians, pick up the B171 to Strengen.
- Don't join the motorway – keep going on the L68 to Flirsch and St Anton.
- Keep going straight as the road becomes the B917.
- At the traffic lights after Rauz, turn right on the L198 to Warth (though if you like hairpins and big views, go left to Stuben, then turn around and climb back up the mountain to rejoin the route).
- Turn right in Warth to stay on the L198 to Reutte.
- In Weißenbach am Lech, turn left on the B199 to Sonthofen. This becomes the B308 when it returns to Germany.
- From Sonthofen, take the B19 towards Kempten. Take the first exit for the B308 to return to Immenstadt.

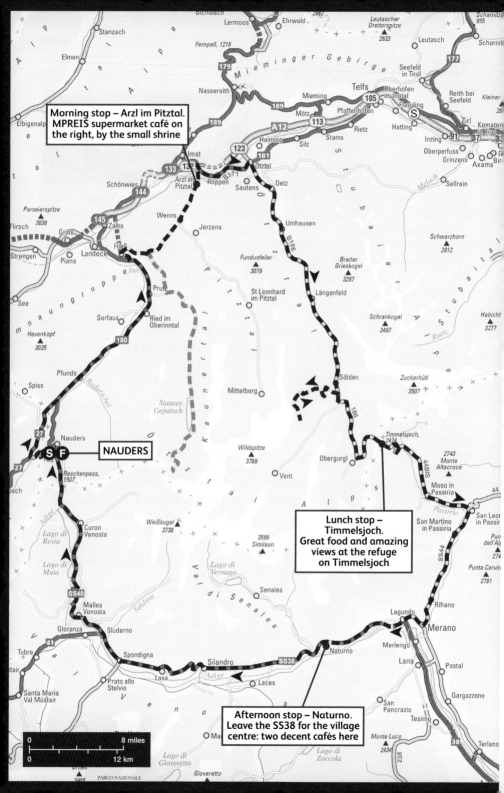

Morning stop – Arzl im Pitztal. MPREIS supermarket café on the right, by the small shrine

NAUDERS

Lunch stop – Timmelsjoch. Great food and amazing views at the refuge on Timmelsjoch

Afternoon stop – Naturno. Leave the SS38 for the village centre: two decent cafés here

75 Timmelsjoch and Ötztal

I admit, I was obsessed with riding all of Europe's highest paved roads. After the famous ones and the easy ones, I ended up here: the Ötztal glacier road, which is the highest, peaking at 2,830 m (trumping France's Cime de la Bonette – the highest non-dead-end road). Not only is this a fabulous ride, but it's also handily on the way to another of Europe's greatest passes, Timmelsjoch. This is already a full day but hardcore mountain

FROM	Nauders
DISTANCE	185 miles
ALLOW	5 hours

fans can extend it with a detour down another dead-end glacier road, Kaunertal. All three of these key roads have tolls, but they're well worth it. The final run down the SS38 is pretty undemanding, making the long day practical (with an early start).

Route

- Leave Nauders on the B185 to Martina.
- In Martina, turn right on Swiss highway 27, back to Austria, where it becomes the B184.
- Turn left on the B180 to Pfunds.
- After 16 miles – as you see the signs for the Landeck tunnel – turn right on the minor road to Fließ and follow the signs for Pitztal.
- Turn left at the T-junction to stay on the back road to Pitztal.
- *For a longer ride, turn right here and follow the signs to Kaunertaler Gletscher (Glacier). It's a dead end, adding 60 miles and 2 hours to the ride, to return to this point.*
- Head through Arzl im Pitztal towards the motorway. Don't get on the A12: instead take the B171 to Telfs and Ötztal.
- After 5 miles, turn right at the roundabout on the B186 to Ötztal.

- Don't miss the right turn, after crossing Sölden, signed for the Rettenbachgletscher and Tiefenbachgletscher.
- After visiting the high points, return to Sölden and continue on the B186.
- Don't miss the left turn at Obergurgl to stay on the B186 to Timmelsjoch. It becomes the SS44BIS (Passo Rombo) in Italy.
- In San Leonardo in Passiria, pick up the SS44 to Merano.
- Cross Merano and pick up the SS38, signed for Forst, Val Venosta and Stelvio.
- Go straight across the roundabout in Spondigna on the SS40 to Resia. This becomes the B180 and returns to Nauders.

Top Motorcycle Museum

Europe's highest bike museum is beside the Timmelsjoch toll barrier. Rebuilt after burning down in the pandemic, it's packed with great bikes. www.crosspoint.tirol

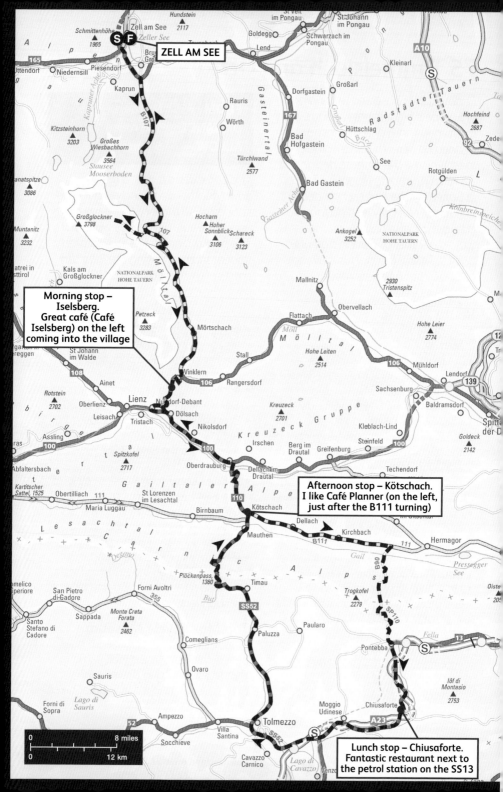

ZELL AM SEE

Morning stop – Iselsberg. Great café (Café Iselsberg) on the left coming into the village

Afternoon stop – Kötschach. I like Café Planner (on the left, just after the B111 turning)

Lunch stop – Chiusaforte. Fantastic restaurant next to the petrol station on the SS13

76 The Großglockner

The Großglockner high alpine road is widely regarded as one of the best biking roads in Europe – and quite rightly. It's long, scenic, packed with amazing corners, studded with great cafés and has a fantastic surface (paid for by the fairly hefty toll…). It's perfectly valid to spend the day just riding the one road – many people do. For me, that's not enough. Not only because the road now has a lowered speed limit but also because it does get busy. So this route fits the Großglockner into a fuller ride –

FROM	Zell am See
DISTANCE	240 miles
ALLOW	6 hours

taking it once in each direction, when it's quieter at the start and again at the end of the day. Just make sure you don't lose the toll ticket: you'll need to show it when you get back for the second run. In between, this route heads out for a loop into Italy using the superb Naßfeld and Plöcken passes.

Route

- Leave Zell am See on the B107. This becomes the Großglockner high alpine road.
- Pay the toll and ride to the end of the road, Kaiser Franz-Josefs Höhe, overlooking the Großglockner glacier.
- Backtrack to the roundabout and turn right on the B107 to Heiliegenblut. Stay on the B107 through Winklern to Lienz.
- On the edge of Lienz, turn left at the roundabout to stay on the B107 to Spittal an der Drau.
- At the B100, turn left to Spittal.
- In Oberdrauburg, turn right (over the bridge) on the B110 to Plöcken Pass.
- In Kötschach, turn left on the B111 towards Villach.

- Don't miss the left turn after 15 miles for the B90 to Naßfeld Pass. This becomes the SP110 when it crosses the border into Italy.
- In Pontebba, turn right after going under the railway, on the SS13 to Udine.
- After 17 miles, bear right on the SS52 to Tolmezzo. Stay on this road back to Austria, over Monte Croce Carnico – also known as Plöcken Pass – as the road becomes the B110.
- Once you get to Kötschach it's a case of retracing your steps: B110 and B100 to Lienz, to pick up the B107 over Großglockner and back to Zell am See.

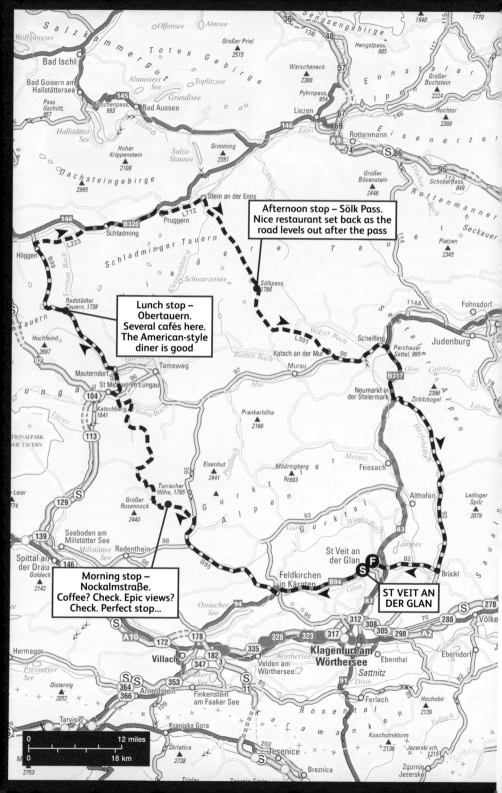

Afternoon stop – Sölk Pass. Nice restaurant set back as the road levels out after the pass

Lunch stop – Obertauern. Several cafés here. The American-style diner is good

Morning stop – Nockalmstraße. Coffee? Check. Epic views? Check. Perfect stop...

ST VEIT AN DER GLAN

77 Nockalmstraße

My last major project before leaving the world of motorcycle magazines – to ride to Australia – was producing the RiDE Guide to Germany *which, like this section of this book, also included Austria. I put together a route around two of my favourite places: the sublime Alpine road Nockalmstraße; and the amazing mountain fortress of Burg Hochosterwitz. I was pretty happy with it, until a helpful chap called Peter contacted me to suggest I could – and should – have included*

FROM	St Veit an der Glan
DISTANCE	205 miles
ALLOW	5 hours

Sölk Pass. That was good advice, as it's produced this new route. It's a relaxed canter through the beautiful mountains of Carinthia and Styria – though it doesn't go into Hochosterwitz. Take a day off the bike to enjoy that properly.

Route

- Leave St Veit an der Glan on the B94 to Feldkirchen in Kärnten.
- Cross Feldkirchen and pick up the B95 to Turracherhöhe and Nockalmstraße.
- Don't miss the left turn 18 miles later for Nockalmstraße. There's no toll at this end – it's as you leave.
- Pay the toll and turn right towards St Michael im Lungau.
- Turn left when this minor road meets the L225, still towards St Michael.
- Go through St Margarethen im Lungau and turn left on the B96 to St Michael, then go straight to join the B99 to Mauterndorf.
- In Mauterndorf, go straight to stay on the B99 towards Salzburg and Radstadt.
- In Höggen, turn right at the roundabout on the L223 to Forstau, which then becomes the L721.
- Turn right after the railway crossing on the B320 to Graz and Schladming.
- After 14 miles, take the exit for Tunzendorf and Pruggern on the L712.
- In Stein an der Enns, cross the river and turn right to Murau and St Nikolai im Sölktal. Though it never seems to get a road number, this becomes the majestic Sölk Pass.
- After 25 miles, turn left on the L501 towards Vienna (Wein), Graz and Scheifling.
- Outside Katsch an der Mur, turn left on the B96 to Scheifling,
- In Scheifling, turn right at the lights on the B317 to St Veit an der Glan.
- *If you're short of time, stay on this road and you'll save half an hour over the full planned route.*
- Otherwise, leaving Neumarkt in der Steiermark, turn left on the B92 to Hüttenberg.
- In Brückl, turn right on the B82 to return to St Veit an der Glan.

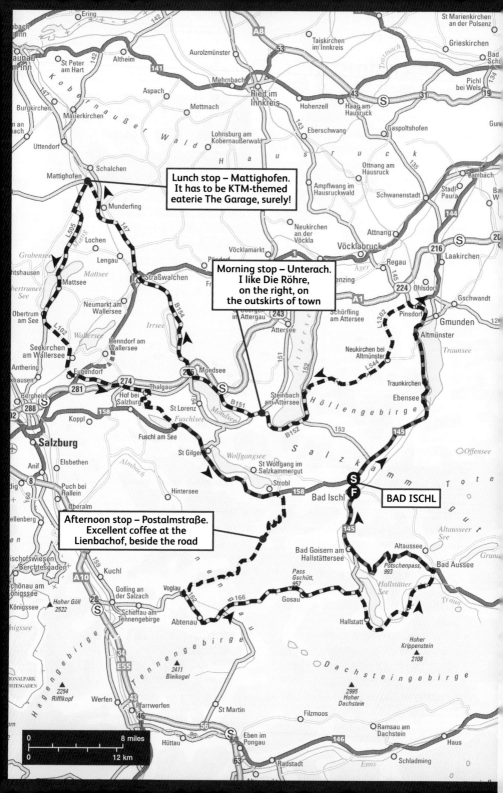

Lunch stop – Mattighofen.
It has to be KTM-themed eaterie The Garage, surely!

Morning stop – Unterach.
I like Die Röhre, on the right, on the outskirts of town

Afternoon stop – Postalmstraße.
Excellent coffee at the Lienbachof, beside the road

BAD ISCHL

78 Austrian Lake Loop

Austria in summer is pretty close to heaven: vivid blue skies, verdant green hills and grey moutains. In the Salzkammergut you can add spectacular lakes into the mix as well, adding an extra element of chocolate-box charm to all the views. There are a lot of memorable views on this relaxed ride that rolls along the shores of ten lakes. It heads out from the pretty mountain resort of Bad Ischl to Mattighofen – the home of KTM. The museum there (see www.ktm-motohall.com) is well

FROM	Bad Ischl
DISTANCE	185 miles
ALLOW	5½ hours

worth a visit, even if you don't have orange blood! The ride continues past Red Bull HQ to the Postalmstraße – a stunning mountain toll road, which for me is on a par with the more-famous passes like Silvrettastraße and Nockalmstraße – before looping round to Hallstatt, one of Austria's most beautiful villages.

Route

- Leave Bad Ischl on the B145 to Gmunden.
- After 13 miles, turn right through Traunkirchen rather than go through the tunnel. Then rejoin the B145 to Gmunden.
- After 6½ miles, turn left at the lights to go into Pinsdorf.
- Turn left just after Pinsdorf station on the L1302 to Neukirchen bei Altmünster.
- Turn right in Neukirchen on the L544 to Steinbach am Attersee.
- In Steinbach, turn left on the B152 to Unterach.
- Leave Unterach on the B151 to Oberburgau and Mondsee.
- In Mondsee, turn right on the B154 towards the motorway and Straßwalchen.
- In Straßwalchen, turn right, then left at the mini-roundabout on the B147 to Mattighofen.
- Leave Mattighofen on the road opposite the KTM Motorhall, the L505 to Mattsee.
- At the Obertrum am See roundabout, turn left on the L102 to Seekirchen am Wallersee and the A1.
- Keep going as the road becomes the L103 and cross the motorway.
- Follow the road from Thalgau as it becomes the L227 to Fuschl am See.
- From Fuschl, join the B158 to Graz and Bad Ischl. Turn right in St Gilgen to stay on this road
- After 8 miles, take the exit for Strobl and turn right to Postalm.
- Cross the bridge In Voglau and turn left on the B162 to Abtenau. Keep going straight as it becomes the B166 to Rußbach.
- Don't miss the right turn 6 miles after Gosau for the L547 to Hallstatt and Obertraun.
- In Bad Aussee, turn left on the B145 to return to Bad Ischl.

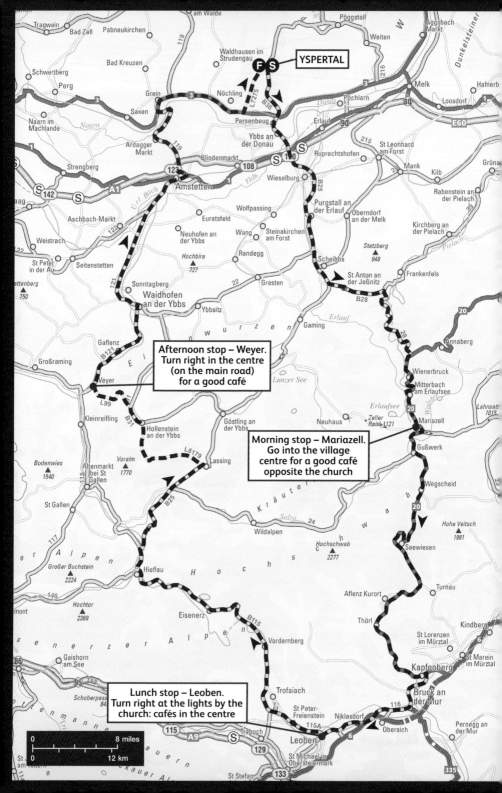

YSPERTAL

Afternoon stop – Weyer.
Turn right in the centre
(on the main road)
for a good café

Morning stop – Mariazell.
Go into the village
centre for a good café
opposite the church

Lunch stop – Leoben.
Turn right at the lights by the
church: cafés in the centre

| 0 | 8 miles |
| 0 | 12 km |

79 Secret Playground

If you want empty roads – where you can ride freely without being held up by other riders or cyclists or camper vans – come to Lower Austria and Styria. These are top-quality mountain roads, with hairpins, miles of great bends and beautiful views. This route

FROM	Yspertal
DISTANCE	215 miles
ALLOW	6 hours

also includes a few miles on the scenic banks of the Danube.

Route

- Leave Yspertal on the B36 to Grein.
- At the B3, turn right then left towards the A3 on the B25 to Ybbs an der Donau.
- Don't get on the motorway: stay on the B25 to Scheibbs.
- Don't miss the left turn, 2 miles south of Scheibbs for the B28 to Mariazell.
- At the B20 junction, turn right to Mariazell.
- Stay with the B20 for about 45 miles, all the way to Kapfenberg.
- You have a choice in Kapfenberg: you can take the dual carriageway B56 towards Graz for four junctions (12 miles), leaving at the exit for Leoben Ost; or you can take the parallel B116 through villages and farmland.
- Leave Leoben on the B115a to Trofaiach. Keep going straight as it becomes the B115 to Heiflau.
- Don't miss the right turn 3 miles after Heiflau for the B25 to Mariazell.

- After 11 miles, turn left in Lassing (opposite the hotel) on the L6179 to Oberkirchen.
- In Hollenstein an der Ybbs, turn left on the B31 to Waidhofen an der Ybbs.
- After a mile and a half, turn left on the L99 to Weyer.
- In Weyer, turn right on the B121 to Waidhofen an der Ibbs. Follow it all the way to Amstetten and the A1
- Don't get on the motorway: take the right exit (or go right at the roundabout with the pears statue) on the B119 to Grein.
- Don't miss the left turn half a mile later to stay on the B119 to Grein.
- Cross the Danube and turn right on the B3 to Grein.
- After 9 miles, turn left (take care: it's a cobbled slip-road) on the L7275 to Yspertal.
- Turn left when it meets the B36 to complete the circular route.

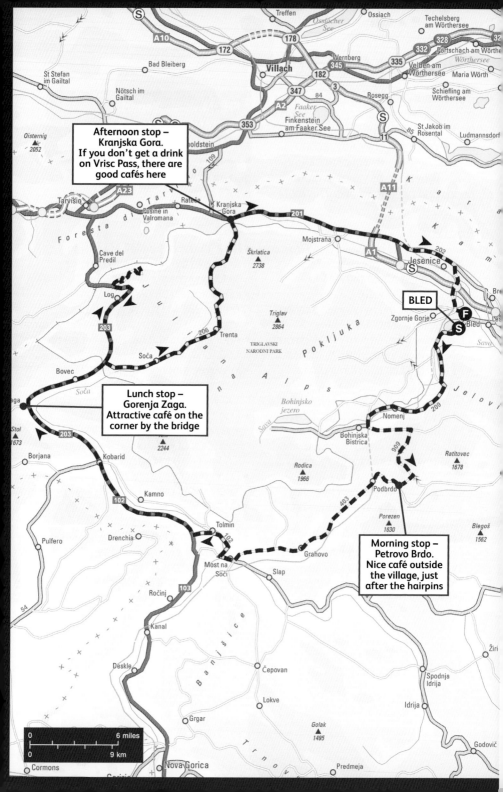

Afternoon stop –
Kranjska Gora.
If you don't get a drink
on Vrsic Pass, there are
good cafés here

Lunch stop –
Gorenja Zaga.
Attractive café on the
corner by the bridge

Morning stop –
Petrovo Brdo.
Nice café outside
the village, just
after the hairpins

BLED

80 Mangart and Vrisc Pass

There are few places prettier than Bled in Slovenia – though for a mountain addict like me, the summit of Mangart Pass just pips it. You can't ride over this saddle, high in the Julian Alps. It's a dead end crowned by a short loop of tarmac with the most staggering views. Not that views are in short supply anywhere on this relaxed daytrip loop. The run south from Bled pops in and out of forests, up and down some steep climbs, though the road surface has seen better days, before settling into the relaxing run to Kobarid. Then after

FROM	Bled
DISTANCE	150 miles
ALLOW	4½ hours

tackling Mangart, the route heads to one of Europe's loveliest and strangest mountain roads: Vrisc Pass. It's famous for a wooden chapel erected by the Russian soldiers who built the road in WWI and many of the fifty hairpins are still cobbled… So this may be a short and laid-back day, but it still has its challenges.

Route

- Leave Bled on the 209, beside the lake.
- In Bohinjska Bistrica, pick up the 909. This is a narrow road in places and the surface has deteriorated. Take it steady on this bit.
- In Petrovo Brdo, join the 403 to Podbrdo.
- Continue along the 403, then join the 102 to Most na Soči. Take the 102 through Tolmin, following signs for Bovec and Kobarid.
- In Kobarid, turn right on the 203 to Vrsno and Bovec. Stay with it for 23 miles, through Bovec, heading towards Italy.
- Don't miss the right-hand turn (as the 203 turns hard left after a bridge) for the 902 to Mangart Pass – look for the brown sign.
- From the top, backtrack to rejoin the 203 heading back towards Bovec.

- After 8 miles on the 203, take the left turn for the 206 to Kranjska Gora.
- This will become the Vrisc Pass. In places it's narrow; in places the surface is poor; some hairpins are cobbled… The Russian Chapel is about 2½ miles down from the summit.
- In Kranjska Gora, pick up the 201 towards Ljubljana and Jesenice.
- Don't join the A2 motorway: keep going straight on the 452 to Jesenice.
- Cross Jesenice and follow the signs for the motorway and Spodnje Gora. Go straight across the A2, on the 634 to Spodnje Gora.
- In Spodnje Gora, turn left on the minor road to Bled.

Switzerland & Italy

Stelvio Pass, Italy (route 84, pages 204–5)

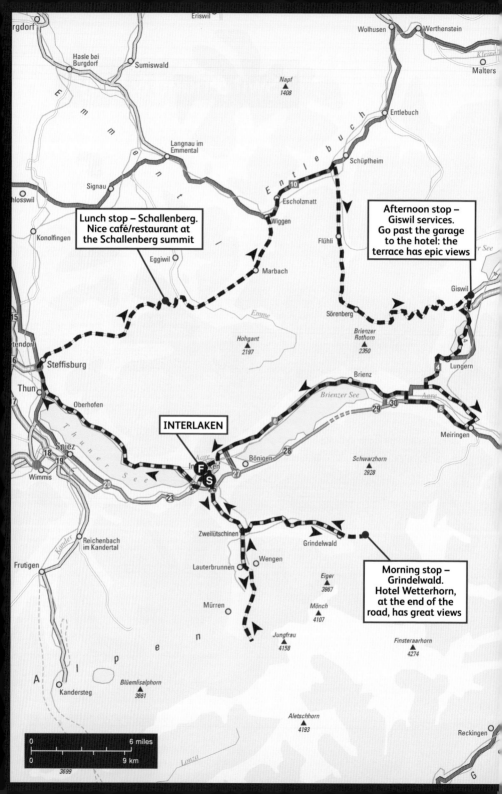

Lunch stop – Schallenberg.
Nice café/restaurant at
the Schallenberg summit

Afternoon stop –
Giswil services.
Go past the garage
to the hotel: the
terrace has epic views

INTERLAKEN

Morning stop –
Grindelwald.
Hotel Wetterhorn,
at the end of the
road, has great views

0   6 miles
0   9 km

81 Interlaken Loop

This short Swiss loop is all about heroic views. Go in late spring or early summer and the dead-end road through Lauterbrunnen passes a succession of dramatic waterfalls. Double back to Grindelwald and you get close to the Eiger, one of the most iconic peaks in the Alps. After this pair of dead ends, the route takes in more traditional touring favourites: the road around Thunnersee, the

FROM	Interlaken
DISTANCE	140 miles
ALLOW	4½ hours

climb over Schallenberg and the Panoramastraße. Then it cuts over the Brunnig Pass to Meiringen – where there's a host of off-bike attractions. It might be a short route, but it can make for a very full day.

Route

- Leave Interlaken following signs for the A8… but go straight over the motorway on the road to Wilderswil and Lauterbrunnen, and take the road as far as you can.
- Backtrack from the end of the road and take the right turn – about 3 miles outside Lauterbrunnen – for Grindelwald.
- From Grindelwald, return to Interlaken and pick up the back road to Thun, along the northern shore of the lake.
- Cross Thun following signs for Bern and then Luzern and Steffisburg.
- Go straight over the roundabout in Steffisburg following the signs for Luzern and Schallenberg.
- In Wiggen, turn right on highway 10 following the signs for Luzern.

- Don't miss the right turn in Schüpfheim for the road to Giswil, Sörenberg and Flühli. This becomes the Panoramastraße.
- In Giswil, turn right on highway 4 to Interlaken. You can short-cut the day by staying with it all the way back (NB: you need a toll vignette to use the Lungern tunnel).
- Don't go through the tunnel by Lungersee – about 2 miles from the recommended coffee stop. Peel off to the right to take highway 4 through Lungern.
- Don't miss the right turn about 4 miles from Lungern for the road to Meiringen (also signed for Grimsel and Susten).
- In Meiringen, pick up highway 6 to Brienz and take it all the way back to Interlaken.

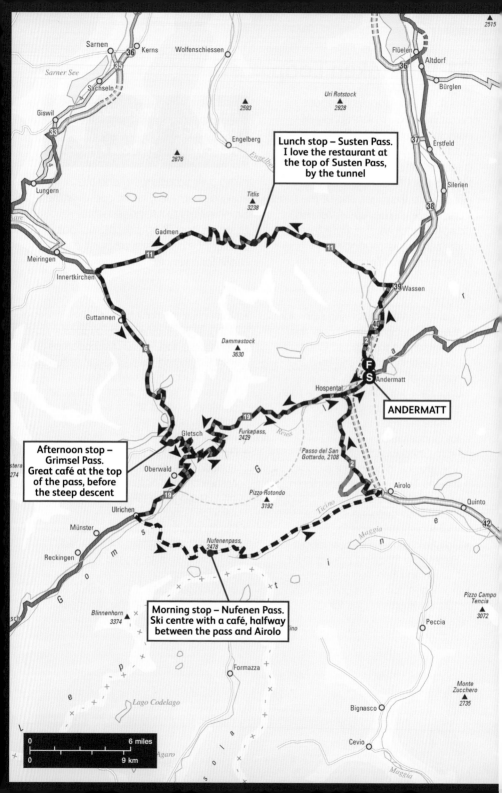

82 The Five Passes

This is one of the great European touring routes, linking the Grimsel, Susten, Nufenen, St Gotthard and Furka passes. There are plenty of possible ways to run it, but I prefer to start and finish in Andermatt, taking Furka Pass east to west as the first road of the day, then riding a giant anticlockwise loop that finishes with Furka ridden from west to east. Every one of these roads is from the top drawer: great to ride and very beautiful. There are lots of cafés

FROM	Andermatt
DISTANCE	140 miles
ALLOW	3½ hours

along the route for as many stops as you like. The St Gotthard has three roads: the motorway; the modern highway 2; and the traditional Tremola, which is cobbled from top to bottom. I like it best as a climb (as here), but prefer highway 2 in the wet.

Route
- Leave Andermatt on Swiss highway 2 to Hospental.
- In Hospental, turn right at the roundabout on the 19 to Brig. This becomes Furka Pass.
- In Ulrichen, turn left on the minor road signed for Airolo and Nufenen. This becomes Nufenen Pass.
- Coming into Airolo, follow the green sign for Passo San Gottardo to join highway 2. If it's raining, maybe stay on highway 2…
- Otherwise, look for the right turn about a mile later signed for Motto Bartola. Turn left at the end of the sliproad (to pass under highway 2). This road becomes the Tremola.
- Rejoin highway 2 at the top and take it past Hospental and Andermatt.
- In Wassen, turn left on highway 11 to Meiringen. This takes you over Susten Pass.
- In Innertkirchen, turn left on highway 6, which becomes Grimsel Pass.
- At the bottom of Grimsel Pass, turn left by the hotel to ride Furka Pass in the other direction, returning to the start of the route.

Reichenbach Falls
Meiringen does a good trade from Sherlock Holmes. The falls where he met his end are real and well worth a visit.
www.grimselwelt.ch

The Alpen Tower
Take the cable cars up from Meiringen for the most amazing views in the Alps.
www.meiringen-hasliberg.ch

Rhone Glacier
Visit the ice caves at the source of the Rhone, beside the Furka Pass Belvedere (as seen in the classic Bond film *Goldfinger*).
www.myswitzerland.com

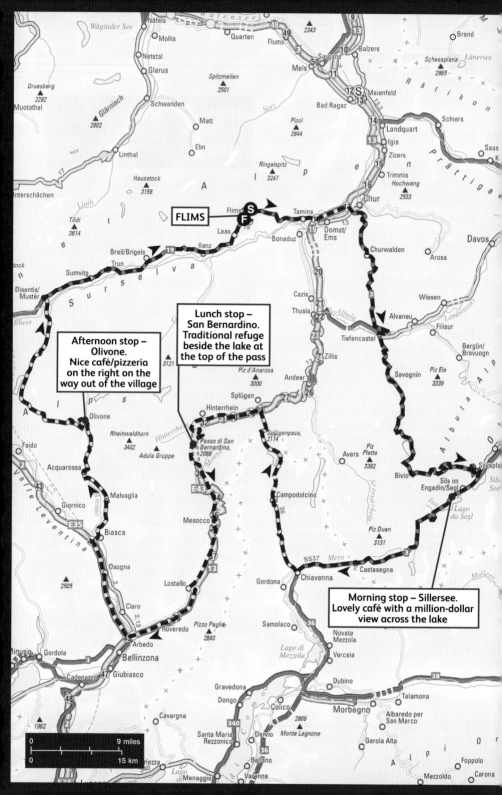

FLIMS

Afternoon stop –
Olivone.
Nice café/pizzeria
on the right on the
way out of the village

Lunch stop –
San Bernardino.
Traditional refuge
beside the lake at
the top of the pass

Morning stop – Sillersee.
Lovely café with a million-dollar
view across the lake

83 Flims Stars

There is so much brilliant riding in the Swiss Alps. This is another quintet of amazing passes that are individually quite well known, but they don't seem to be linked together in the public imagination as a single route like 'The Five Passes' (see route 82). That's a tragedy, really. That might be because this is a fuller day, or maybe it's because making this route work does require using some stretches of Swiss motorway (for which an

FROM	Flims
DISTANCE	**225 miles**
ALLOW	**6 hours**

expensive vignette is required). It's worth it to be able to ride the Julier, Majola, Splügen, San Bernardino and Lukmanier passes together – in one amazing day. The question is, which is your favourite pass? They're all stars in my book.

Route

- Leave Flims on Swiss highway 19 to Chur.
- Join the A13 for one junction, leaving at J17 for Chur Süd.
- From Chur, take highway 3 to Lenzerheid.
- In Tiefencastle, turn left towards St Moritz and Julier Pass to stay on the 3.
- In Silvaplana, turn right at the roundabout on the 3 towards Majola Pass. This becomes the SS37 when it crosses the border to Italy.
- In Chiavenna, turn right at the roundabout on the SS36 to Madesimo and Passo Spluga (aka Splügen Pass).
- Don't miss the left turn in Splügen (just before the bridge) to join the A13 towards San Bernardino.
- After 6 miles, take the exit (J32) for San Bernardino Pass on highway 13.
- On the far side of the pass, the 13 runs parallel to the motorway (which is a two-lane road, not even a dual carriageway, until Soazza). Join the motorway after Cabbiolo and take the A13 to Bellinzona.
- At J45 (Bellinzona Nord), join the A2 to San Gottardo and Airolo.
- Leave the A2 at J44 for Biesca.
- Cross Biesca following the signs for Lucomagno. Despite being the main road over Lukmanier Pass, there's no road number.
- In Disentis, turn right on the 19 to return to Flims.

Europe's highest bungee jump

If you want to test your nerve, head to the Verzasca Dam outside Locarno for the 220 m plunge...
www.trekking.ch

Chur

Look past the modern outskirts and there's a lovely historic town nestled in the centre. The modern art gallery is good too.
www.kunstmuseum.gr.ch

Cable car

For some amazing Alpine views, take the cable car from the centre of Chur to the slopes of Brambrüesch.
https://chur.graubuenden.ch

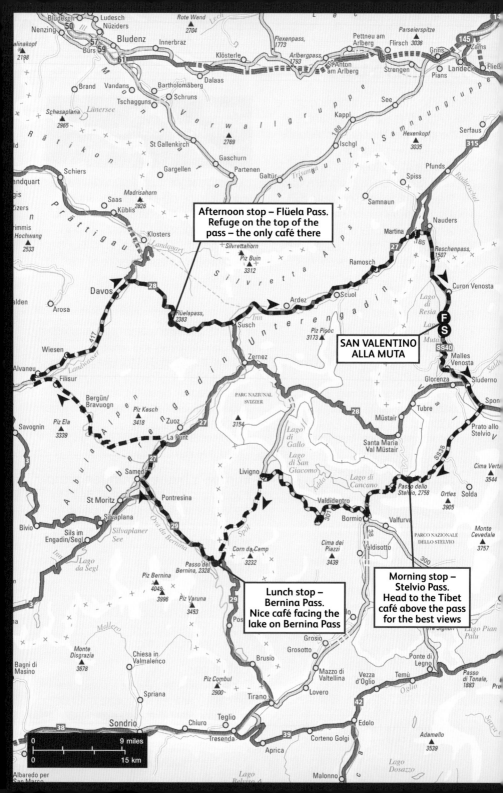

Afternoon stop – Flüela Pass.
Refuge on the top of the pass – the only café there

SAN VALENTINO ALLA MUTA

Lunch stop –
Bernina Pass.
Nice café facing the lake on Bernina Pass

Morning stop –
Stelvio Pass.
Head to the Tibet café above the pass for the best views

0   9 miles
0   15 km

84 Not Simply Stelvio

Stelvio is perhaps the most divisive pass in the Alps. Italy's highest road is famed for its hairpins – forty-eight of them on the northern side alone. At 2,757 m high, it's the second-highest pass in the Alps, just 7 m lower than Col de l'Iseran. It's high, it's tough, it's the two-wheeled Everest and people come to ride it, just because it's there. That can be the problem. Stelvio gets busy – with pushbikes and sports cars as well as motorbikes. And it's a hard road: it's long, the surface can be far from immaculate in places, and all those hairpins make it hard to get into a rhythm, especially if

FROM	San Valentino alla Muta
DISTANCE	190 miles
ALLOW	5½ hours

there's lots to overtake. It's a difficult road and some riders just don't enjoy it. I absolutely love it: I love the challenge of it and the satisfaction that comes from getting a good, clean run over it – which is easier to do in the early morning or at the end of the day. I recommend riding this route twice – once in each direction – to fully experience Stelvio.

Route

- Leave San Valentino alla Muta on the SS40 heading to Malles Venosta, over Reschen Pass.
- At the Spondnga roundabout, turn right on the SS38 to Prato allo Stelvio and keep going: this becomes Stelvio Pass.
- Coming into Bormio, look for the right turn (on a hairpin) for the SS301 to Livigno.
- After 21 miles, coming into Livigno, don't miss the left turn (going straight on at a hairpin) towards Switzerland on the minor road over the Forcola Pass.
- Turn left at the border crossing on Bernina Pass (highway 29) to St Moritz.

- Go straight over the roundabout by the airport on highway 27 to Scuol and Zernez.
- After 4 miles, turn left in La Punt Chaumes to Albula. There's no road number, but it becomes Albula Pass.
- After 22 miles (half a mile after going under the railway bridge), turn right to Davos on Swiss road 417.
- Go through Davos and pick up highway 28, signed to Flüela Pass.
- In Susch, turn left on the 27 to Martina.
- In Martina, turn right (by the customs post) to Nauders. This becomes the B185 in Austria, on the other side of the bridge.
- In Nauders, turn right on the B180 to Resia and Italy, where it becomes the SS40 to San Valentino alla Muta.

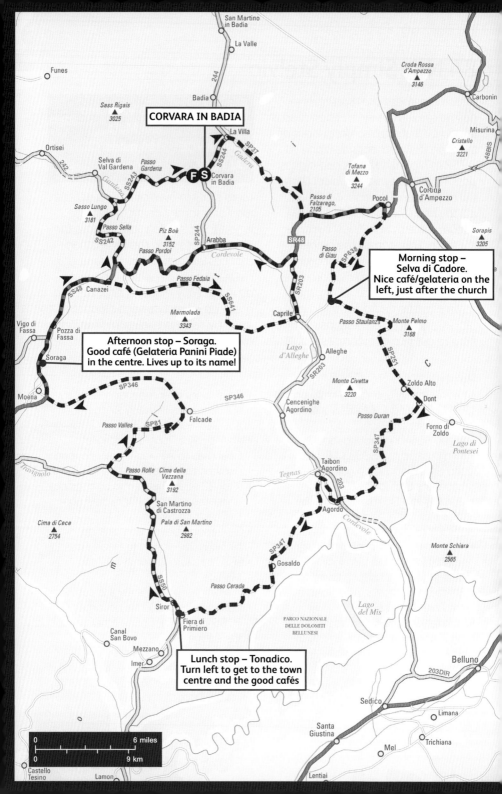

85 Dolomite Daze

The Dolomites are so beautiful and have so many brilliant roads that I could fill a book with routes here and never tire of riding all the variations. The catch is that lots of people feel the same, so the roads can be busy and many now have (well-enforced) lower speed limits. The most famous section is known as the Sella Ronda, the four passes that orbit the Sella Massif: Campolongo, Pordoi, Sella and Gardena. But there's much more

FROM	Corvara in Badia
DISTANCE	180 miles
ALLOW	6 hours

to see than just these four passes – there are thirteen on this day's ride alone. I've spent ages trying to get this route just right and at the point where I was about to say, 'the perfect Dolomite day trip doesn't exist…', it finally all clicked.

Route

- Leave Corvara on the SS244 towards Brunico
- In La Villa, turn right at the roundabout on the SP37 over Valparolla Pass.
- When this meets Falzarego Pass, turn left on the SR48 to Cortina d'Ampezzo.
- After 6 miles, turn right in Pocol on the SP638 to Caprile, over Giau Pass.
- Go straight when it meets the SP251 to Selva di Cadore (also signed for the motorway to Venice) over Staulanza Pass.
- Don't miss the right turn in Dont (really) for the SP347 to Agordo, over Duran Pass.
- In Agordo, go through the town centre to stay on the SP347 to Voltago Agordino and Cerada Pass.
- In Tonadico, turn right on the SS50 to the Rolle Pass.
- Don't miss the savage right turn, 4 miles from the top of the Rolle Pass, for the SP81 to Falcade, over Valles Pass.
- At the SP346, turn left to Moena over San Pellegrino Pass.
- At the SS48 roundabout, turn right to Canazei.
- Keep going straight through Canazei to pick up the SS641 to Belluno over Fedaia Pass.
- In Caprile, turn left on the SR203 to Cortina.
- At the SR48, turn left to Arabba and stay on it over Pordoi Pass.
- Don't miss the right turn, on a hairpin about 4 miles down from the Pordoi summit, for the SS242 to Sëlva (also signed for the A22 to Brennero), which takes you over Sella Pass.
- Don't miss the right turn, about 3 miles from the top of the pass, for the SS243 to return to Corvara over Gardena Pass.

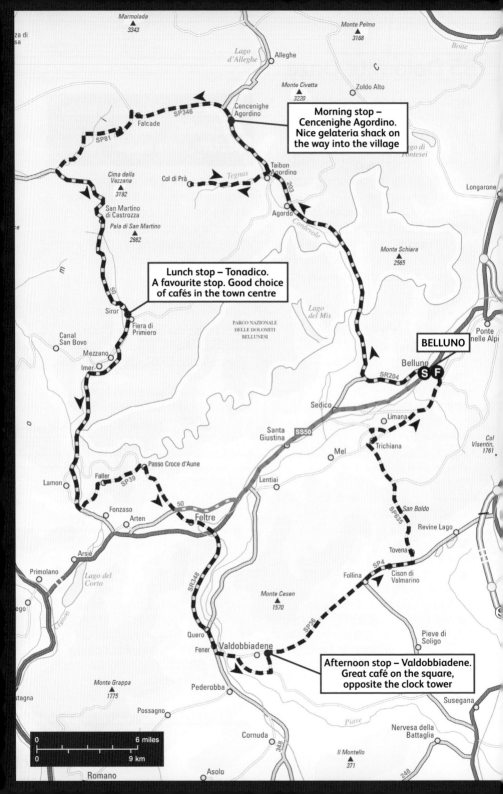

Morning stop –
Cencenighe Agordino.
Nice gelateria shack on
the way into the village

Lunch stop – Tonadico.
A favourite stop. Good choice
of cafés in the town centre

BELLUNO

Afternoon stop – Valdobbiadene.
Great café on the square,
opposite the clock tower

0   6 miles
0   9 km

86 Col di Prà and San Boldo

The Dolomites are, quite frankly, stunning. Not just the roads: when you get off the bike, you find the most amazing things… like the secluded pool and waterfall at the end of the Col di Prà road. From there, this relaxed ride takes in some touring favourites – Passo Rolle and Passo Valles – before looping south over Passo Croce d'Aune before tackling the crazy climb to San Boldo, with

FROM	Belluno
DISTANCE	145 miles
ALLOW	5 hours

hairpins in tunnels. Just another of the amazing things you find in the Dolomites. This southern edge of the mountains is far quieter than the famous Sella Ronda area.

Route

- Leave Belluno on the SR204 to Agordo.
- Go straight over the SR203 roundabout, still following signs for Agordo.
- Rather than going into Agordo town centre, turn left towards Arraba and Cencenighe Agordino, still on the SR203.
- Don't miss the left fork – half a mile past the second Agordo roundabout – for Taibon Agordino.
- Turn left by the church and take the road through the centre, following signs for Valle de San Lucano.
- After visiting Col di Prà, backtrack to Taibon Agordino and rejoin the SR203.
- Turn left in Cencenighe Agordino on the SP346 to Bolzano and Falcade.
- Don't miss the left turn – a mile after Falcade Alto – for the SP81 over Passo Valles, signed for San Martino di Castrozza.
- At the SS50 T-junction, turn left to San Martino and Feltre over Passo Rolle. Stay on the SS50 for 30 miles.
- Don't miss the tight left turn (doubling back on yourself) into Faller on the SP39, just after crossing the river at Lamon.
- After 6 miles, take the easy-to-miss right turn for Passo Croce d'Aune.
- Turn right in Passo Croce d'Aune and decend to Pedavena and Feltre.
- *Want a short day? Take the SS50 back to Belluno from Feltre.*
- For the full route, continue south from Feltre on the SR348 to Treviso and Padova.
- Cross the village of Fener and turn left at the roundabout on the SP36 to Segusino and Valdobbiadene. On the far side of the bridge, turn right to Valdobbiadene.
- Turn left to follow the one-way system through Valdobbiadene and stick with the SP36 to Follina, picking up the SP4.
- At the SP635 junction, turn left to Tovena and take it over Passo San Boldo.
- From Trichiana, pick up the SP1 to return to Belluno.

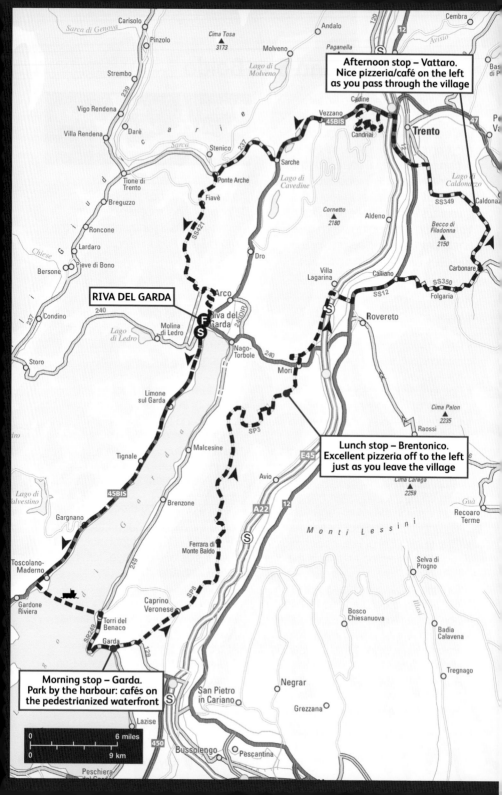

Afternoon stop – Vattaro.
Nice pizzeria/café on the left
as you pass through the village

RIVA DEL GARDA

Lunch stop – Brentonico.
Excellent pizzeria off to the left
just as you leave the village

Morning stop – Garda.
Park by the harbour: cafés on
the pedestrianized waterfront

87 Riva Ride

There's a lot of great riding around Riva del Garda and it's enhanced by the sheer beauty of the surroundings. This route uses a ferry to cut out the busier southern end of the lake, then runs along the spine of the mountains on the eastern shore – with some single-lane, nerve-testing roads. The

FROM	Riva del Garda
DISTANCE	160 miles
ALLOW	5½ hours

roads looping out to Folgaria, skirting Trento and on to Ponte Arche are broader but just as rewarding.

Route
- Leave Riva del Garda on the SS45BIS to Limone and Brescia.
- Turn left by the church in Maderno, at the waterfront, to the ferry (traghetti).
- Take the ferry across Lake Garda.
- Get off the ferry in Torri del Benaco and turn right to Garda on the SR249.
- In Garda, turn left at the roundabout on the SP8 to Costermano. Stay with this road through Caprino Veronese and Ferrara di Monte Baldo.
- Stay on the one road all the way to Mori – it does become narrow and changes its number, to become the SP3.
- Turn right in Mori on the SS240 to Rovereto and the autostrada. Turn right to go under the motorway (don't get on it).
- In Rovereto, turn left on the SS12 towards Trento.
- Don't miss the right turn in Calliano for the SS350 to Folgaria.
- In Carbonare, turn sharp left just before the church on the SS349 to Vattaro.
- Coming into Trento, follow the signs for the motorway – but before getting there, join the parallel SS12 towards Bolzano.
- When the SS12 hits a major roundabout, turn left on the SS45BIS to Arco and Riva.
- Don't miss the left turn 1 mile later, just after a tunnel, for the SP85 to Sardagna.
- In Candriai, turn right (on a hairpin) to stay on the SP85 to Sopramonte.
- In Cadine, rejoin the SS45BIS towards Riva.
- In Sarche, go straight over the roundabout on the SS237 to Madonna de Campiglio. Turn left at the roundabout to stay on the SS237.
- In Ponte Arche, turn left at the roundabout on the SS421 to return to Riva del Garda.

Lake Garda
My favourite of the Italian lakes. Plenty of sailing and watersports-type activities to try around Riva, or just enjoy the amazing views.

Strada della Forra
This spectacular road (SP38) starts in a tunnel then cuts through a narrow gorge beside the lake. Adding it into the day extends it by half an hour.

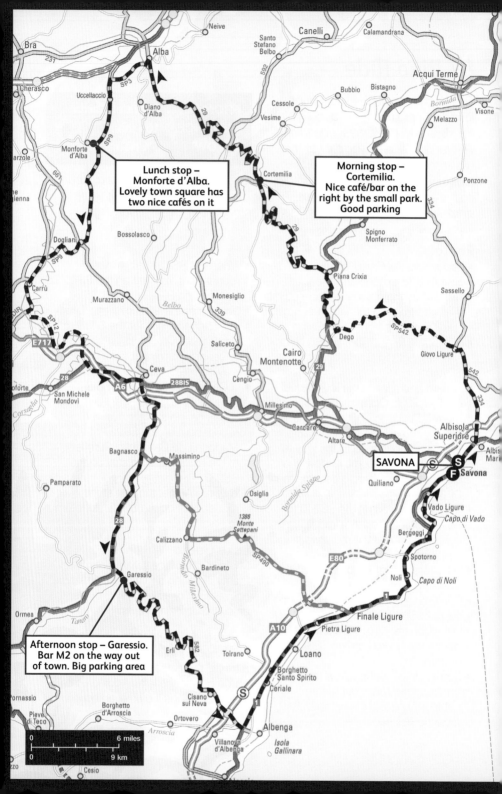

Morning stop –
Cortemilia.
Nice café/bar on the
right by the small park.
Good parking

Lunch stop –
Monforte d'Alba.
Lovely town square has
two nice cafés on it

Afternoon stop – Garessio.
Bar M2 on the way out
of town. Big parking area

SAVONA

88 Aurelia and Friends

Piemonte and Liguria have some amazing riding, but being so close to the Alps means these regions are definitely overshadowed. That's a huge shame – because heading here in summer means sunny days on twisty roads, without the tourist traffic of the holiday hotspots. Well, that's not entirely true of all of this route… The inland stretches are blissfully quiet, but from Albenga to Savona

FROM	Savona
DISTANCE	160 miles
ALLOW	6 hours

it follows one of Italy's oldest roads, Via Aurelia. This coast-hugging epic is beautiful but you may have to share it with fellow sunseekers. It's worth it for one of the most spectacular rides in this book.

Route

- Take the SS1, Via Aurelia, through Savona until you can turn left on the SP334 to Acqui Terme (also signed to the autostrada).
- In Giovo Ligure, turn left on the SP542 to Pontinvrea.
- In Dego, turn right to Alessandria.
- One mile later, turn right to join the SP29 to Piana Crixia and Acqui Terme.
- Don't miss the left turn 3 miles later to stay on the SP29 to Alba (also signed to Torino). This becomes the SP429. Take it all the way into Alba town centre.
- Cross Alba following signs for Torino and Asti-Cueno to pick up the SP3.
- In Uccellaccio, turn left on the SP9 to Monforte d'Alba.
- In Dogliani, turn right, then left (past the impressive church) towards Savona. About a mile out of town, go straight on at the hairpin to stay on the SP9 towards Farigliano.
- Don't miss the right turn, just outside Farigliano, signed to Piozzo. Then turn left to join the SP12 towards Mondovi and Carrù.
- When the SP12 is running parallel to the A6, turn left at the roundabout back under the motorway – on the SS28 to Ceva.
- Stick with the SS28 around Ceva.
- *For a shorter day, turn left in Bagnasco on the SP490 to Finale Ligure and turn left on the SS1.*
- Otherwise, turn left in Garessio (across the railway line) on the SP582 to Albenga.
- In Albenga, pick up the SS1, the Via Aurelia, and take it along the coast to Savona.

Savona

The modern port lacks the charm of the old bits. The Priamar fortress is a must-see.
www.comune.savona.it

Alba

Famous for its truffles and for its wines, the old town is stunning with a lovely cathedral.
www.comune.alba.cn.it

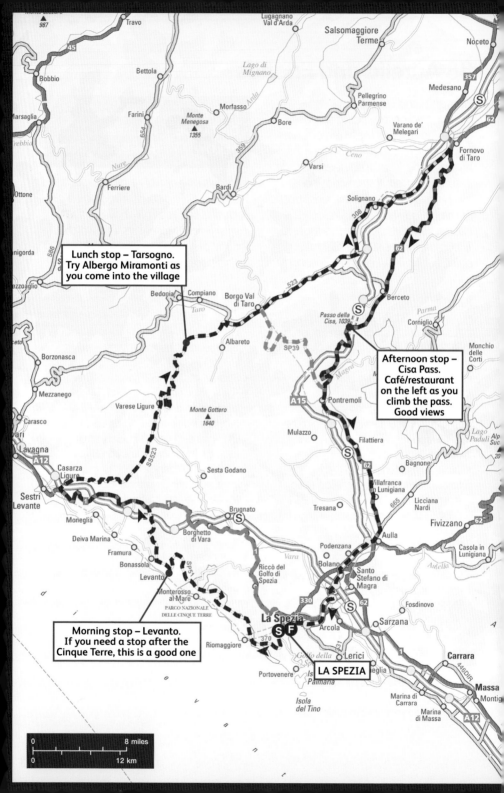

Lunch stop – Tarsogno. Try Albergo Miramonti as you come into the village

Afternoon stop – Cisa Pass. Café/restaurant on the left as you climb the pass. Good views

Morning stop – Levanto. If you need a stop after the Cinque Terre, this is a good one

LA SPEZIA

89 The Cinque Terre

If you like Amalfi, you'll love the Cinque Terre. The five towns of Riomaggiore, Manarola, Monterosso al Mare, Vernazza and Corniglia cling to cliffs above azure waters – all linked by a narrow but brilliantly serpentine road. Spending time off the bike exploring all five of them in a day means riding the very shortest route, looping back to La Spezia on

FROM	La Spezia
DISTANCE	165 miles
ALLOW	5½ hours

Via Aurelia. As lovely as the towns are, that would be a shame, as there's great riding heading inland towards Parma, then back to the coast over the Cisa Pass.

Route

- Leave La Spezia on the SP370 to Portovenere and the Cinque Terre. This becomes the SP51 along the Cinque Terre.
- At the SP38 T-junction, turn left to Genoa and Levanto.
- From Levanto, take the SS332 to Genoa and Bonassola.
- At the SS1, Via Aurelia, turn left to Genoa.
- *For a very short ride, turn right on the SS1 to return to La Spezia.*
- Go into Sestri Levante and pick up the SS523 to Parma and Varese Ligure.
- *Short of time? Turn right in Borgo Val di Taro on the SP20 to Pontremoli, which becomes the SP30. This saves just over an hour.*
- For the full route, continue on the SS523 – and after 8 miles, bear left towards Parma and the motorway as it becomes the SP308 to Solignano, Parma and the motorway.
- Don't get on the motorway: stay on the SP308 for 17½ miles.
- At the roundabout after the petrol station, turn right on the SS62 towards Berceto and Pontremoli.
- Stay on the SS62 over the Cisa Pass, all the way to Aulla.
- You can keep going on the SS62 from Aulla to La Spezia, but it's increasingly suburban. For me it's better to join the A15 and get back to La Spezia quickly.

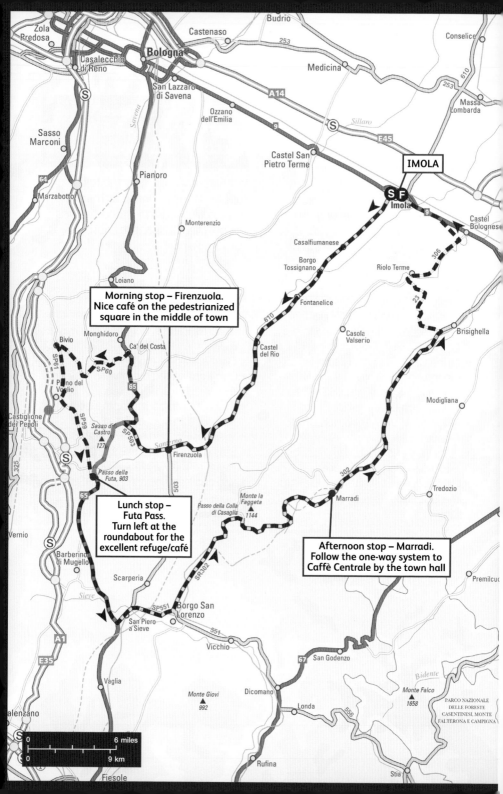

Morning stop – Firenzuola.
Nice café on the pedestrianized
square in the middle of town

Lunch stop –
Futa Pass.
Turn left at the
roundabout for the
excellent refuge/café

Afternoon stop – Marradi.
Follow the one-way system to
Caffè Centrale by the town hall

IMOLA

90 Imola and Mugello

Even more than the amazing roads, it's the way motorcycles are part of the national consciousness that makes Italy a wonderful place to ride. You get a real sense of how bikes are a central part of the life of the nation if you visit Imola for a World Superbike weekend or if you join the enthusiastic crowds at Mugello for a MotoGP race. This route heads out from Imola, not quite to the Mugello circuit – though it's a very short detour

FROM	Imola
DISTANCE	140 miles
ALLOW	4½ hours

from Borgo San Lorenzo if you want to visit. Along the way it crosses the Futa Pass, my favourite of the passes in the low mountains that form the border between Tuscany and Emilia Romagna, returning over the Casaglia Pass.

Route
- Leave Imola on the SP610 to Firenze (Florence). It is a bit suburban to start with, but bear with it...
- When the road forks, go straight on, into Firenzuola. Follow the signs for the A1 to Bologna to pick up the SP503 (Giogo Pass).
- At the SS65, turn right towards Bologna.
- *For a shorter ride, turn left here and ride directly to the Futa Pass.*
- In Ca' del Costa, turn left on the SP60 to San Benedetto.
- In Bivio, turn left on the SP61 to Pian del Voglio (also signed for the A1 to Firenze, but don't get on the motorway). Stick with the SP61 as it becomes the SP59.
- At the roundabout, turn right on the SP65 to Firenze over Futa Pass.
- Stay on the SP65 all the way to pick up the SP551 to Borgo San Lorenzo.
- Skirt the edge of Borgo San Lorenzo and turn left on the SR302 to Faenza and Palazzuolo sul Senio. It eventually becomes the SP302.
- In Brisighella, turn left on the SP23 to Riolo Terme and Zattaglia.
- In Riolo Terme, turn right to Faenza on the SP306.
- At the SS9, turn left to Imola.

Bologna
The capital of Emilia Romagna is 20 miles from Imola and is home to Ducati. A visit to the museum is a must for bikers.
www.ducati.com

Racing
There's nothing like watching a bike race in Italy. For tickets and info for Mugello, see
www.mugellocircuit.com
or for Imola, www.autodromoimola.it

More passes
As well as the Futa, and Casaglia passes used on this route, the Muraglione and dell'Abetone passes are worth riding if you have time. Get the locally pressed olive oil on Muraglione: it's amazing.

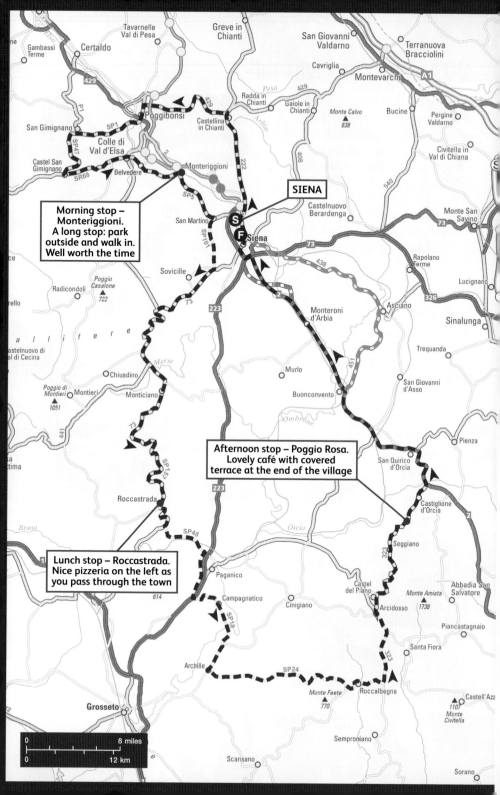

SIENA

Morning stop – Monteriggioni. A long stop: park outside and walk in. Well worth the time

Afternoon stop – Poggio Rosa. Lovely café with covered terrace at the end of the village

Lunch stop – Roccastrada. Nice pizzeria on the left as you pass through the town

0   8 miles
0   12 km

91 Siena Thriller

Tuscany is an amazing place for a bike trip: beautiful countryside dotted with charismatic towns and villages… and some awesome riding. This route distils all of that magic down into 200 highly concentrated miles. Just don't spend too much time looking round the historic villages at the start, as there's a lot of ground to cover.

FROM	Siena
DISTANCE	200 miles
ALLOW	6 hours

Route
- Leave Siena on the SR222 to Ouercegrossa and Castellina in Chianti.
- In Castellina, turn left on the SR429 to Poggibonsi and San Gimignano.
- Cross Poggibonsi and take the SP1 to San Gimignano.
- In San Gimignano, turn left on the SP47 to Montauto and Volterra.
- In Castel San Gimignano, turn left to Colle di Val d'Elsa and Siena on the SR68.
- Cross Colle di Val d'Elsa following signs for Siena and the motorway – but at the roundabout in La Colonna, turn right on the SP5 to Monteriggioni. This becomes the SR2.
- Don't miss the right turn in San Martino for the SP101 to Santa Colomba.
- At the SP73, turn right to Rosia. This eventually becomes the SP157.
- Don't miss the left turn (going straight when the SP157 turns right) about 2½ miles after Roccastrada for the SP48 to Paganico.
- In Paganico, take the SP64 towards Grosseto (parallel to the dual carriageway).
- After 3 miles, turn left on the SP18 to Arcille and Campagnatico. Turn right at the T-junction to stay on this road.
- In Arcille, turn left on the SP24 to Baccinello and Cana.
- In Santa Caterina, turn left on the SS323 to Roccalbegna and Arcidosso.
- At the SR2, turn left to Siena. Take this road all the way back to the city.

Want more?
- For a longer ride, turn right in Buonconvento on the SP451 to Asciano.
- At the roundabout in Asciano, turn left on the SP438 to return to Siena.

Siena
Fantastic historic walled city. Crazy-busy when the Palio horse race is on, but always genuinely fabulous. www.terredisiena.it

San Gimignano
This lovely Tuscan hilltop town, crowned with fourteen towers, is a UNESCO World Heritage site. Worth an off-bike day trip. www.sangimignano.com

Monteriggioni
From a walled city to a walled town to this perfectly preserved walled village. It starred in the *Assassin's Creed* video games. www.visittuscany.com

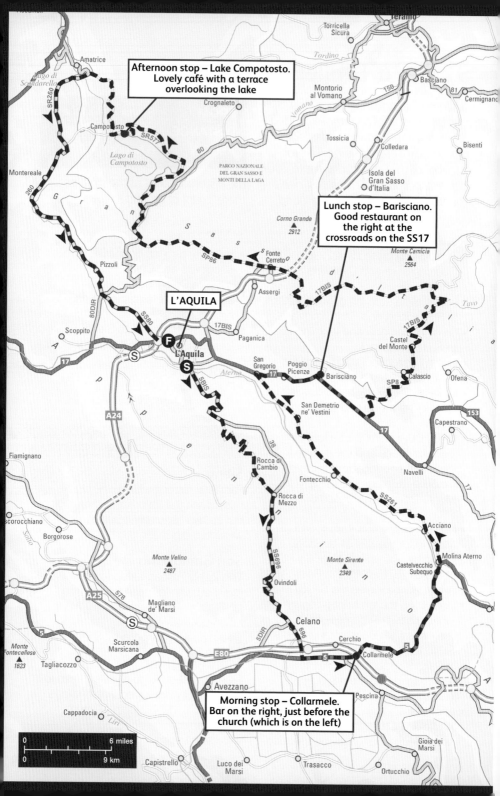

Afternoon stop – Lake Compotosto. Lovely café with a terrace overlooking the lake

Lunch stop – Barisciano. Good restaurant on the right at the crossroads on the SS17

L'AQUILA

Morning stop – Collarmele. Bar on the right, just before the church (which is on the left)

92 L'Aquila Slammer

The great thing about exploring by bike is the sense you get of discovering places – like L'Aquila. Obviously, the Roman ruins and baroque palazzos and general bustle of modern life suggest other people have known it was here for some time, but it seems that it's not so well known outside Italy. That's a shame, because as well as being a fine city it's also the gateway to the Gran Sasso, a rugged section of the Apennine Mountains.

FROM	L'Aquila
DISTANCE	195 miles
ALLOW	5½ hours

High enough for skiing in winter, in summer it's a hiking and biking paradise – crossed by the kind of quiet, scenic, twisty roads that can make any motorcyclist very happy indeed. Why not come and discover them for yourself?

Route

- Leave L'Aquila on the SS5BIS to Avezzano. Keep going straight as it becomes the SS696.
- Stay on the SS696 around Celano.
- Go under the motorway and turn left on the SR5 towards Pescara.
- Don't miss the left turn a mile outside Castelvecchio Subequo (after the railway line) for the SS261 to Molina Aterno and L'Aquila.
- In San Gregorio, turn right at the roundabout on the SS17 to Popoli.
- After 8 miles, when you see an overpass, take the exit and turn left at the top of the slip road on the SP8 to Calascio.
- In Castel del Monte, turn left on the SS17BIS towards Pescara.
- Don't miss the right turn a mile past Fonte Cerreto for the SP86 to Teramo.
- At the SS80, turn right to Teramo.
- After 2½ miles, turn left on the SR577 to Amatrice.
- In Amatrice, turn left on the SR260 to L'Aquila. This becomes the SS260.
- When the road merges with the SS80, bear left to return to L'Aquila.

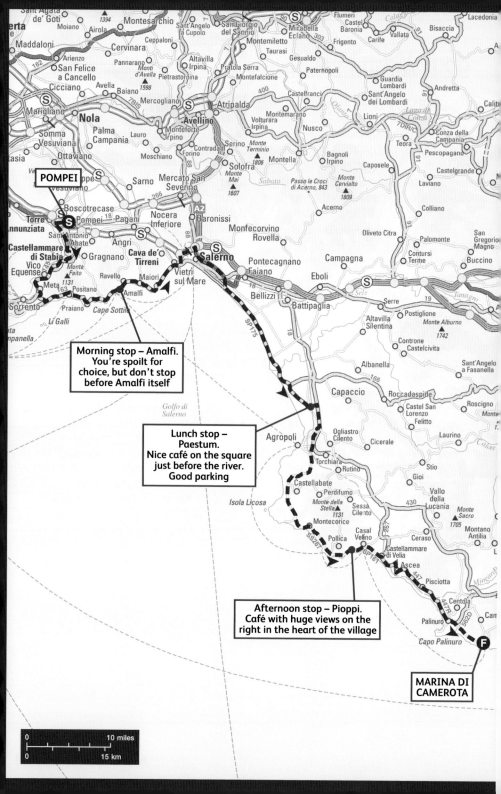

POMPEI

Morning stop – Amalfi.
You're spoilt for
choice, but don't stop
before Amalfi itself

Lunch stop –
Paestum.
Nice café on the square
just before the river.
Good parking

Afternoon stop – Pioppi.
Café with huge views on the
right in the heart of the village

MARINA DI
CAMEROTA

0 __ 10 miles
0 __ 15 km

93 Amalfi and More

The Amalfi Drive is famous for being one of Europe's most beautiful roads. It's also – whisper it – one of the craziest, thanks to the local drivers (ever been overtaken by a scooter, ridden three-up, on the pavement? Come round a blind corner to find a man leading donkeys down the middle of the road? Welcome to Amalfi...). Don't be put off: it's well worth it. This route drinks in the scenery, then heads down a quieter

FROM	Pompei
TO	Marina di Camerota
DISTANCE	135 miles
ALLOW	6 hours

stretch of coast, past the Greek ruins at Paestum... 15 per cent less dramatic on the landscape front, 150 per cent calmer on the traffic one. It's two great rides for the price of one.

Route
- Leave Pompei on the SS145 to Castellammare di Stabia. This will go through two tunnels.
- Just over half a mile from the end of the second tunnel (just past a petrol station on the left), take the exit on the right, signed to Vico Equense – rather than going into a third tunnel. Confusingly, this is also the SS145…
- In Vico Equense, turn right at the roundabout towards Sorrento. Keep following the signs for Sorrento to rejoin the, ahem, SS145 as it emerges from the tunnel.
- In Piano di Sorrento, turn left to Positano to pick up the SS163 (if you want to go into Sorrento, keep going straight and follow the SS145 until it meets the SS163).
- Take the SS163 all the way along the Amalfi coast to Vietri sul Mare.
- Turn right on the SS18 towards Salerno then follow the (green) signs for the Tangenziale and join the A3.
- Take the first exit for Salerno Est.
- After 5 miles, take the exit for Stadio Arechi. Turn right at the end of the slip road.

- At the second roundabout, turn left to Agropoli on the SP175.
- A mile outside Paestum, join the SS18 towards Agropoli.
- After 5 miles, take the exit for Agropoli Sud and Castellabate. Turn right at the end of the slip road.
- Turn left at the roundabout on the SS267 to Santa Maria, San Mauro and Montecorice. Follow the SS267 along the coast.
- At Marina di Casal Velino, cut through town on the SP161.
- In Castellammare di Velia, pick up the SR447 to Palinuro and Pisciotta. Keep going straight as it becomes the SR447racc.
- In Palinuro, turn left on the SR562 and stay on it around the coast to the route's end in Marina di Camerota.

Pompeii & Herculaneum
Don't try to fit the Roman ruins into a riding day. Give yourself a day in shorts and sunscreen. To do them justice, take a tour.
www.pompeii-tickets.com

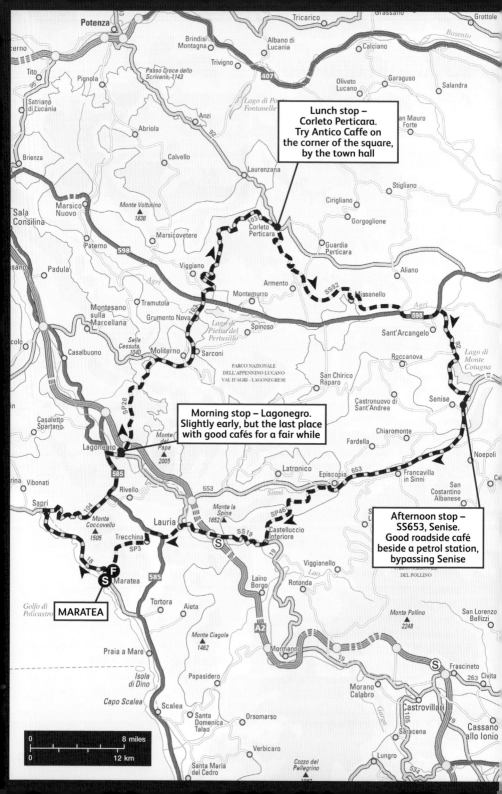

Lunch stop –
Corleto Perticara.
Try Antico Caffe on
the corner of the square,
by the town hall

Morning stop – Lagonegro.
Slightly early, but the last place
with good cafés for a fair while

Afternoon stop –
SS653, Senise.
Good roadside café
beside a petrol station,
bypassing Senise

MARATEA

94 Maratea Miles

Secrets. Everybody has them – and sharing them with the select few makes all concerned feel great. Let's face it, that's the principle on which this book is based, after all. But then I thought Britain's biggest gift to espionage, James Bond, had blown a great big hole in this secret route by setting the opening scene of No Time To Die *in Maratea. I did think it was odd that the iconic action franchise didn't feature the thing that first drew me here – and earns Maratea its place in this section of the book: the gigantic statue of Christ the Redeemer, perched on the top of a promontory at the end of a hairpin-heavy dead-end road. It's up to you whether you visit it at the start or end of the ride, though I'd suggest going*

FROM	Maratea
DISTANCE	180 miles
ALLOW	6 hours

early, before it gets busy. Then the route starts with the scenic coastal drive (which does actually appear in the movie) to Sapri before heading inland. One stretch of road was in a poor condition last time I visited (the SP26), but that was offset by others that had been freshly resurfaced with immaculate tarmac. This full day in the beautiful Basilicata countryside is an absolute blockbuster of a route – though in fact that Bond action sequence wasn't filmed here but in nearby Matera, so this is just our little secret...

Route

- Leave Maratea on the SS18 to Sapri.
- Turn right by Sapri harbour on the SP104 to Lagonegro and Potenza.
- Turn left to Lagonegro on the SS585.
- Go into Lagonegro and follow the signs for the hospital to pick up the SP26 to Moliterno. (NB: It's a narrow road and the surface may be in a poor state in places.)
- Join the SP103 towards Moliterno and stay on it for 30 miles.
- Cross Corleto Perticara and pick up the SS92 to Sant'Arcangelo.
- Join the SS598 towards Sant'Arcangelo and Taranto.
- After 5 miles, turn right to continue on the SS92 towards Senise.
- Join the SS653, signed for the A3 motorway to Reggio Calabria.
- Don't miss the exit signed for Agramonte, 17 miles later. Turn right at the end of the slip road, then left to pick up the SP46.
- At the SS19, turn right to Lagonegro and Potenza (also signed for the motorway).
- Stay on the SS19 to Lauria and pick up the SP3 to return to Maratea.

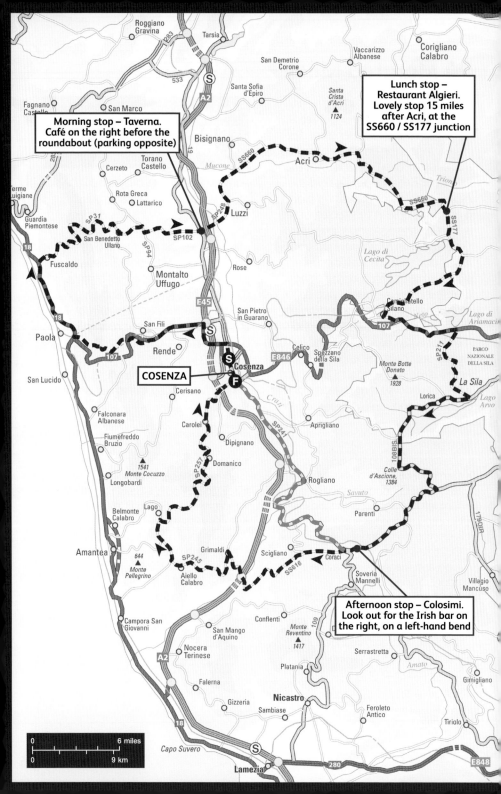

Morning stop – Taverna.
Café on the right before the
roundabout (parking opposite)

Lunch stop –
Restaurant Algieri.
Lovely stop 15 miles
after Acri, at the
SS660 / SS177 junction

COSENZA

Afternoon stop – Colosimi.
Look out for the Irish bar on
the right, on a left-hand bend

0   6 miles
0   9 km

95 Cosenza Countryside

It takes a bit of commitment for riders from the northern fringes of Europe to get to the far south of Italy – especially as there's a lot of high-quality riding to hold their attention along the way. It's worth persevering, though. What you find down here is a sun-drenched land where crazily twisty roads rise and fall through farmland and forest, dropping down

FROM	Cosenza
DISTANCE	180 miles
ALLOW	6½ hours

to the sparkling sea. It's quiet, too… almost eerily so in places. Some minor roads can be challenging, but the better-maintained ones deliver some truly astonishing rides.

Route

- Leave Cosenza on the SS107 to Paola.
- Take the first left turn after the tunnel on the SP35 to San Fili.
- When it meets the SS107 again, turn right to Paola.
- In Paola, turn right on the SS18 to Salerno.
- After 4½ miles, in Marina di Fuscaldo, turn right on the SP31 to Fuscaldo.
- Don't miss the sharp left turn – doubling back on yourself – in San Benedetto Ullano for the SP100 to Triscoli.
- At the SP94, turn right towards Montalton Uffugo and Cosenza, then keep going straight as the road becomes the SP102 to Cosenza and the motorway.
- In Taverna, turn left at the roundabout then take the first right for the SP248 to Bisignano, Acri and Luzzi.
- Keep going straight as the road becomes the SS660. Take it for about 30 miles.
- At the SS177 roundabout, turn right towards Cosenza.
- In Camigliatello Silano, turn left (then go straight) on the SS107 to Crotone.
- After 6 miles, take the exit for Lorica. Turn left at the end of the slip road and then immediately right on the SP211 to Colosimi.
- At the SS108BIS, turn right to Lorica and Catanzaro. Stay on this road for 36 miles – it becomes the SS16 at Coraci.
- *For a shorter ride, turn right in Coraci on the SP241 and take that all the way back to Cosenza (saving 45 minutes).*
- Otherwise, take the SS616 to the motorway: don't get on it… go straight on, towards Grimaldi and Maione.
- Don't miss the left turn, 2 miles after the motorway, for the SP57 to Grimaldi.
- In Grimaldi, turn left on the SP245 to Aiello Calabro and Campora.
- In Aiello, turn right on the back road to Lago. After a mile, turn right to Lago.
- In Lago, turn right on the SP257 and take it all the way back to Cosenza.

Mediterranean islands

Some of Europe's finest riding isn't on the mainland, but on the islands. Grab a ferry and see for yourself.

ISLAND	FERRIES FROM...
Corsica	Civitavecchia, Genoa, Livorno, Naples, Nice, Marseille, Toulon, Sardinia
Elba	Piombino, Corsica
Mallorca	Barcelona, Dénia, Valencia
Malta	Pozzallo (Sicily)
Sardinia	Barcelona, Civitavecchia, Corsica, Genoa, Livorno, Marseille, Naples, Nice, Palermo, Toulon
Sicily	Civitavecchia, Naples, Reggio Calabria, Sardinia, Villa San Giovanni

SS1 Via Aurelia, Liguria (route 88, pages 212–3)

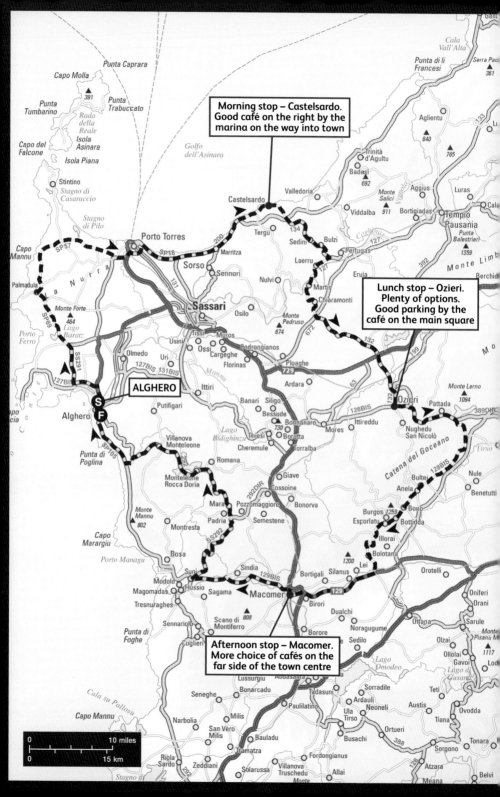

Morning stop – Castelsardo.
Good café on the right by the marina on the way into town

Lunch stop – Ozieri.
Plenty of options.
Good parking by the café on the main square

Afternoon stop – Macomer.
More choice of cafés on the far side of the town centre

ALGHERO

0   10 miles
0   15 km

96 Alghero Miles

Whenever I'd meet an Italian bike tester on a motorcycle launch, I'd ask them where the best roads in Italy were or where they went to ride for pleasure. I always got the same answer: Sardinia. Some favoured the north, some the centre, some the south… but everyone raved about the riding here. This long loop from

FROM	**Alghero**
DISTANCE	**220 miles**
ALLOW	**6½ hours**

Alghero starts with a scenic seaside run before heading inland for some of the finest roads – not just in Sardinia but in Italy and possibly all of Europe.

Route

- Leave Alghero on the SS291DIR towards the airport. When it hits a T-junction, turn right on the SS291 to Sassari.
- Turn left at the lights to Neptune's Grotto.
- After a mile and a half, turn right on the SP69 to Palmadula and Lago Baratz.
- At the SP18, turn left to go into Palmadula and turn right in the village on the SP4 to Stintino. Keep going as it becomes the SP57.
- When the SP57 meets the SP34, turn left to Porto Torres and follow the signs for Castelsardo to pick up the SP81 that runs along the north coast.
- In Marritza, turn left on the SS200 to Lu Bagnu and Castelsardo.
- Keep going through Castelsardo and past Elephant Rock as the road becomes the SS134 to Sedini.
- Turn right on the SS127 to Laerru.
- In Martis, turn left on the SS132 to Ozieri.

- From Ozieri, take the SS128BIS to Pattada. Stick with it as it loops round through Bultei and Bono (where the streets have no names).
- In Bottidda, turn right (when you see the church tower) on the SP78 to Esporlatu. After a mile turn left on the SP111.
- At the SP17, turn left to Bolotana.
- Don't miss the right turn, south of Bolotana, for the main SS129 to Macomer.
- Go into Macomer for coffee and then leave on the SS129BIS to Sindia and Bosa.
- At Suni, pick up the SS292 to Padria and Villanova Monteleone.
- Don't miss the left turn, about 3 miles after Villanova Monteleone, for the minor road signed for Alghero litoranea.
- At the SP105 T-junction, turn right to return to Alghero.

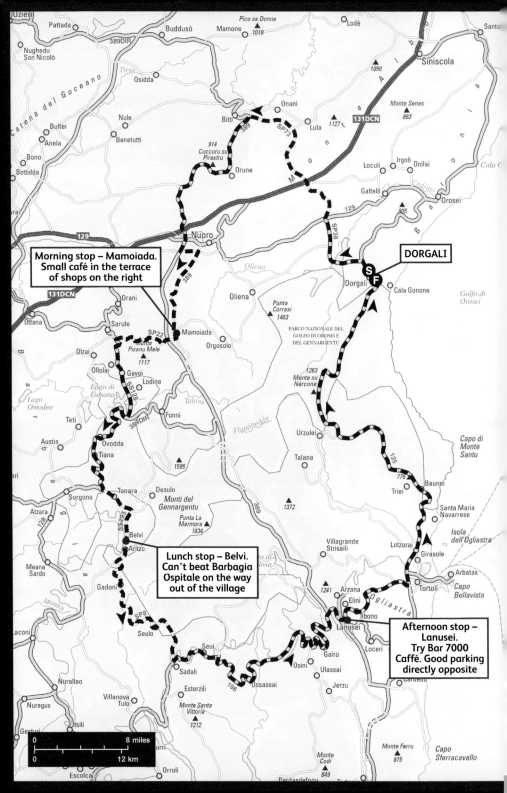

Morning stop – Mamoiada. Small café in the terrace of shops on the right

DORGALI

Lunch stop – Belvì. Can't beat Barbagia Ospitale on the way out of the village

Afternoon stop – Lanusei. Try Bar 7000 Caffé. Good parking directly opposite

| 0 | | 8 miles |
| 0 | | 12 km |

97 Eastern Promise

One of the most famous roads in Sardinia is the Strada Orientalis, following the line of the eastern coast (even though it's often not in sight of the sea). For me, it's up there with the established touring greats like Route Napoleon, California's Pacific Coast Highway or even the North Coast 500. It has everything: massive views over an unspoilt landscape; endless sweeping bends and plenty of tighter turns; and of course, as it's in Sardinia, most of the time it's bathed in glorious sunshine. In other words,

FROM	Dorgali
DISTANCE	205 miles
ALLOW	6½ hours

it's a perfect touring road. The thing is, you could say that about a lot of the roads here. This route through the mountains of central Sardinia could make your head spin with the quality of the riding. It's bend after amazing bend, as the route builds up to my favourite stretch of the Orientalis.

Route

- Leave Dorgali on the SS125 then, after about half a mile, turn left on the SP38 to Nuoro and Oliena.
- After 10 miles, turn right towards Nuoro and Siniscola, then keep going straight to Bitti on the SP73.
- In Bitti, turn left on the SS389 to Nuoro and Orune.
- At Nuoro, join the ring road (circonvallazione sud) following signs for Mamoiada. Go through the tunnel and take the first exit, towards the city centre. Then take the third exit for the SS398ex to Mamoiada.
- Cross Mamoiada and take the right fork to the SP22 to Sarule.

- At the SS128, turn left to Ollolai and Fonni.
- About 4 miles outside Tiana, turn left (after crossing a bridge) on the SS295 to Tonara and Belvì.
- Don't miss the left turn 2½ miles outside Belvì on the SP8 to Gadoni and Seulo.
- At the SS198, turn left to Lanusei and Seui. Stay on this road all the way to the coast.
- Coming into Tortolì, turn left to join the SS125 to Olbia and Urzulei. Take it all the way back to Dorgali.

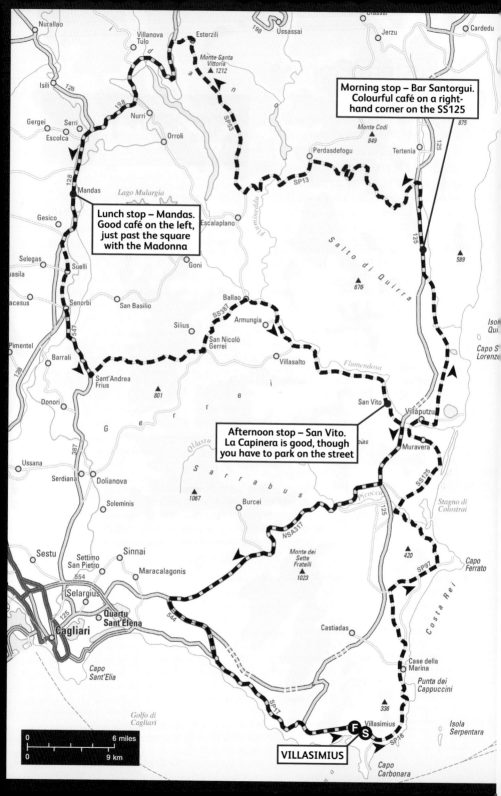

Morning stop – Bar Santorgui. Colourful café on a right-hand corner on the SS125

Lunch stop – Mandas. Good café on the left, just past the square with the Madonna

Afternoon stop – San Vito. La Capinera is good, though you have to park on the street

VILLASIMIUS

98 Southern Bella

As with so many outings on Sardinia, this trip around the charming seaside resort of Villasimius blends amazing mountain riding with some staggering coastal views (the SP17 that makes up the final leg is particularly lovely). Naturally, as it's on the eastern side of the island, this ride also uses the famous Orientalis – both the twistier, hillier original road

FROM	Villasimius
DISTANCE	210 miles
ALLOW	6½ hours

and the flatter, faster modern one that takes most of the traffic, keeping the old road nice and quiet. If you have time, it's worth a side trip to Capo Ferrato to soak up the views.

Route

- Leave Villasimius on the SP18 to Muravera.
- At the SP97 junction, turn right to San Priamo and Muravera.
- Stay on the road through Capoferrato - it gets quite narrow and bumpy for about a mile. After it crosses a river, turn right on the SS20.
- After 500 m, turn right to join the SS125 – the original Orientalis. Stick with it through Muravera and Villaputzu, heading north towards Olbia.
- Eventually, the road will reach a roundabout (4 miles after the suggested coffee stop). Turn right on the ex SS125 – back on the old Orientalis again.
- Don't miss the right turn a mile later for the minor road to Perdasdefogu.
- In Perdasdefogu, turn left on the SP13 to Escalaplano.
- After 9 miles, take the right turn for the SP53 to Esterzili and Sadali.
- At the SS198 junction, turn left towards Serri and Mandas.

- Turn left on the SS128 towards Cagliari and Mandas.
- After 11 miles (about 7½ miles after Mandas), turn left at the roundabout on the minor road to Senorbì.
- Cross Senorbì and pick up the SS547 to Sant'Andrea Frius.
- Turn left by the church in Sant'Andrea Frius on the SS387 to Ballao. Stay on this one road for 32 miles, all the way through Ballao and down to San Vito.
- Join the SS125var towards Cagliari for one junction, following the signs for Burcei on the NSA371 (which some maps will still call the SS125, as it's another piece of the original Strada Orientalis).
- After 21 miles, when you see the motorway bridge ahead, turn left to join the SS544BIS / SS125VAR towards Villasimius and the Tortolì-Arbatax ferry.
- Keep going straight as the road becomes the SP17, which returns to Villasimius.

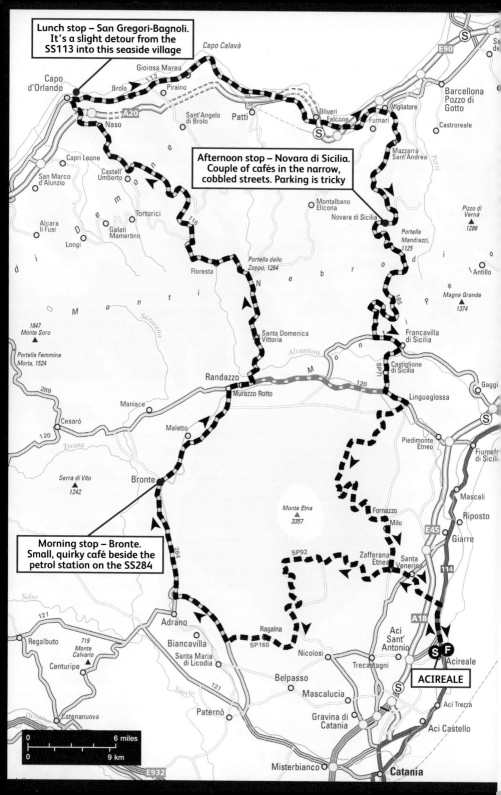

Lunch stop – San Gregori-Bagnoli.
It's a slight detour from the
SS113 into this seaside village

Afternoon stop – Novara di Sicilia.
Couple of cafés in the narrow,
cobbled streets. Parking is tricky

Morning stop – Bronte.
Small, quirky café beside the
petrol station on the SS284

Capo Calavà

E90

Gioiosa Marea

Capo
d'Orlando

Brolo

Piraino

Oliveri
Falcone

Vigliatore

Barcellona
Pozzo di
Gotto

A20

Naso

Sant'Angelo
di Brolo

Patti

Furnari

Castroreale

Mazzarrà
Sant'Andrea

Capri Leone

San Marco
d'Alunzio

Castell'
Umberto

Montalbano
Elicona

Novara di Sicilia

Pizzo di
Vernà
1286

Alcara
li Fusi

Galati
Mamertino

Tortorici

Portella
Mandrazzi,
1125

Longi

116

Antillo

Monte Soro
1847

Floresta

Portella dello
Zoppo, 1264

185

Magna Grande
1374

Portella Femmina
Morta, 1524

Saracena

Santa Domenica
Vittoria

Alcantara

Francavilla
di Sicilia

289

SP7I

Castiglione
di Sicilia

Randazzo

120

Linguaglossa

Gaggi

Maniace

Murazzo Rotto

Cesarò

Troina

Maletto

Piedimonte
Etneo

120

Serra di Vito
1242

Fiumefr
di Sicili

Bronte

Fornazzo

Mascali

Monte Etna
3357

Milo

Riposto

E45

Giarre

284

SP92

Zafferana
Etnea

Santa
Venerina

114

Adrano

Ragalna

SP160

Nicolosi

Aci
Sant'
Antonio

A18

S F

Acireale

121

Biancavilla

719
Monte
Calvario

Regalbuto

Santa Maria
di Licodia

Trecastagni

ACIREALE

Centuripe

Belpasso

Mascalucia

Aci Trezza

121

Paternò

Gravina di
Catania

Aci Castello

| 0 | | 6 miles |
| 0 | | 9 km |

Catenanuova

Salso

Simeto

Misterbianco

Catania

E932

99 Mount Etna and More

Picture the scene: Sicily, a sunny day, your bike and miles of amazing roads – plus the added attraction of the otherworldly landscape of Mount Etna. Appealing, isn't it? This long day's ride won't really be practical if you take the cablecar to the top of Etna. If you do, cut the route short

FROM	Acireale
DISTANCE	205 miles
ALLOW	6½ hours

from Randazzo, but that would be a shame as for me the best riding is across the mountains to the coast.

Route

- Leave Acireale on the SS114 to Messina.
- Don't miss the left turn after 5 miles for the SP49i to Zafferana Etnea.
- Go through the centre of Santa Venerina as the road briefly becomes the SP4, then turn left on the SP59i to go into Zafferana.
- Follow the one-way system around Zafferana to pick up the SP92 to Etna.
- 8 miles after the visitor centre, turn right on the SP120 to Belpasso.
- At the SP160 roundabout, turn right to Ragalna.
- Turn right in Ragalna to stay on the SP160 towards Catania and Paterno.
- After 2½ miles, turn right to Adrano on the SS284 and stick with it for 23 miles.
- At Murazzo Rotto, turn right on the SS120 to Randazzo.
- *Short of time? Stay on the SS120 to Linguaglossa for a rapid circuit of Etna.*

- For the full tour, cross Randazzo and turn left on the SS116 to Santa Domenica Vittoria and Floresta, taking it all the way to the coast.
- In Capo d'Orlando, turn right on the SS113 to Messina and take it along the coast.
- Don't get on the motorway at Marina di Patti: stick with the SS113.
- Don't miss the right turn in Vigliatore, signed for the SS185 to Novara di Sicilia. Cross the river and turn right to join the SS185 and stay on it for 30 miles.
- Turn right at the lights in the centre of Francavilla di Sicilia on the SP7i to Castiglione di Sicilia.
- In Linguaglossa, turn right when you see a brown sign for 'Etna nord' (easy to miss) and take the minor road through the forest.
- Turn right in Fornazzo on the SP59i towards Zafferana and then retrace your steps through Santa Venerina on the SP49i and SS114 to return to Acireale.

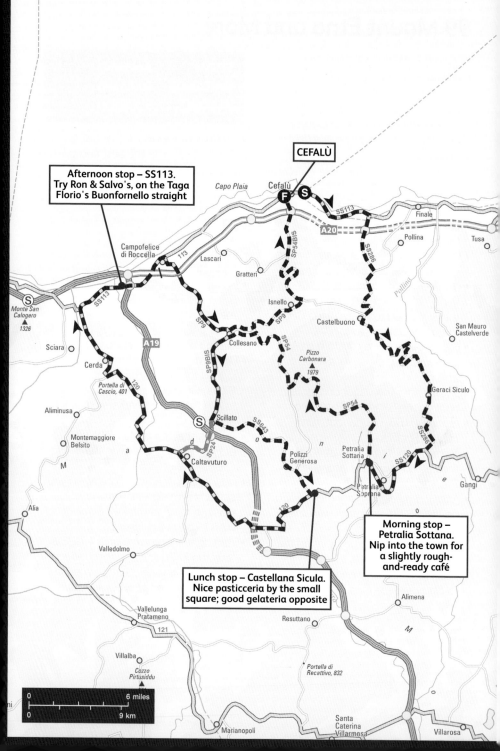

CEFALÙ

Afternoon stop – SS113.
Try Ron & Salvo's, on the Taga
Florio's Buonfornello straight

Lunch stop – Castellana Sicula.
Nice pasticceria by the small
square; good gelateria opposite

Morning stop –
Petralia Sottana.
Nip into the town for
a slightly rough-
and-ready café

Capo Plaia
Cefalù
Finale
Pollina
Tusa
A20
Campofelice
di Roccella
Lascari
Gratteri
Isnello
Castelbuono
San Mauro
Castelverde
Monte San
Calogero
1326
Collesano
Pizzo
Carbonara
1979
Geraci Siculo
Sciara
Cerda
Scillato
Polizzi
Generosa
Petralia
Sottana
Aliminusa
Caltavuturo
Petralia
Soprana
Gangi
Montemaggiore
Belsito
Alia
Valledolmo
Alimena
Vallelunga
Pratameno
Resuttano
Villalba
Cozzo
Pirtusiddu
Portella di
Recattivo, 832
Marianopoli
Santa
Caterina
Villarmosa
Villarosa

Portella di
Cascio, 401

0   6 miles
0   9 km

100 Targa Florio Butterfly

The Targa Florio was once one of the world's toughest races – the four-wheeled equivalent of the Isle of Man TT, contested under the fierce sun of a Sicilian summer. It ran from 1906 until the late 1970s using a variety of courses, from a full lap of the island to the 45-mile 'Circuito Piccolo delle Madonie' from Cerda to Campofelice to Collesano and Caltavuturo. This is my homage to this great race, using

FROM	Cefalù
DISTANCE	150 miles
ALLOW	5 hours

as many roads from different versions of the course as possible. If you take the SP24 from Scillato to Caltavuturo, to ride all of the Madonie circuit, you'll save 25 miles – but the longer route is a better full-day ride.

Route

- Leave Cefalù on the SS113 towards Sant'Ambrogio.
- After crossing the railway line, turn right towards the A20 to Palermo, on the SS286 – but don't get on the motorway. Keep going straight on the SS286 to Geraci Siculo and Castelbuono, staying on this road for 25 miles.
- At the SS120, turn right towards Palermo.
- After 6½ miles, turn right on the SP54 signed for Petralia Sottana and Collesano.
- At the SP9 T-junction, turn left to Collesano and Scillato.
- Cross Collesano on the SP9BIS to Scillato.
- *To follow the Madonie ciruit, turn right at SS643 T-junction to Scillato, then take the SP24 to Caltavuturo, turning right onto the SS120 to rejoin the route.*
- For the full ride, turn left at the SS643 T-junction to Polizzi Generosa.
- At the SS120, turn left to Castellana Sicula (for fuel and lunch).
- From Castellana Sicula, backtrack past the SS643 junction and stay on the SS120 for more than 30 miles, passing through Caltavuturo and Cerda until you reach Floriopoli – the Targa Florio grandstands.
- Turn right on the SS113 to Campofelice di Roccella.
- Leave the SS113 for the SP9 into Campofelice and stay on it, back through Collesano, all the way to Isnello.
- Don't miss the left turn – on a hairpin a mile after Isnello – for the SP54BIS to Gratteri. Stay on this road back to Cefalù.

thanks to...

The biggest thanks must go to my partner Ali for encouraging me to start prepping my European routes, as first collected in the two self-published *Bikers' Europe* volumes. Picking those up and turning them into this much more polished, practical collection couldn't have been done without the team at HarperCollins: Vaila Donnachie, Rebecca Shulga, Gordon MacGilp, Karen Marland and Julianna Dunn.

However, over the years a great many people have helped stoke my obsession, introducing me to many of the more obscure but brilliant pieces of European tarmac. Great recommendations have come from, among others, Robert Adams, François Barrois, Mark Comer, John Cundiff, Paolo Fenati, Simon Hargreaves, Chris Hood, Mark Hucke, Tony Lang, Neil Leigh, David Lopez, Richard Millington, Richard Nash, Lorraine Nevill, Simon Rice, Pieter Rykaert, Kev Raymond, Kevin and Julia Sanders, Paul Travers – plus of course all the manufacturers who took me off on launches, and Bauer, which sent me off across the Continent accompanied by Weeble to generate content for *RiDE*.

More than anything else, this book owes a lot to the countless riders I've met over the years who have shared their passion for riding and helped me fine-tune these routes. If you'd like to get in touch – to share a good road or to give feedback – please contact me at www.simonweir.co.uk.